Jonathan Swift
IN THE COMPANY OF WOMEN

A portrait of Jonathan Swift, in the boardroom of St. Patrick's Hospital. On each side it is flanked by a portrait of a woman: Stella on the Dean's right, Vanessa on his left. Photo by Davison and Associates, Dublin, with permission given by St. Patrick's Hospital, Dublin.

Jonathan Swift

in the Company of Women

LOUISE BARNETT

OXFORD
UNIVERSITY PRESS

2007

OXFORD
UNIVERSITY PRESS

Oxford University Press, Inc., publishes works that further
Oxford University's objective of excellence
in research, scholarship, and education.

Oxford   New York
Auckland   Cape Town   Dar es Salaam   Hong Kong   Karachi
Kuala Lumpur   Madrid   Melbourne   Mexico City   Nairobi
New Delhi   Shanghai   Taipei   Toronto

With offices in
Argentina   Austria   Brazil   Chile   Czech Republic   France   Greece
Guatemala   Hungary   Italy   Japan   Poland   Portugal   Singapore
South Korea   Switzerland   Thailand   Turkey   Ukraine   Vietnam

Published by Oxford University Press, Inc.
198 Madison Avenue, New York, New York 10016

www.oup.com

Oxford is a registered trademark of Oxford University Press

Library of Congress Cataloging-in-Publication Data
Barnett, Louise K.
Jonathan Swift in the company of women / Louise Barnett.
  p. cm.
Includes bibliographical references.
ISBN-13 978-0-19-518866-0

1. Swift, Jonathan, 1667–1745—Criticism and interpretation.
2. Swift, Jonathan, 1667–1745—Relations with women.
3. Misogyny in literature. 4. Vanessa, 1690–1723.
5. Johnson, Esther, 1681–1728. I. Title.
PR3728.W6 2006
828'.509—dc22 2006007047

9 8 7 6 5 4 3 2

Printed in the United States of America
on acid-free paper

For Nicholas, Alec, and Harry

ACKNOWLEDGMENTS

Immersing myself in Swift over the course of a professional lifetime has been a sustaining pleasure. I have been intrigued by this great figure of world literature since my graduate school days, when I remember longing impatiently for the third volume of Irvin Ehrenpreis's biography of Swift to appear. In writing this book my greatest debts are to a long line of illustrious writers on Swift, and most notably those who have so meticulously assembled the editions of primary texts that others build upon. Additionally, the new scholarship on the history of women has given us a much fuller understanding of the lives of women during Swift's time.

Some parts of this book have appeared in print, and I am grateful to the University of Delaware Press and *1650–1850: Ideas, Aesthetics, and Inquiries into the Early Eighteenth Century* for permission to cannibalize the essays that originally appeared in their publications: "Swift, Women, and Women Readers" in *Representations of Swift*, edited by Brian A. Connery (University of Delaware Press, 2002: 181–94), and "'Betty's Freckled Neck': Swift, Women, and Women Readers," in a special issue of *1650–1850* edited by Jim Thorson (4 [1998]: 233–45).

My work was significantly aided by fellowships from the Beinecke Rare Book and Manuscript Library and the Huntington Library, whose staffs were unfailingly helpful and gracious. And once again, I needed and received much timely help from Mary Shelly and other members of the Interlibrary Loan Department of Franklin and Marshall College.

I wish to offer my heartfelt thanks to the following people for help of various sorts: Julia Bader, Brian A. Connery, Nora Crow, Donald C. Mell, C. Earl Ramsey, Claude Rawson, George Starr, and Jim and Connie Thorson. The two anonymous readers of my manuscript at Oxford University Press generously gave me the benefit of their knowledge and saved me from a number of embarrassing errors. My editor, Shannon McLachlan, her assistant, Abby Russell, and production editor

Linda Donnelly all contributed their efficient expertise to the publication process. The frontispiece photograph requires almost as many individual thank-you's as the entire book: first, to St. Patrick's Hospital, Dublin, for its permission to take the photograph and its patience as the project required successive efforts; next, to Robert Mahony and William McCormack—who, in a spirit of friendship and collegiality, did their best to take the photo themselves; and lastly, to Andrew Carpenter for connecting me with Davison and Associates, whose professionals succeeded in producing the photo used in the book.

Robert J. Barnett, Jr., my husband, has always been the last word in matters of style: he has never failed to improve a sentence I have brought to him. He has, as always, my grateful appreciation.

Stephen Kennamer, my brother, went far beyond the call of sibling loyalty to read my entire manuscript and advise me on everything from hyphens and commas (many more needed) on up to the most vexing questions about Swift and women. His rigor has made this a better book. I can't thank him enough, nor, indeed, any of the people who have contributed to my writing of this book.

Finally, I wish to acknowledge the importance of my family to any work that I do: my husband Robert; my two sons and their wives, Rob and Laura and Greg and Sylvia; and my grandsons, Nicholas, Alec, and Harry. They have, as always, my love and gratitude.

CONTENTS

ABBREVIATIONS

I have listed below editions of Swift's writings and other frequently-cited works, along with the abbreviations used to refer to them. Not all volumes of the Woolley edition of Swift's correspondence have yet been published, so I have cited the older Williams edition for later letters.

BP   Barber, Mary. *The Poetry of Mary Barber.* Edited by Bernard Tucker. Lewiston, Maine: Edwin Mellen Press, 1992.

C   *The Correspondence of Jonathan Swift.* Edited by Harold Williams. 5 vols. Oxford: Clarendon Press, 1963–65.

CP   *Jonathan Swift: The Complete Poems.* Edited by Pat Rogers. New Haven: Yale University Press, 1983.

E   Irvin Ehrenpreis. *Swift: The Man, His Works, and the Age.* Vol. 1, London: Methuen, 1962; vols. 2 and 3, Cambridge, Mass.: Harvard University Press, 1967, 1983.

JS   *Journal to Stella.* Edited by Harold Williams. 2 vols. Oxford: Clarendon Press, 1948.

N   David Nokes. *Jonathan Swift, A Hypocrite Reversed.* Oxford: Oxford University Press, 1985.

OED   *The Oxford English Dictionary.* 2nd ed. 20 vols. Oxford: Clarendon Press, 1989.

P   Laetitia Pilkington. *The Memoirs of Mrs. Laetitia Pilkington.* Edited by A. C. Elias, Jr. 2 vols. Athens: University of Georgia Press, 1997.

PS   *The Poems of Jonathan Swift.* Edited by Harold Williams. 2nd ed. 3 vols. Oxford: Clarendon Press, 1958.

PW   *The Prose Works of Jonathan Swift.* Edited by Herbert Davis. 14 vols. Oxford: Clarendon Press, 1937–68.

W   *The Correspondence of Jonathan Swift, D.D.* Edited by David Woolley. 4 vols. Frankfurt am Main: Peter Lang, 1999–.

Jonathan Swift
IN THE COMPANY OF WOMEN

It is said of the Horses in the Vision, that their Power was in their Mouths and in their Tails. What is said of Horses in Vision, may be said of Women in reality.

—*Thoughts on Various Subjects*

I cannot call to mind that I ever once heard her make a wrong judgment of persons, books, or affairs. Her advice was always the best, and with the greatest freedom, mixt with the greatest decency. She had a gracefulness somewhat more than human in every motion, word, and action. Never was there so happy a conjunction of civility, freedom, easiness and sincerity.

—*On the Death of Mrs. Johnson*

Introduction

Jonathan Swift's relations with women, and certain representations of women in his writings, have elicited strong reactions and tempted speculation from his own time to ours. Swift never married, and, although opinions differ, there is no evidence that he ever had a sexual relationship. Sexual pleasure is not alluded to in his writing, much less valorized, and implicit references to sex are negative: the commercial sex of prostitution, with its attendant diseases; the passion of wellborn women for socially inferior men or elderly men for young women; the lust of the female Yahoo for Gulliver.[1]

As a satirist, Swift is often didactic, but when he turns his attention to a couple's wedding night and sermonizes about proper marital behavior, sex is eclipsed by excretion. The closest thing to an embrace of ordinary eroticism in Swift comes from the highly problematic speaker of *The Lady's Dressing Room*:

> Should I the queen of love refuse,
> Because she rose from stinking ooze? (*CP* 452)

Swiftian references to gods and goddesses are usually ironic, but even if "queen of love" is accepted as a positive allusion to Aphrodite, the image is immediately undercut by "stinking ooze," an expression that forcibly recalls the smelly shit that has been the endless subject of the second half of the poem. While the amorous voyeur who has toured the lady's dressing room is overcome both literally and metaphorically by her excrement, lamenting "Oh! Celia, Celia, Celia shits!" (*CP* 451), the speaker does not disavow the association of women with various kinds of filth; he merely observes that it can be disregarded—"If Strephon would but stop his nose"—in order to obtain pleasure. Like Strephon, he agrees that women are "gaudy *tulips* raised from *dung*" (*CP* 452). Both Strephon and the speaker represent familiar male points of view, one an immature romanticism that inevitably leads to disillusionment, the other a willingness to use women while deprecating them.

Swift's writings contain many negative representations of women like that of Celia in *The Lady's Dressing Room*, some of which simply reflect the common consensus of his world while others cross the line into misogyny. Probably one of the most reliable portraits of what Swift disliked in women on a visceral level occurs in his polemical essay *The Story of the Injured Lady*: personifying Scotland, he writes, "She hath a stinking Breath, and twenty ill Smells about her besides; which are yet more unsufferable by her natural Sluttishness; for she is always lousy, and never without the Itch" (*PW* 9:3). The primary emphasis is on violations of cleanliness, especially those that produce unpleasant odors—which, as the poems about excreting and decaying women illustrate, Swift regards as worse offenses in women than in men.

In addition to specifics, Swift often deployed numbers in aid of his arguments, as he does when the modest proposer buttresses his case for cannibalism with statistics. A similar computation produces the number of upper-class sons who are "tolerably educated, with a sufficient share of good sense"—a mere thousand. Of comparable women, he believed there were only five hundred, signifying that half the men of sense must "couple themselves with women for whom they can possibly have no esteem; I mean fools, prudes, coquettes, gamesters, saunterers, endless talkers of nonsense, splenetic idlers, intriguers, given to scandal and censure" (*PW* 4:228). The unfinished essay ends abruptly with this typically Swiftian catalogue of pejorative labels, which may obscure the realization that Swift finds half of marriageable daughters acceptable—and wishes his society would produce more.

At the same time that he castigated women as a sex and as a gender, Swift also compiled a positive record of friendship with and approbation of individual women. The closest and most satisfying of his relationships with women was with Esther Johnson, an intimate friendship that endured from youth into middle age and ended only with her death. Swift's relationship with Esther Vanhomrigh, governed above all by its clandestine nature, seemed to follow the course of a passionate love affair in which Swift constantly assured her of his esteem while also tiring of her demands. Socially, he always saw a large number of women and liked many of them. It would be difficult to prove that he was more demanding in his choice of close female friends than male: he was discriminating about both. Moreover, he wrote of the desirability of educating women and the ungendered nature of virtue and vice.

As epigraphs to this book I have juxtaposed two passages that exemplify Swift writing in propria persona, owning his words (although, in the first instance, not publicly) as those of the man, Jonathan Swift, rather than attributing them to a created character or disembodied voice. The second passage, a generous appreciation of a woman's character, comes from his memorialization of Esther Johnson,

"Stella," written immediately after her death and under some evident physical and psychological duress. It illustrates that side of Swift that valued particular women—not only Stella but others whose company he enjoyed and who sought him out as friends, admirers, and protégées. In these women he found praiseworthy qualities of character and intellect that, he believed, set them apart from the ordinary run of women. Throughout his mature life Swift had such women friends, and to those who aspired to literary attainments he could be remarkably generous. He depended on Stella, during their more than a quarter century association in Ireland as his "greatest friend," the person who was an integral part of his social circle in Dublin, nursed him when he was ill, transcribed his poems, and received all the news of his life when he was away in London, including his most personal hopes and fears.

The other passage, drawn from Swift's unpublished writings, reflects the sharply different feelings he had when he thought of women not as individuals he knew and liked but as a gender. Here they are reduced to a crude physical stereotype of mouths and genitals, a representation that was commonplace in the seventeenth century.[2] Such tracts as George Webb's *The Arraignment of an Unruly Tongue* (1619) and Robert Harper's *The Anatomy of a Woman's Tongue* (1638) exemplify the criticisms of women whose speech violated decorum, a condition that portended more serious missteps:

> A Wretched Woman strove to wear the Breeches,
> And, to her Husband, us'd uncivil Speeches.[3]

These two activities of women, uncivil speaking and usurping male prerogatives, went together in the patriarchal social vision of Swift's time.[4] Conversation, unlike the "Ill Words [that] are worse than Poison now and then," is an ordered, civil kind of speech in which, ideally, nothing is said to discomfit a participant.[5] Swift's references to Stella are full of praise for her conversation, the only conversation, he once wrote, that made life tolerable. To her suitor he asserted that "I never saw that person whose conversation I entirely valued but hers" (W 1:53). Continuing, he described what made her conversation so appealing: "I have no-where met with a humour, a wit, or conversation so agreeable, a better portion of good sense, or a truer judgment of men and things" (W 1:154). Stella's conversation, then, is an example of ideal civilized speech: agreeable, sensible, truthful. Unlike the stereotype of women's unchecked chattering, her speaking manifests no agenda of preempting male authority.

For Swift, the power of the tail, sexuality, would be another form of illegitimate female power. It represented a feeling capable of destroying both reason and order, ultimately causing men to abdicate their authority in allowing themselves "to be undone, by the Vanity, the Folly, the Pride, and Wantonness of their Wives, who under their present Corruptions seem to be a kind of animal suffered for our sins to be sent into the world for the Destruction of Familyes, Societyes, and Kingdoms" (*PW* 12:80). This sweeping charge is made in Swift's anonymously published *Answer to Several Letters from Unknown Persons*, but there is no reason to think of the speaker as other than Swift. He published subversive tracts anonymously to avoid prosecution, not to advance views he did not hold. On the contrary, anonymity gave him freedom to express his own positions strongly.[6] To get people's attention, especially to move them to overcome inertia and change their behavior, any activist will paint the situation in the most apocalyptic colors, and Swift is no exception: exaggeration is part of his stock in trade as a satirist and a polemicist. His characterization of ungoverned wives as "the highest Indignity to human nature" is hyperbolic, but this does not mean that he does not see them as potential agents of societal ruin. The satirist of the Irish tracts is not engaging in comic exaggeration: he is a bitter prophet of doom.

To better examine Swift's multiform attitudes and writings about women, I intend to place him in the context of seventeenth- and early-eighteenth-century writers on women—most, like himself, clergymen—and, occasionally, in the company of Daniel Defoe, the great writer of fiction and fellow propagandist of the Harley ministry who was his close contemporary.[7] It has been overly tempting for critics to join Swift and Pope in light of their friendship and collaborative publications, but in many respects they are not well suited to such assimilation. Born twenty-one years after Swift, Pope is a true man of the eighteenth century, who also belonged to the minority Catholic culture of his time. Although both writers had long involvements with women they did not marry, the two situations differ: most significantly, Pope probably wanted to marry "Patty" Blount; Swift was content with a companionate relationship with Esther Johnson.[8] Further, where the posthumously born Swift was virtually an orphan, spending some years of infancy away from his mother and then placed by her in his uncle's large household, Pope remained first with his parents and then with his mother alone almost until his own death. Swift generally had no love of his relations; Pope was part of a warm extended family from birth. These are significant differences.

Most tellingly, Pope could express a strong sympathy for women who were mistreated by husbands or male guardians. As Valerie Rumbold writes, "His passionate advocacy of oppressed wives in a society where the rights of a husband were paramount implies considerable moral courage."[9] Swift's moral courage was reserved for other venues: he tended to respond harshly to women who transgressed, regardless of the provocation. When he intervened in a marriage, it was in the form of a letter to a young bride, sternly, even contemptuously, advising her on how she must behave to remain of interest to her husband. Pope's intervention in the marital conflicts of the Westons and the Copes was entirely on the side of women he perceived to be injured.

Swift and Defoe were not friends: disliking dissenters of all stripes, Swift once referred to the author of the *Review* as one of two "stupid, illiterate scribblers, both of them fanatics by profession" (*PW* 3:13). Defoe was not actually a fanatic, but, as John Ross concludes, "Swift simply and automatically regarded Defoe as a being of another and inferior world."[10] His dislike was impersonal, both religion- and class-based, and as a tradesman's son Defoe always felt vulnerable to such judgments. He demonstrated his inability to forget or forgive by taking hostile swipes at Swift throughout his career. As late as 1726, in a pamphlet on Peter, the wild boy discovered in Germany, Defoe makes a sudden turn to attack Swift:

> I am mighty willing to leave it to the learned Dr. S——; for he that can Preach and read Prayers in the Morning, write Baudy in the Afternoon, banter Heaven and Religion and write prophanely at Night, and then read Prayers and Preach again the next Morning, and so on in a due Rotation of Extremes; is much fitter than I am for turning the Tears of the Unhappy into a Ballad, and making a Mock of human Misery.[11]

Defoe's attack captures Swift's unsettling ability to play both subversive and orthodox roles that many of Swift's contemporaries distrusted, the same quality that informs his writing about women. (Swift ignored all of Defoe's provocations.)

However much they disagreed on religious doctrine, the two writers can be fruitfully compared on the subject of women. In an illuminating essay entitled "The Feminism of Daniel Defoe," Katharine Rogers compares Defoe to Fielding, Steele, Lord Halifax, Richardson, and Astell, yet many of the feminist positions she ascribes to Defoe could equally be found in Swift.[12] On moral issues in general, Swift is close to such Puritans as Milton and Defoe; all three are passionate believers in intellectual companionship as an integral part of marriage. When Defoe writes that "Chastity is a virtue much talked of, little practised," he expresses a cynicism that Swift embodies in a full-scale fantasy of feeding brides who only pretend to chastity to hungry lions.[13] The two also share a concern with what is proper in the marriage relation, a concern that surfaces fitfully in Swift but was addressed by Defoe in a book of 406 pages, *Conjugal Lewdness*. Swift has lately been hailed as a proponent of equality for women, an area in which his ideas are outstripped not only by contemporary women, like Mary Astell and Bathsua Makin, but by Defoe.[14]

Swift's assertion in a letter to Stella that "Order governs the world. The Devil is the author of confusion" merely prefaces an explanation of his system for filing letters (*JS* 72), but it functions in his thought and writings as a foundational principle. Swift was devoted to order, which he ascribed to God as both its source and enforcer. He regarded religion as the means by which unruly humanity can be threatened and cajoled into some semblance of orderly existence. Religion is therefore the dominant political issue for him, and he brings to it all the intolerance and acrimony of the century of his birth and education. Lacking any authoritative parental figure, Swift found stability in the teachings and institutionalism of the Church of England, the one constant in his life.

A desire for order manifests itself everywhere in Swift, from a scrupulous adherence to "proper" behaviors on a personal level to the categorizing and controlling of social groups wherever possible. He strenuously opposed the participation of dissenting Protestants and Catholics in civil life, and he wished to have Irish beggars wear badges indicating their parish of origin.[15] Women, in Swift's view, were a special danger when they escaped the fixed sphere of their prescribed existence and arrogated to themselves various male prerogatives.[16] By freely circulating in society, they eluded male hegemony and thus required severe measures.[17]

Women in Swift's writings are also represented as unruly bodies that inappropriately urinate and defecate, produce ordinary substances like snot, and exhibit running sores, but Swift never names or alludes to the bodily discharge exclusive to the female body—menstrual blood. That other feminine fluid, breast milk, also does not appear but may be inferred by references to breast-feeding. Maternity is most notable in its absence from Swiftian texts. Those references that exist are almost entirely unsympathetic and even unfeeling. Finding so much of humankind culpable in one way or another, Swift seems to have felt that most reproduction was also blameworthy.

If Swift had been a religious thinker rather than a cleric who saw religion as an essential pillar of state and society, his sermons might have been memorable vehicles of his commitment to order. Instead, his genius was satiric, which meant that he was always writing about, even at times wallowing in, those subversive and disorderly materials his texts condemned. His extraordinary visual imagination and his appetite for detail, wedded to the power of his writing, resulted in such vivid and energetic descriptions of disorder that some critics have believed him to be secretly or unconsciously on the side of chaos. But embracing these materials in literature is not the same thing as embracing them in reality.

The first part of my book will have a biographical focus, because Swift's deep and long-term relationships with Esther Johnson and Esther Vanhomrigh (Stella and Vanessa), the earlier, ill-fated engagement to Jane Waring (Varina), and the later association with women who became part of his circle furnish useful ideas about what qualities Swift approved in women—and the distance he needed to impose between himself and even a highly valued woman. Although no strict separation is possible, Part II emphasizes Swift writing about women as a gender, taking up first his attitude toward maternity, then the continuing issue of misogyny, and finally his history as a subject of criticism by women.

What Swift as a satirist most objects to are departures from an order of human affairs established by reason and traditional pieties. In his view, some of the most persistent violators of order are women, but the major part of what is negative in his attitude toward women, or in his literary representations of them, is quite orthodox religious and social doctrine of his time. It would be unfair to label Swift a misogynist merely because he has the gift to express this received wisdom with such creative verve and energy, but it is worthwhile distinguishing between those ideas that characterized his time and those that exhibit a peculiarly Swiftian animus.

Recent advances in women's history have provided far more detailed evidence about the lives of women in Swift's time than was available to previous generations of critics and biographers. But this is only one part of the equation: in every society, whatever its gender premises, some men have liked and valued women as a sex while others have regarded them with loathing. Swift continues to fascinate readers because he holds both of these attitudes without any sense of contradiction. At first glance this might seem resolvable by Swift's granting favored women the status of exceptions to the general rule: he knew and liked women who were sensible and intelligent, and not surprisingly, their habits of mind and conversation reminded him of men. But even these women had female bodies, and Swift perceived such bodies as disgustingly other, the "nauseous unwholesom living Carcase" that he inveighs against in one of his bitter Irish tracts (*PW* 12:80). No doubt for his own psychic comfort, Swift kept these two views of women in rigorously separated compartments, an artificial separation that has led some critics in various eras, including our own, to privilege one of his ideas of women and ignore the other. It has been easy for both sides to produce supporting data: outraged defenders of womanhood have no difficulty finding misogyny, while male defenders of Swift and their new feminist allies are equally adept at flourishing evidence of Swift's respect and admiration for a number of women friends. If this dichotomy leads to a skewed perspective, the twentieth-century predilection for neat psychological formulas presents another way of misreading Swift. I hope to keep these temptations in mind while examining all aspects of Jonathan Swift in the company of women.

Part I

JONATHAN SWIFT IN THE COMPANY OF WOMEN

She delighted him with love, but did not tempt him with lust; she pleased him with discourse and sweet societie, yet provoked him to no libidinous desire.

—Thomas Heywood, Gynaikeion

1

*L*ove Dramas

The great statesmen who fretted their busy hour upon the stage of life have sunk
into the gulf of nothingness—but the pale, beautiful, shadowy forms of Stella and
Vanessa are still beside us, even as they passed from this life weeping.

—Lady Wilde

Swift's general condemnations of women as a frivolous sex provide a context for
his praise of the two women with whom he had long and admiring relationships,
Stella and Vanessa;[1] in fact, he praises the two favored women only by imagining them as different from all other women, who are, for him, appalling Others:
monkeys,[2] disgusting female Yahoos, a tribe of bold, swaggering, rattling ladies,
unclean belles, or decaying prostitutes. The women Swift liked and approved
for their nonphysical attributes had bodies, too, but he preferred to look away
from this reality and foreground those character traits that qualified them for his
friendship. References to the beauty of Stella and Vanessa are abstract and hurriedly presented; in the poems for Stella, allusions to her physical person typically
draw attention to the effects of age. Swift intends to draw a sharp line when he
tells Vanessa that compared to her other women are *bestes en juppes*, but of course
Vanessa, too, is an animal in skirts, that is, a physical being underneath her clothing—even if Swift is determined to ignore it. *Why* he wanted to ignore it seems
clear enough on a surface level: bodies suggest the sexual relationship Swift did
not want to have with Stella or Vanessa, or indeed, once the pattern of his adult
life was established, with any woman.

Where this reluctance originally came from is less obvious. Earlier centuries
were content to ascribe all of Swift's peculiarities to some dark defect that ultimately manifested itself in madness. Or, less melodramatically, to conclude, following Swift's own early description of himself as hard to please and possessed of
a cold temperament, that he was constitutionally unsuited to matrimony.[3] Swift's
major twentieth-century academic biographers, Irvin Ehrenpreis and David

Nokes, have been more inclined to psychological explanations based on his father-lessness.[4] As a posthumous child Swift was indeed fatherless, but during the criti-cal years of early childhood he was also motherless, removed from his mother for at least two years during infancy, the critical period of maternal bonding, and then, as a small boy, placed in his uncle Godwin Swift's household when his mother left Ireland for Leicester—taking his older sister with her.[5] This was, from an eigh-teenth-century standpoint, perfectly reasonable. The impecunious widow would have seen the opportunity to position her son in an affluent relative's household as desirable; most likely, a girl could not have been similarly placed, and in any case the connection between Abigail Swift and her daughter, uninterrupted from birth, was arguably more emotionally powerful. For all of its lack of nurturing, belong-ing to his uncle's family gave Swift access to the education he needed to make his way in the world.

The great difficulty with the conclusion that Swift was predisposed to celibacy from an early age is what we know of his history as a young man. When he spent several months with his mother in 1689, he apparently worried her by a serious flirtation with one Betty Jones.[6] This was followed by a significant relationship with Jane Waring, the cousin or sister of one of his Trinity College classmates and the modestly well-off daughter of a deceased clergyman, living in Belfast with her widowed mother and some seven siblings. Swift not only proposed marriage to the woman he styled "Varina," he wrote to her impatiently to urge an immediate betrothal, presumably to be followed by marriage as soon as this was financially possible. And although it is conventional to characterize Swift as young at the time, the better to dismiss the episode, he was almost twenty-nine when he wrote the only such confession of erotic feeling to be found in his writings: "A violent desire is little better than a distemper, and therefore men are not to blame in looking after a cure. I find myself hugely infected with this malady" (W 1:124). The language of disease is markedly unfelicitous, but Swift seems to be genuinely possessed of the very urgency he had criticized four years earlier in those "hon-est young men, who perhaps are too litteral in rather marrying than burning" (W 1:105). His strongest attempt to move Varina is through a lightly veiled allusion to sexual pleasure, a unique positive reference:

> Surely, Varina, you have but a very mean opinon of the joys that accompany a true, honourable, unlimited love; yet either nature and our ancestors have hugely deceived us, or else all other sublunary things are dross in comparison. Is it possible you can be yet insensible to the prospect of rapture and delight so innocent and so exalted? Trust me, Varina, Heaven has given us nothing else worth the loss of a thought. Ambition, high appearance, friends, and fortune, are all tasteless and insipid when they come in competition. (W 1:126)

Not only does Swift never write like this again; his other treatments of sex are bru-tally satiric and cynical. Yet in spite of the unusual content of this passage, the accu-satory tone is recognizably Swiftian: he is hectoring and denunciatory throughout the letter, effectively overwhelming the few expressions that suggest affection:

It was your pity opened the first way to my misfortune; and now your love is finishing my ruin. . . .

. . . By Heaven, Varina, you are more experienced, and have less virgin innocence than I. . . .

. . . The little disguises, and affected contradictions of your sex, were all (to say the truth) infinitely beneath persons of your pride and mine; paltry maxims that they are, calculated for the rabble of humanity. . . . No, Madam, I will give you no more of my unhappy temper, though I derive it all from you. (W 1:126–27)

There is a particularly bitter accusation, probably alluding to the Waring family's understandable concern over Swift's slender finances: "One settlement of separate maintenance, well engrossed, would have more charms than all the wit or passion of a thousand letters. And I'll maintain it, any man had better have a poor angel to his rival than the devil himself if he was rich" (W 1:125). The conclusion is a threat: "Only remember, that if you still refuse to be mine, you will quickly lose, for ever lose, him that is resolved to die as he has lived, all yours" (W 1:127). Waring did not accept Swift's ultimatum, but in spite of his threat their relationship continued: several other letters, now lost, survived for a time, as well as the presumably final letter of 1700.[7] One of these was written only two months after Swift vowed that a negative response would lose his love forever (W 1:128n).

Above all, the first of the two surviving letters suggests anger at the woman addressed. In the five-thousand-year tradition of her sex, according to Swift, Varina has induced him to love her, only to contrive his ruin; she is governed by "paltry maxims" that place material considerations over the physical and emotional satisfaction of marriage; all her wrongheaded concerns are delaying their union. The letter contains some endearments, but they are overwhelmed by the hostility of the language; compared to Swift's later affectionate utterances to both Stella and Vanessa, the brief invocations of positive feeling for Varina appear forced.

More than any of Swift's own explanations for avoiding marriage—his "cold" temperament, his lack of sufficient income—this letter explains why he would never marry in spite of his sermonizing on the joys of the marriage bed. In his eyes, women, and this particular woman, are too deeply flawed; even in the grip of a strong sexual desire Swift cannot conceal his exasperation. Like some contemporary writers of advice manuals, and like the majority of those who satirize women at this time, Swift prefers enumerating female defects to any other form of engagement. And so he is deflected from writing a love letter that praises the beloved to composing an accusatory bill of particulars: like others of her treacherous sex, Varina has done *this* while failing to do *that* and in the process come close to forfeiting his love. Only an immediate submission to his will in the form of accepting his proposal, he writes, will save their relationship. Otherwise, he concludes dramatically, she can expect never to see him again.

Critics have often found the second of Swift's two surviving letters to Varina cruel or brutal in its deprecating references to her personal cleanliness, slurs on her family, and list of demands, but it is scarcely more insulting and peremptory than the first letter. Still, the idea embraced by some biographers that Swift never seriously wanted to marry Jane Waring is unpersuasive. The first letter reveals the stimulus of feeling, however much the rhetoric repels. In all likelihood, Swift had never written a proposal of marriage before and was torn between his desire and the strictures imposed by both the conventions of courtship and his own inflexible temperament. He had already identified a destructive paradigm in the behavior of young men he knew, one that his friend Thomas Sheridan, reflecting on his own unhappy marriage, would describe succinctly: "I was in the mad years of life when [I] marryed & mad to marry, & almost mad after I had marry[ed]."[8] Swift had said in his letter to John Kendall that he was determined to avoid a mistake that he had amply observed in others (W 1:104–5).

After the collapse of her relationship with Swift, Jane Waring did not marry either, but this may not have reflected her wishes. Her years of greatest marriageability were part of a period in English history when there was a notable difference between the number of marriageable men and women, to the disadvantage of women.[9] And, as the anonymous *Woman Triumphant* (1712) observed, women were not the initiators of courtship: "Men court the women, and not women the men; which is a shrew'd token of the bashfulness of the one, and the boldness of the other: For maids, if they are so unfortunate as to fall in love, will rather choose to die, than to declare it to the person, so great is their modesty."[10]

The second letter to Jane Waring, dated Dublin, May 4, 1700, seems to be a response to a letter of hers complaining of Swift's neglect and wondering if another woman has claimed his attention—proof that their relationship had continued beyond the deadline Swift had imposed in 1696 and had endured for a number of years.[11] In his reply, Swift is eager to demonstrate that he has been right in all the issues where they have disagreed and been guilty of nothing in his behavior toward her. For him to deny the existence of another woman seems untruthful: less than a year later he would persuade Stella to move to Ireland, and in 1704 he would tell William Tisdall that if he had ever thought of marriage himself, she would have been his choice (W 1:153).

The cold letter to Waring, in which she is no longer addressed as Varina but only as "madam," subjects her to a barrage of criticism that once again masquerades as part of a reasonable discourse between a couple considering marriage: "I had used a thousand endeavours and arguments to get you from the company and place you are in. . . . All I had in answer from you, was nothing but a great deal of arguing, and sometimes in a stile so very imperious, as I thought might have been spared, when I reflected how much you had been in the wrong" (W 1:140–41). A similar accusation was to be made some twenty years later about Stella, in *To Stella, Who Collected and Transcribed His Poems*:[12]

> And when a friend in kindness tries
> To show you where your error lies,
> Conviction does but more incense;
> Perverseness is your whole defence:
> Truth, judgement, wit, give place to spite,
> Regardless both of wrong and right. (*CP* 206)

The poetic rendition of Stella's "*only* fault" is cushioned by compliment, but it consumes more than half the poem, including the telling conclusion. In the last stanza Swift suggests that Stella may fail to copy the lines of criticism or worse, destroy them:

> Whene'er they burn, if burn they must,
> They'll prove my accusation just. (*CP* 207)

The interruptive clause is swallowed up by the progress of the sentence that surrounds it, which has the effect of confirming Stella's destruction of the offensive lines *and* the accuracy of Swift's criticism. Stella is thus doubly placed in the wrong in spite of the praise that precedes the "accusation."

The similar charges leveled against Waring—being in the wrong and not admitting it—are proffered more sternly than those aimed at Stella because Swift's relationship to Varina is more adversarial, more a contest of social and economic worth. Since matrimony is in prospect, more depends upon his victory. Endearments are absent: when Swift refers to their union, it is in the unfeeling terms of a contractual arrangement in which the addressed party must fulfill certain conditions: "These are the questions I have always resolved to propose to her with whom I meant to pass my life; and whenever you can heartily answer them in the affirmative, I shall be bless'd to have you in my arms, without regarding whether your person be beautiful, or your fortune large" (W 1:143). Because Waring's fortune was *not* large, Swift's comment is an unsubtle reminder that for all her hesitation over his financial resources, she has no fortune that would recommend her to him. The expression of indifference to her physical attractiveness is also a gratuitous unkindness. Swift's final words baldly communicate his sense of having been ill treated: "I singled you out at first from the rest of women, and I expect not to be used like a common lover" (W 1:143). Jane Waring might not have appreciated the honor bestowed upon her, or thought that her differences of opinion from Swift constituted an affront, but he had been deeply offended, so much so that he would never again place himself in a position of such vulnerability. No more transparent statement of Swift's feelings exists in his writings than this closing of his accounts with Varina.

Jane Waring fits uneasily in the biographical patterns generally imposed on Swift's life: only by doing violence to the evidence can she be dismissed as a nonserious interest. At the time of their courtship, Swift was an inexperienced suitor: while the letters to Varina reveal his rhetorical skill and the force of his personality, they are not the polished performances of a man who willingly submits to the conventions of the genre. Ironically, in a way the mature Swift would have hated, the letters are variations on a lover's lament of the mistress's abuse, a genre Vanessa was to perfect from the point of view of the neglected mistress. What they finally reveal about Swift is his need to control—to be acknowledged as in the right, to be met with acquiescence rather than argument—and his strong sense of injury because he has not received this submission. Swift's last words to Varina assert that she has not responded to the signal honor of being chosen by him and has instead treated him like a "common lover," something he will not stand for. He will give no other woman the opportunity to humiliate him in this fashion.[13]

Varina is the first of the three love interests in Swift's life to be placed by some biographers, notably Ehrenpreis and Nokes, in the category of "frail and fatherless." For Ehrenpreis, Swift's loss of his father before birth is crucial: "On those whom he loved, he would bestow, as his best gift, a fatherliness too stern for their needs, or a father's direction where they looked for a lover's softness" (E 1:32–33). Frailty enhanced the woman's vulnerability and need for a substitute father. By the writing of the third volume of his biography of Swift, Ehrenpreis describes Swift's proclivity as "his addiction to first-born, fatherless girls in poor health and much younger than himself" (E 3:391).

Observing that the two women with whom Swift formed long relationships were both frail and fatherless inevitably suggests that part of what attracted Swift to a particular woman was this conjunction, yet there are problems with both designations. Gentlewomen of the period overwhelmingly presented themselves as frail or delicate because it was a class convention of femininity, and both men and women often thought of women as "the frail sex." Bernard Mandeville, in his medical treatise on hypochondria and hysteria, observed that "Women are not of that robust Constitution as Men are. . . . Their Frame, tho' less firm, is more delicate."[14] Female indispositions were magnified rather than diminished, in keeping with the notion that only coarse natures were strong and healthy. At the same time, due to the still primitive condition of medicine, poor nutrition and sanitation, and other factors bearing on health, many women were prey to real illnesses of all sorts and were regarded as "more susceptible to ailments than men."[15] Their general reputation for poor health seems to have been socially and culturally determined: men, because of their multiple public roles, might be less likely to take to their beds; upper- and middle-class women would find it more acceptable to indulge their indispositions. Mandeville thought that in addition to many errors of diet, "their idle Life, and Want of Exercise" predisposed women to hysteria, a catchall diagnosis for a range of symptoms. He concluded that their "innumerable Disorders" were, above all, the consequence of "the menstural Flux, and the whole *Uterus*."[16]

We have no data suggesting that Vanessa was particularly frail or ill until late in her life, when she probably became tubercular as a result of long exposure to her dying sister. Given the extremely contagious nature of the disease, an entire family might succumb once one member became infected. It is possible, as Sybil le Brocquy suggests in *Cadenus*, that this was the case with the Vanhomrighs. Mrs. Vanhomrigh and her four children all died within a span of time suggestive of serial tubercular infection.[17] Jane Waring's health is referred to as one of the reasons for delaying her marriage to Swift, but his letters are too unspecific to reach a conclusion about the nature or severity of her illness.

If Swift desired to play the father to a frail and fatherless woman, the daughter figure would naturally be younger than himself. That Swift regarded a susceptibility to younger women as a danger he might be predisposed to is borne out by those curious resolutions he made at the age of thirty-two entitled "When I come to be old." He resolved "not to marry a young Woman" or "conceive I can be loved by a young woman" (*PW* 1:xxxvii–viii), but after Stella's death in Swift's sixty-first year he became fond of a series of much younger women: among others, Laetitia Pilkington, Mary Kelly, Anne Acheson, and Mary Pendarves. Swift always had younger male friends as well. His closest Irish friends, Patrick Delany and Thomas Sheridan, were a generation younger, as were Alexander Pope, John Gay, and Charles Ford. Andrew Fountaine and Bolingbroke were younger than Swift by a decade or more.

Jane Waring, however, was only five years younger than Swift, hardly enough—given the habits of marriage of the time—to qualify as a preference for a younger woman. Even the age difference between Swift and first Stella (fourteen years) and then Vanessa (twenty-one years) would hardly be unusual in marriage partners: although an extreme disparity might be commented on, factors other than age were usually regarded as more critical to marital unions. Moreover, Swift himself was not old when he contracted the intimate relationships with Stella and Vanessa that would last their lifetimes.

Following Ehrenpreis, Nokes represents Swift as enjoying with Varina "the form that suited him best, in which he was part father, part lover, and part tutor" (N 30). Ehrenpreis's belief that a fatherless man would seek to be a father to others ignores a larger social and cultural phenomenon: that women, recipients of such inferior educations vis-à-vis men, were always to some extent in the position of pupil or daughter figures to adult males, to whom they were expected to be subservient and respectful. Beyond their accepted subordinate status, women were always more limited in knowledge and experience—hence the natural assumption of a didactic and paternalistic stance on the part of men in their social sphere.

The biographical emphasis on fatherless girls assumes that Swift was consciously or unconsciously drawn to this aspect of their condition, either through the common bond of fatherlessness he shared with them or through a desire to play the role of father himself. In my opinion this is a misleading inference. Loneliness and proximity probably caused the attachments to Jane Waring and Stella to flourish, but there was no advantage to Swift in Waring's fatherlessness, since she was firmly embedded in her large family. That Swift wished to remove her from that space and place her in his own, as he succeeded in doing with Stella, is no more than any prospective husband might reasonably intend.

That Varina, Stella, and Vanessa all happened to be fatherless appeared more significant to twentieth-century critics than it would have to Swift's contemporaries. Fatherlessness, which Swift and his sister shared, was a common condition for both sexes in the late seventeenth and early eighteenth centuries, "an age of heavy mortality among men in their early prime."[18] In 1696, Gregory King suggested that there were as many as 250,000 widows in England and Wales, constituting an unusually high one-sixth of the adult female population and clearly comprising far more than elderly women.[19] Varina and Vanessa had lost their fathers as teenagers; only Stella had lacked a father much earlier, and only Stella was instructed by Swift from childhood, perhaps accounting in some measure for her greater tractability in conforming to his wishes. Equally important, as far as is known, Swift never had any conflict with Stella's remaining family, her mother and sister. His relations with them, as references in the *Journal to Stella* attest, appear to have been cordial, and there is no evidence that Stella's mother tried to interfere in her daughter's adult life, a prime source of disagreement between Swift and Varina.[20] Swift's constant presence in the Vanhomrigh house in London testifies as well to a positive relationship with Vanessa's widowed mother.

A traditional father would have kept Stella or Vanessa from entering Swift's orbit without some recognized declaration: each young woman would have remained under the paternal roof, protected from irregular arrangements of the sort that Swift came to have with both in Ireland. Yet the differences between Stella's and Vanessa's circumstances would seem to outweigh the similarities. Had Vanessa's father been alive, this would not have prevented Swift, as a distinguished guest in the household, from "instructing" her or becoming the inadvertent object of her passion. It would instead have saved him from a situation in which Vanessa had all too much freedom of action.

Rather than being attracted to fatherlessness in others and eager to play the role of the absent father, Swift remained a needy son well into his adult life, pinning his hopes on a series of older mentor figures. This is nowhere more starkly expressed than in his letter of May 18, 1727, to Archbishop King, where, angered into recklessness, he complained of a long series of slights: "From the very moment of the Queen's death, your Grace hath thought fit to take every opportunity of giving me all sorts of uneasiness, without ever giving me, in my whole life, one single mark of your favour, beyond common civilities" (W 3:87). King never recognized Swift as a surrogate son: while Swift longed for some sign of approval or tangible help from him, the archbishop aided his own blood relatives.

Monck Berkeley refers to Stella and Vanessa as "those two celebrated females, who bartered happiness for immortality."[21] The pairing of the two women is inevitable, an acknowledgment that both were connected to Swift in mysterious long-term relationships that tease the critic into speculation. In Berkeley's case, the word *barter* suggests an intentionality and calculation that we know are inappropriate: neither woman could have seen her life or the future in these terms. But Berkeley's attempt to impose a pattern, however far-fetched, is merely one example of many such efforts to find meaning in this peculiar triangle.[22] Following the more moralizing conclusion of the Earl of Orrery's *Remarks on the Life and Writings of Dr. Jonathan Swift*, Sir Walter Scott romantically attributes the deaths of the two women to their "disappointed hopes and ill-requited affection." As le Brocquy conjectured, it is more likely that Vanessa caught tuberculosis by nursing her fatally ill sister. Stella's complaint, which deprived her of appetite and was evidently painful, has never been specifically identified, although David Venturo rather puzzlingly claims that she was suffering from breast cancer.[23] In Orrery's early biography of Swift, Stella died "absolutely destroyed by the peculiarity of her fate," while Vanessa, a culpable party in the Earl's opinion, "perished ... under all the agonies of despair."[24] Thomas Beddoes, a late-eighteenth-century physician, also interpreted the deaths of Stella and Vanessa as brought about by their relations with Swift: "That the ladies themselves looked towards ordinary, solid, matrimonial love is too shockingly evinced by the shortened life of one, and the embittered death of the other."[25]

In life as in death: both women were devoted to Swift, but Stella accommodated herself to his strict requirements while Vanessa persistently—and sometimes violently—chafed against them. The situation invokes certain familiar male-perspective paradigms: the patient wife versus the tempestuous mistress; the selfless and reliable, if unexciting, partner opposed to the attractive but volatile temptress. Yet neither relationship was sanctioned by the legal recognition or social custom that contained the lives of most eighteenth-century women within the institutions of the family and marriage. If Swift did not confer the official status of marriage on Stella, he nevertheless found a way to integrate her into his respectable life; there was no such way for Vanessa. Her self-indulgent passion posed the constant threat of violating the boundaries Swift had drawn and creating the kind of scandal that he feared. Their relationship was marked by constant negotiation over when and under what circumstances he would see her, over her effort to instill obligation and his to escape it.

Down through history male critics have gallantly lauded Stella and condemned the importuning Vanessa as a usurper.[26] A view of the women as moral opposites jelled early. Shortly after Vanessa's death in 1723, Bishop Evans of Meath, an enemy of Swift, wrote to the Archbishop of Canterbury that Vanessa had died after discovering that the Dean was married to "Mrs. Johnson, a very good woman." Of Vanessa, he related, "'Tis generally believed that she lived without God in the world" and on her deathbed had turned away her parish clergyman.[27] The image of Vanessa as a sexually aggressive woman besieging the well-meaning Dean has also been remarkably long-lived, beginning with Bishop Berkeley's assurance to Dr. Delany that the Swift-Vanessa correspondence reflected badly on her and not on Swift.[28] Herbert Davis is in this tradition when he says of Vanessa, "She was of a very different temperament [than Stella]; and she failed him."[29] As Denis Johnston observed, "It is Vanessa who always has to pay, to keep Swift right with the world."[30]

No one has been more vehement in this camp than William Makepeace Thackeray, whose encomium to Stella is punctuated with several uses of the prized Victorian adjective *manly*. Addressing Stella directly, he claims, "You have had countless champions, millions of manly hearts mourning for you."[31] The "manly heart," Thackeray implies, will acknowledge Stella's claim to sympathy. While both women were "injured" by Swift, Vanessa is the interloper whose sexual aggression offends the nineteenth-century sensibility; Stella is the ideal woman and wife. "It is hardly surprising," Johnston writes, "that several generations of male Victorians have wept their great hearts out over Stella."[32] Yet Thackeray followed his celebration of Stella by noting that women of his acquaintance preferred Vanessa.[33] Perhaps these women responded to Vanessa's obvious unhappiness; they might also have admired her subversive self-assertion.

Critics have tended to accept at face value Swift's extravagant praise of Stella as a repository of virtues:[34] "She had an elevated understanding, with all the delicacy and softness of her sex. Her voice, however sweet in itself, was still rendered more harmonious by what she said."[35] This is Orrery, who, without any personal experience of either woman, began the predictable tradition of representing Stella and Vanessa as antipodal figures. If Stella is the perfect companion, accomplished but unassertive, happy within her circumscribed sphere, Vanessa is the interloper whose negative qualities foretell a fall from virtue: "fond of dress: impatient to be admired: very romantic in her turn of mind: superior, in her own opinion, to all her sex: full of pertness, gaiety, and pride."[36] Vanessa is dangerously unrestrained and ambitious: her sad end will be no surprise—will even, to the censorious Orrery, seem to some degree merited: "Thus perished at *Selbridge* . . . Mrs. Esther Vanhomrigh; a miserable example of an ill-spent life, fantastic wit, visionary schemes, and female weakness."[37] Yet the deserving Stella fares no better in Orrery's account: her lot is a longing for death to end her protracted suffering.

In examining Swift's relationship with Stella and Vanessa, I do not assume, as Nora Crow does, that "women bring to the interpretation of Swift certain gender-specific advantages over men."[38] I believe, however, that there is at times a gender difference in the evaluation of some data concerning Stella and Vanessa arising from the general premise that men and women may differ on the subject of what makes an exemplary female life. In his unfinished essay entitled *Of the Education of Ladies*, Swift touches on this point himself, describing a difference of opinion between men and women on the prudence of marrying a woman who has some qualities other than the domestic.[39]

Rather than focusing on dissimilarities of temperament, a feminist perspective would place Stella and Vanessa within the gender rubric of disadvantage and the significant difference that socioeconomic status made in their lives. Nevertheless, for Ann Cline Kelly, the two women are assimilated into one category, alike in independence. "Without husbands or fathers," she writes, "they manage their own money and have their own houses. Far from being trapped by home, hearth, and heritage, both women pull up stakes from England and move to Ireland."[40] For both women, the move was sensible: Stella could live less expensively in Ireland, while Vanessa had a considerable property there. And beyond these practical considerations, proximity to Swift beckoned, although he had tried to discourage Vanessa from coming. But neither woman had prospects in England that would counsel remaining there. That both lived "independently" blurs differences in circumstance that would have weighed heavily in their world. Stella had a household, shared with Rebecca Dingley, but she moved from one modest rented lodging to another; Vanessa owned a substantial house and surrounding acreage at Celbridge. Nor is it clear to what extent either woman managed her own money. Stella had very little, supplemented by Swift after she moved to Ireland. Vanessa was affluent, but she probably left most financial matters in the hands of her (male) lawyers and accountants: she often importunes Swift for his help, or pity, because of the tangled nature of her inheritance.

Stella had an acknowledged public role as Swift's friend, yet we know more about Vanessa, whose relationship to him was clandestine. In addition to what Vanessa's correspondence with Swift reveals of her nature and concerns, her family was prominent in Dublin: they can be placed more confidently than Stella's obscure antecedents. The very lack of any evidence of Stella that has not been channeled through Swift should be one of the most salient facts of her history. Marginalized in Swift's life, after her death, insofar as it was within his power, she was deliberately erased as an independent voice. Bridget Hill has observed this same process of erasure for the entire category of spinsters in the late seventeenth and early eighteenth centuries: "The possibility of a woman remaining unmarried was not acknowledged. It is this that makes spinsters such shadowy figures, often difficult to identify."[41] However different their circumstances, Stella and Vanessa were both spinsters.

Posterity would have much more of a sense of Stella's personality today if Swift had preserved even a few of the sixty-two letters she wrote to him between the spring of 1708 and June 6, 1713.[42] Stella is ironically memorable for this erasure—for the absence of enough information about her to form an opinion or reach a conclusion, and, above all, for the silence of her own voice except for its intermittent reflection in Swift's. Vanessa was also a target of erasure, but because of her independence of both class and spirit, the effort was only partially successful. Her correspondence was not within Swift's control, and although it was not published immediately, as she had instructed, it was preserved and later published. The poem Swift wrote for her, *Cadenus and Vanessa*, appeared in 1726, three years after her death.

While "Stella" and "Vanessa" are, in Swift's poetry, ideal literary heroines matched against both inferior real women and the falsely romantic creations of earlier bards, they are also individuals who were the first audience of the poems written for and about them. Considered together, the poems for both women yield more than they do when regarded separately. Swift wrote only two poems for Vanessa, but one of them is the longest of his poetic oeuvre; he wrote eleven poems for Stella, but all are relatively short: *Cadenus and Vanessa* is 897 lines, with the additional *Verses to Vanessa* contributing another twenty-six. Stella's eleven poems have a total of 764 lines.

The obvious differences between the poems for Stella and Vanessa are outweighed by what they have in common. All are compliments to their respective subjects, who are praised in much the same way; that is, as exceptional women with certain admirable masculine qualities. And both have the underlying aim of pacifying by means of praise the woman addressed or described. The differences in length, many short poems versus one long poem, reflect the differing challenges of the two endeavors. Although the poet's relationship with Stella is threatened by external forces (particularly the effects of time), his mastery, and the harmony between them, can always surmount all obstacles—even when one subtitle states that he was sick in bed at the time the poem needed to be produced. In *Cadenus and Vanessa*, the poet tackles a dangerously unstable situation and an intractable dilemma generated by the incompatible desires of the two protagonists. This struggle to resolve an impossible situation is a likely explanation of the poem's length and scope.

Swift is unusual for his day (and ours) in emphasizing other qualities than the physical in his poetic mistresses. Yet he does not disregard the physical entirely; he pays Stella and Vanessa the traditional compliment of beauty, but then indicates that qualities of mind and character are more praiseworthy and more enduring. Beyond this, he wants to eschew the usual language of the genre because, as Nora

Crow Jaffe writes, "it is trite, insincere, and effectively immoral."[43] While disavowing the common practice of poets of describing a woman as a goddess, Swift himself is willing to misrepresent his subject's age. But when he refers to Stella as "thirty-four (We shan't dispute a year or more)" (*CP* 187) when she is actually thirty-eight, the assertion becomes a playful joke, far removed from the untruths of the romantic apostrophe:

> So Maevius, when he drained his skull
> To celebrate some suburb trull;
>
> .   .   .   .
>
> Had gone through all the commonplaces
> Worn out by wits who rhyme on faces;
> Before he could his poem close,
> The lovely nymph had lost her nose. (*CP* 205–6)

To celebrate his unworthy subject Maevius must shuffle through the clichés that have already been invoked by a long line of poets whose subject is restricted to the physical. His stale untruths become farcical when the woman extolled becomes a grotesque, even as he is writing—a striking illustration of the impermanence of beauty and the lack of congruence between signifier and signified in conventional love poetry. Yet, just as Swift takes care not to truly denigrate Stella's appearance, he is guilty of the same kind of exaggeration that he loathes in descriptions of physical beauty when he extols her character:

> Heroes and heroines of old,
> By honour only were enrolled
> Among their brethren of the skies,
> To which (though late) shall Stella rise.
> Ten thousand oaths upon record,
> Are not so sacred as her word. (*CP* 202)[44]

Swift was primarily an occasional poet, and the occasion for seven of his poems for Stella was her birthday. How the tradition began is not known, but once the initial poem was produced for her birthday of March 13, 1719, verses on Stella's succeeding birthdays became obligatory. By the third year, Swift is referring to the poem as an "annual tribute," which he accepts as a task and Stella expects. By the next year, the tribute seems to be expected among their friends as well. Swift's playful narrative petitions Apollo for aid to save his face:

> I told him what the world would say
> If Stella were unsung today;
> How I should hide my head for shame,
> When both the Jacks and Robin came;
> How Ford would frown, how Jim would leer;
> How Sheridan the rogue would sneer. (*CP* 256)

The poet concludes this section: "Nor do I ask for Stella's sake; / 'Tis my own credit lies at stake" (*CP* 257). A similar enumeration of friends in Swift's poem *To Charles Ford, Esq. on His Birthday* also emphasizes the close-knit circle of kindred spirits that gathered around Swift:

> I throw into the bargain, Jim:
> In London can you equal him?
> What think you of my favourite clan,
> Robin and Jack, and Jack and Dan? (*CP* 255)[45]

In his effort to reconcile Ford to living in Dublin, Swift welcomes him into this group and proposes local counterparts for every London attraction, including Stella as a "middle-agéd charmer" to substitute for an English lady Ford admired. The poem's conclusion summonses the group to a game of whist. Stella was an established member of this happy company that shared so many amusements—exchanges of puns and satiric verses, card-playing, dining, and conversation—all of which relaxed merriment Vanessa was excluded from.

The other four poems for Stella also have specific but not recurring occasions: those that do not mark her birthday are dedicated to particular and identifiable activities suggested by their titles: *A Receipt to Restore Stella's Youth, Stella at Wood Park, To Stella, Who Collected and Transcribed His Poems,* and *To Stella, Visiting Me in My Sickness.* Two of these non-birthday poems place Stella outside Dublin and away from Swift's company in homes belonging to friends; the other two represent her as the poet's deeply valued friend who performs the practical and unromantic tasks of transcribing texts and administering medicine. Collecting and transcribing texts is a secretarial chore, while taking care of a sick person is nursing, but when assumed by a close friend rather than a paid worker, both are labors of love. Like the birthday poems, these two texts describe a comfortable equilibrium very different from the tension of the elaborate romantic narrative of *Cadenus and Vanessa. A Receipt to Restore Stella's Youth,* in which Stella is compared to a cow who needs to be rejuvenated through fattening up, is similarly unimaginable as a poem intended for the sensitive Vanessa, whom Swift rarely teases in his letters. In keeping with his different relationships with the two women, Swift would publish some of the Stella poems and resent the original publication of *Cadenus and Vanessa,* intended, like his letters to Vanessa, for no eyes but her own.

Like a significant group of Shakespeare's sonnets, the birthday poems establish the poet's mastery over the effects of time, although Swift's strategy is pointed toward the present while Shakespeare's is centered on the future. Shakespeare asserts the power of his art to preserve the subject's youth and beauty when its reality has been destroyed by time: "Yet do thy worst, old time; despite thy wrong / My love shall in my verse ever live young" (Sonnet 19).[46] Swift does not say that his poetry can outwit death or preserve a vanished beauty. His assertions are more modest and therefore more poignant: while Stella lives, he can find ways of minimizing the importance of aging, some of which, like the argument that his failing eyesight cannot see her wrinkles, are ingenious. Swift does not deny the wrinkles; he merely says that because of his weak eyes, he cannot see them and thus will not credit their existence. Time is acknowledged and then disarmed by its own effects, as if even absolute universal laws can be made to serve the Swift-Stella rapport. When Stella is dying, the poet simply reminds her that her life has been lived well. He makes no claims for the power of his art to preserve Stella in verse because that is irrelevant to his purpose: what is of primary importance to Swift is Stella herself, the person who distinctively makes his world in the here and now rather than serving as the occasion for a display of poetic expertise.

What has endeared the Stella poems to generations of readers and made them partisans of the woman Swift called his "truest, most virtuous, and valuable friend" (*PW* 5:227) is the human dimension of the relationship memorialized. These poems all embody paradox in one form or another and create suspense over whether the poet will be able to render his annual tribute, but they celebrate a stable and harmonious relationship. However peculiar the terms of their intimacy, however beset by problems in real life, as inhabitants of the world created by the poet, Swift and Stella are completely suited to each other, as Swift and Vanessa could never be.

Both Shakespeare and Swift also correct the misguided conventions of love poetry. Shakespeare ends his sonnet 130, *My mistress' eyes are nothing like the sun*, with a triumphant reversal by proclaiming that in spite of not illustrating the conventional tropes of love poetry his mistress is as fair as those women falsely praised. Swift concludes that his subject is not that fair ("an angel's face, a little cracked"), but she is still the most attractive woman because her intangible charms outweigh the physical. Just as Shakespeare conjures up antiromantic images such as "if hairs be wires, black wires grow on her head," Swift projects the effects of age into the future to create an even more extreme vision to triumph over:

> When Stella's locks must all be grey
> When age must print a furrowed trace
> On every feature of her face. (*CP* 224)

Climactically, Swift represents Stella at fourscore attracting men away from youthful women by means of her intellect and virtue. Like Shakespeare, Swift embraces a reality opposed to romantic rhetoric, but where Shakespeare makes his case in terms of the falsity of that rhetoric, Swift shifts the ground of value. Shakespeare's mistress is conventionally fair, while Swift's is defined in nonphysical terms:

> So little is thy form declined;
> Made up so largely in thy mind. (*CP* 187)

Swift's use of romantic conventions is not always a matter of simple mockery. The reference to Stella as a nymph in *Stella at Woodpark* is enveloped by a context of compliment and straightforward speaking that makes it an endearment rather than a token of foolish exaggeration. Similarly, *On Dan Jackson's Picture*, addressed to Dan Jackson, concludes with the line "Thy nose outshining Celia's eyes" (*CP*

183). Here, a feature neglected by romantic hyperbole is comically assimilated to a conventional romantic topos so that the aggressive proselytizing for an either/or distinction—truth or romantic rhetoric—does not apply.

The often hard-won equilibrium of the birthday poems may be not only literary but personal: Swift's acknowledgment that he owes Stella something while so often focusing on the difficulties of providing it suggests that, like Cadenus in his relationship with Vanessa, he is not suited to what a woman would most want from him. The clearest example of propitiary verse is *Stella at Woodpark*, written after Swift returned from the long trip to the south of Ireland that he began immediately after Vanessa's death. During that period he did not communicate with Stella, who went to Charles Ford's house at Woodpark for an extended stay. The poetic matter is a comic contrast between the luxury of Woodpark and the more modest life Stella leads in Dublin. Reluctantly quitting the country, Stella "strove in vain to ape Woodpark" but soon exhausted her resources:

> She fell into her former scene.
> Small beer, a herring, and the Dean. (*CP* 262)

Swift presents himself, disarmingly humble, assimilated to the plain fare as part of the lesser world that Stella must now inhabit. The lines can also be read as a peace offering in which Swift reminds Stella that he, too, has returned to his, their, "former scene," and his climactic presence in the line will make acceptable the simple food and drink of the first part of it. Stella's visit to Woodpark, like Swift's travels, was a departure from the norm; the larger departure from the norm was his long-term involvement with Vanessa, which has been ended by her death.

After a period whose lack of communication may have meant estrangement, *Stella at Woodpark* seeks to reestablish their relationship, first through Swift's typical raillery, and then through direct explanation. "Thus far in jest" (line 73) signals a shift from the comic narrative to the serious commentary in which Swift claims a poetic privilege, elsewhere condemned, to write what is false:

> But poets when a hint is new
> Regard not whether false or true. (*CP* 262)

After rewriting his description of Stella's table in a complimentary fashion, he concludes with a moral that reinscribes Stella's value in his life:

> We think you quite mistake the case;
> The virtue lies not in the place:
> For though my raillery were true,
> A cottage is Woodpark with you. (*CP* 262)[47]

"We" brings in, as is so often the case in the jocular Stella poems, the sense of the Dublin social circle who echo Swift's admiration of Stella. In the last two lines, the shift from a collective to a singular point of view invokes intimacy most forcefully by creating a vision of domesticity inhabited by Stella and the poet.

The final section of *Stella at Woodpark* shows, according to some commentators, that Swift "could not take for granted Stella's response to his raillery."[48] Perhaps, but this kind of concluding section occurs repeatedly in Swift's poetic narratives, a stepping back to furnish a moral or epilogue. Rogers points out that the passage is "closely comparable to the earlier poem *To Mr Delany*" (*CP* 732n). Its seriousness also links it with the conclusion of *Strephon and Chloe*, whereas a similar final stanza in *The Lady's Dressing Room* seems mischievous rather than sincere. The forthright message of the conclusion of *Stella at Woodpark* also merits comparison with the lack of narrative closure in *Cadenus and Vanessa*:

> But what success Vanessa met,
> Is to the world a secret yet:
>
> .　.　.　.　.　.　.　.　.　.
>
> Must never to mankind be told,
> Nor shall the conscious muse unfold. (*CP* 151)

Had Vanessa pondered these lines, she must have realized that Swift never intended to acknowledge their relationship in any public way.

If the Stella poems all have an intimate and quotidian tone, *Cadenus and Vanessa* has the artificial feel of mock-epic with its satiric sweep of society, its court of gods and goddesses, and its grandiose treatment of the human situation at its center. Venus tricks Pallas into endowing a female infant with manly qualities, thereby creating Vanessa as the ideal Swiftian woman, but one who, predictably, has nothing in common with the superficial world of belles and beaux she is forced to inhabit. Cupid shoots Vanessa while she is reading the "feeble volume" of her tutor's "poetic works," and the damage is done. Given the infusion of masculinity in her character, Vanessa takes the initiative in making her love known to Cadenus, whose first thought is his own reputation. The poem is more sad evidence that the innocent real-life Vanessa, like her poetic counterpart, must have been puzzled by the resistance of an unmarried man who had given her proofs of affection over a period of years. Just as Vanessa is the presence that haunts the *Journal to Stella*, Stella is the invisible obstacle to Vanessa's happiness in *Cadenus and Vanessa*. Cadenus vainly offers the substitute of friendship; Vanessa counters with instruction about love. Their real-life counterparts were to continue in this stalemate until Vanessa's death. Although Swift's objective was to appease Vanessa, it was impossible for him to resolve the narrative in a way that would have achieved this goal. And so he labors on and on, unwilling to entirely commit the poem to one course or its opposite, a mirror of his attenuated but inconclusive history with Vanessa:

> For sixteen years the cause was spun,
> And then stood where it first begun. (*CP* 133)

Thus, what is most remarkable about Swift's longest poem is its lack of resolution.

Above all, the subject of *Cadenus and Vanessa* is self-exculpation, following the model of Swift's two letters to Varina, which blame her for all problems and exonerate him. In *Cadenus and Vanessa*, the impulse of self-justification is disguised and evasive[49] because the text is a poem with an elaborate fiction rather than a letter. Leaving the sublunary world "at six and seven" replicated his relationship with Vanessa, a guilty pleasure that could not be assimilated into the order of Swift's life and which always made him fearful of discovery.

As Stella approached her end, Swift's correspondence with close friends gave many proofs of his anguish, but as much as any other written evidence, lines he penned in desperation a few months before her death, as he waited impatiently at Holyhead to return to Ireland, demonstrate that Stella was the woman whose centrality in his life made her loss unthinkable:

> But now the danger of a friend
> On whom my hopes and fears depend,
> Absent from whom all climes are cursed,
> With whom I'm happy in the worst,
> With rage impatient makes me wait
> A passage to the land I hate.
> Else, rather on this bleaky shore
> Where loudest winds incessant roar,
> Where neither herb nor tree will thrive,
> Where nature hardly seems alive,
> I'd go in freedom to my grave,
> Than rule yon isle and be a slave. (*CP* 330)

No place seems more desolate than Holyhead, a kind of sterile hell emblematic of Swift's despair over Stella and over Ireland; yet, ten years later, when he composed instructions on his death for his cousin, Martha Whiteway, Swift directed his executors to pay the cost of transporting his body to Holyhead "and for my Burial in the Church of that Town, as directed in my Will."[50] This surprising decision, made at a time when Swift had been Dean of St. Patrick's for more than twenty years, reflects the enduring nature of his hatred of Ireland as a site of misery and enslavement. What seems in the poem to be a perverse variation on several famous formulas—Satan's in *Paradise Lost* and Achilles' in the *Odyssey*—becomes in the instructions a meaningful symbol.[51] Death is the price of freedom, but it is preferable to being king of Ireland.

The wish to be buried at Holyhead may also refer less obviously to Stella. Poised on the edge of Britain and headed for Ireland, Swift must always have thought of those dual conditions of his life: the unhappiness of living in Ireland coupled irrevocably with the pleasure of Stella's company. As unpromising a place as Holyhead was, where a day seemed longer than a week, Swift wrote in his *Holyhead Journal*, "Here I could live with two or three friends in a warm house, and good wine—much better than being a slave in Irel^d" (*PW* 5:207). In death he would escape Ireland by choosing burial at Holyhead, the place where he had confronted those conflicting feelings so often in his life.

If Stella is controlled or under control, able to occupy happily or unhappily the delimited area that represented a prescribed distance from Swift, Vanessa is always disturbingly close, always threatening a scandalous disruption. Swift saw Vanessa alone, as he refused to do with Stella: no third party enters here to restrain the expression of an intimacy charged with eroticism. As the Swift-Vanessa correspondence demonstrates, Vanessa is controlled with difficulty and never permanently. The conflict that permeated their relationship is almost everywhere present: her advances, his retreats; her rages and reproaches, his attempts to pacify; his rages and reprimands, her attempts to pacify; above all, her attempts to alter their relationship which never succeeded in effecting any change.

In the boardroom of St. Patrick's Hospital, a portrait of Jonathan Swift, whose bequest made the hospital possible, is, fittingly, the focal point of the room. On each side it is flanked by a portrait of a woman: Stella on the Dean's right, Vanessa on his left. Like so much about these women, the authenticity of their portraits cannot be vouched for.[52] This, too, seems fitting, a representation of relationships that were significant to Swift but largely beyond the domain of record. Literally, then, the room exhibits in public space what was private, even secret, during Swift's lifetime: the metaphoric love triangle that has captured so many imaginations.

The rigid constraints that Swift placed on his intercourse with Vanessa he ascribed to a need to avoid occasion for gossip, but such prescriptions also answered his need—both psychological and practical—to control their relationship. As Vanessa pointed out in a letter of December, 1714, responding to a lengthy lecture on secrecy, Swift's worship of propriety is hard to square with his role as a truthteller to society: "You once had a maxime (which was to act what was right and not mind what they world said) I wish you would keep to it now." She adds, rather innocently, "Pray what can be wrong in seeing and advising an unhappy young woman I cant imagine" (W 2:101). What Vanessa may not have known so early in her new life in Ireland was the existence of Stella, who probably constituted a more powerful motive for secrecy than any other. Swift's precautions may also speak to his deep-seated sense of vulnerability as a man without powerful family connections to fall back upon and with little status as his world reckoned it. Richard Cave has observed that Swift's mind was "trapped in a labyrinth of guilt of its own devising that betrays itself to ever subtler forms of irrationality in its efforts to avoid confronting the necessary irrationality of so much human behaviour."[53] If Stella and Vanessa suffered from Swift's cramped vision of relationships between men and women, he was its victim as well, unable to alter the temperament that imprisoned him as much as them.

Our understanding of the two relationships can never be equal, however, for one was open and known to many people while the other was concealed. Swift often referred to Stella in his correspondence: when she was dying, he expressed his feelings at length and without subterfuge to several of his closest friends. To Thomas Sheridan he wrote in the unmistakable accents of genuine grief: "I look upon this to be the greatest Event that can ever happen to me, but all my Preparations will not suffice to make me bear it like a Philosopher, nor altogether like a Christian. There hath been the most intimate Friendship between us from her Childhood, and the greatest Merit on her Side that ever was in one human Creature to another" (W 3:2). About Vanessa there could be no such confession, even to intimates. Upon her death Swift hurriedly left Dublin, telling no one where he could be found, "so that not even the clergy of his own Cathedral could contact him."[54] He remained uncommunicative for two months, a "fugitive Dean," as le Brocquy calls him, until he wrote to Sheridan that he would be returning in a few weeks to take up the threads of his familiar life again. He wrote nothing that we know of to memorialize Vanessa, nor could he have without compromising the respectability he cherished.

For the man who desired so strongly to avoid scandal and gossip about his personal life, the world's enduring interest in Swift's relations with Stella and Vanessa is a supreme irony. As Robert Mahony's meticulous study, *Jonathan Swift: The Irish Identity*, documents, in every historical period since Swift's death, his reputation as a patriot and writer has been overshadowed by his reputation as a man of unconventional relations with two women.[55] Lady Wilde reflected, after reviewing Swift's achievements, "But, above all, the love-drama of Swift's life has helped to make his name immortal."[56] That personal history has provoked a wide range of supposition as well as the most sweeping of condemnations. At bottom the two relationships remain only partially understandable, emblems of Swift's own elusiveness, and of the even greater lacunae in our knowledge of both women.

In a particularly sweeping condemnation, Anna Jameson writes of Swift's relations with Stella and Vanessa that "he had not sufficient humanity, honor, or courage, to disclose the truth of his situation."[57] But honesty might have been the crueler course. Both women preferred some relationship with Swift to none at all, and he was evidently incapable of giving them more. The history of Swift and these two women, insofar as we know it, was a course that Swift undoubtedly did not plot or imagine in its entirety at the moment of each relationship's inception. He did not foresee the suffering of either woman or produce it intentionally. Perhaps in Stella's case he did not even imagine it.

2

Stella

"A Conjugall love without any Conjugall act"

A scholar who has devoted his professional life to studying Swift begins an essay on "Stella's Books" with the following statement: "About Esther Johnson, better known to the world by the name of Stella, we know next to nothing. After two hundred and fifty years, we are still in the dark about her parentage, her childhood, and her removal to Ireland, as well as about the nature of her relationship with Jonathan Swift."[1] What little is known of the woman who was Swift's particular friend in Ireland for some twenty-seven years comes primarily from Swift himself. Of the people who knew Stella personally, the only other writer to set down his opinions—briefly, and almost thirty years after her death—was Patrick Delany.[2] Delany agreed with the laudatory portrait of Stella Swift draws in the essay he began writing the night Stella died, *On the Death of Mrs. Johnson*.

Modern scholarship has done little to verify or dispute Swift's sketchy account of Stella's early life in this essay, a moving testament to her loss. Bridget Johnson and her child Esther, who was born in 1681, belonged to the household of Sir William Temple, which Swift joined, probably in 1689 (E 1:102–4). He played some part in her education and ultimately formed her taste in, one is tempted to say, everything. So she affirms in her poem *To Dr. Swift on his birth-day, November 30, 1721*, describing him as "my early and my only guide," and thanking him for teaching her the lesson that "wit and virtue" are powerful substitutes for fading physical charms (*PS* 2:737).[3] We know that Stella was a winning child, whom Sir William Temple treated with special affection and generosity, and she became an attractive, if delicate, young woman, one who could reasonably expect to marry, albeit—given the ordinariness of her antecedents and her lack of fortune—modestly. With Swift's encouragement she and an older companion, Rebecca Dingley, moved to Ireland after Swift received a parish there, and he partially supported the two women in Ireland for the rest of their lives.[4] Like Sir William Temple and his sister Martha Giffard, or William and Dorothy Wordsworth, Swift and Stella became close companions without being physically intimate. And, at some point, rumors that they actually were brother and sister began to circulate.[5]

It is at least plausible that Stella followed Swift's advice to move to Ireland because she thought that one day they would be married.[6] A young woman would naturally have hoped to marry in a time when "marriage and motherhood were regarded as the norm, spinsterhood and infertility as a blight."[7] In the social hierarchy, single women would always be made aware of their low status: the boundaries between the single and the married were delineated in everything from church seating to modes of address.[8] The young Lady Mary Wortley Montagu, writing to her friend Philippa Munday, memorably expressed a visceral repulsion to remaining unmarried that equates grim effects of age with growing old alone: "I have a Mortal Aversion to be an old Maid, and a decaid Oak before my Window, leavelesse, half rotten, and shaking its wither'd Top, puts me in Mind every morning of an Antiquated Virgin Bald, with Rotten Teeth, and shaking of the Palsie."[9] The picture of decrepit age Lady Mary paints could serve just as well for aging wives—and husbands, for that matter—but in her mind this horror is exclusively the province of spinsterhood.

As for the theoretical value of celibacy, Wetenhall Wilkes, in *A Letter of Genteel and Moral Advice to a Young Lady*, distinguishes between a "superannuated virginity" of necessity, which is both an "affliction" and "a kind of imputed scandal," and a free choice made for spiritual reasons, which may be called "a life of angels."[10] Swift wrote of Stella to William Tisdall, her suitor—"time takes off the lustre of virgins in all other eyes but mine" (W 1:153)—but a less meticulous person might not have made such a fine distinction between the abhorrent and saintly forms of spinsterhood. In covering the topic of "old maids" exhaustively in a three-volume work later in the eighteenth century, William Hayley enumerates the defects commonly attributed to spinsters—curiosity, credulity, affectation, envy, and ill nature—and remarks the insulting fact that widows are overwhelmingly preferred to old maids, according to the popular rhyme:

> Strings never try'd some harshness will produce;
> The fiddle's harmony improves by use.[11]

In spite of the support of friends and family, the common currency of negative stereotypes about her condition must have felt demeaning to an unmarried woman growing old. If spinsters were also identified with certain positive qualities—ingenuity, patience, and charity—these could be read as natural outgrowths of a life of "perpetual and ever varying hope," hope destined to be repeatedly disappointed.[12] Once his own intention to remain single had been formed, Swift must have expatiated on the desirability of celibacy in the clergy, and Stella, who acquired his handwriting and his values, followed suit. Her will specified that after the deaths of her mother and sister, who received the life interest of her income, her money should be used to support a chaplain at Steevens Hospital, Dublin. It also required that this chaplain be single and that if he were to marry, he be dismissed.[13] Stella was fortunate at least in having a modest financial independence: those women dependent upon allowances from a male relative might find their maintenance paid grudgingly and irregularly.[14] She was also more fortunate than most single women in having her own household: in England at this time, never-married women under the age of forty-five were predominately classified as daughters and servants.[15]

Swift himself had no impressive family lineage and no fortune: he was just beginning his career on the lowest rung of the church when Stella and Dingley arrived in Ireland. Stella could well have imagined that there was no insuperable obstacle to a future marriage with someone who had urged her to change her country in order to be near him. Instead, they settled into a special friendship in which, as Virginia Woolf comments, "they knew each other in and out; the good and the bad, the deep and the trivial."[16] Stella lived with this unofficial status from her arrival in Ireland in 1701 until her death in 1728. However she felt about it, her position, as a woman, was inscribed as reactive: she could have withdrawn from Swift's company but not proposed marriage to him.

Although evidence of Stella's state of mind is only anecdotal, speculation has been an irresistible temptation to readers of Swift. Two main camps can be distinguished: those like Orrery, who see her as an example of a wretched and unhappy existence, and those like Harold Williams, who states that "Stella, there is every reason to believe, save for unfulfilled desires which she probably succeeded in laying aside, was happy in their friendship" (*JS* xxx). What unites these divergent views of Stella's condition is swallowed up in the long awkward middle of the sentence, those undefined grounds for dissatisfaction that Williams believes Stella overcame and commentators of the Orrery persuasion believe made her miserable. The arrangement between Stella and Swift endured, and therefore, Williams concludes, neither party desired to change it, an argument that would be found insufficient if applied to almost any relationship involving a difference in power.

Many other critics have been confident that they knew Stella's state of mind. For Anna Jameson, she lived "in pale contented sort of discontent," while in Joseph Manch's opposing view, "there is nothing which might lead us to believe that Stella was unhappy about her situation. She accepted it willingly."[17] Stanley Lane-Poole, even more of a proponent of Stella's happiness than Manch, believes that she "would not have changed her lot with the happiest wife in Christendom."[18] William Lecky is optimistic but puzzled. He finds Stella "admirably suited both for social life and for sustained friendship"—in other words, for the kind of life she led. "But," he continues, "she appears to have . . . acquiesced very placidly during her whole life in a kind of connection which few women could have tolerated."[19] Lecky can only call attention to the mystery of Stella's agreeing to such a curtailed and morally suspect position; he cannot explain it. Once again, the endurance of the arrangement becomes the evidence that Stella accepted it "very placidly."

However Stella felt, the continuation of this relationship with Swift over time indicates its importance in her life as well as in his. Their social circle in Ireland also acknowledged it, as does Stella's poem for Swift's birthday. From the poems he wrote in her honor and the impressive correspondence known today as the *Journal to Stella* she had reason to believe that he regarded her in the same light. In those letters, with their playful "little language" and extravagantly expressed affection, Stella still seems to be the adored little girl of their first acquaintance. And when she became aware of a rival, if we can believe Dr. Delany, she penned the poem *Jealousy*, which protests against "This Tyrant that imbitters all my Hours" (*PS* 2:738), but does so in measured lines.

Swift was a little more than thirteen years older than Stella, so in 1721, when she was thirty-three, writing a poem for Swift's birthday, she took for granted that she would outlive him:

> Late dying may you cast a shred
> Of your rich mantle o'er my head;
> To bear with dignity my sorrow,
> One day *alone, then die to-morrow*. (*PS* 2:738)

Only a few years later Stella's own health declined, and she experienced a progressive wasting illness in which she was often denied the comfort of Swift's presence. Phobic about death, and this death in particular, Swift wanted to be away when it happened, apparently unable to adhere to his own ideas of rational behavior in the face of what he called "the greatest Tryal I ever had" (W 3:8).

Preoccupation with his own approaching loss seemed to eclipse concern for Stella's feelings. Perhaps his buying her a watch at the end of her life only honored her desire for such a present, in which case it would have been a thoughtful rather than a tactless gesture. It cannot have been a token of denial, since, as his correspondence reveals, Swift was well aware that Stella was dying. And what must Stella have thought as Swift prayed over her "to raise up some other in her place, with equal disposition and better abilities"? (*PW* 9:254).

Swift insisted that Stella be moved out of his deanery lest by dying there she should implicate him in scandal. Surely whatever had been said about Swift and Stella was by now stale news, more than a quarter century old. Stella and Dingley had lived in the deanery routinely and openly while Swift was away. And yet, in 1727, when he was sixty years old and had no realistic hope of further advancement, the risk of a scandal was apparently enough to justify treating this treasured companion of so many years unceremoniously. And worse, unfeelingly: Swift wrote to Sheridan that he avoided Stella's deathbed because "I could not behave myself tolerably, and should redouble her Sorrow" (W 3:2). The sign of Swift betraying emotion at her state would no doubt have touched Stella, while his absence at the last must have been painful. At the end of her life she must have wanted to see the man she had devoted it to.

Even in Stella's final moments Swift could not put her feelings first, nor could he forbear making excuses for himself, justifying the transference of a terminally ill woman from one place to another and claiming that he refrained from seeing her because his own lack of composure would make her feel worse for *him*. This is of a piece with the last birthday poem for Stella (1727), which begs her not to take out her illness on her friends, namely himself. He goes on to plead in the poem's conclusion:

> Me, surely me, you ought to spare,
> Who gladly would your sufferings share;
> Or give my scrap of life to you,
> And think it far beneath your due;
> You, to whose care so oft I owe,
> That I'm alive to tell you so. (*CP* 315)

Maurice Johnson, author of the first book-length study of Swift's poetry, describes these lines as "hardly 'Swiftian,'" whereas I read them as quintessentially Swiftian.[20] The poet's powerfully rendered anguish at Stella's imminent demise and the poignant balance of her preservation of his life with his willingness to sacrifice that life for her are both overshadowed by the unconscious egotism of his need to portray his own nobility. The final couplet contains two references to *you* enclosing two to *I*, a positioning that at first glance emphasizes the *you* figure. But the emphasis is instrumental rather than absolute. Stella's care kept Swift alive; ultimately, she has not been the valuable person but someone who has sustained a valuable person. And Swift tells her this, assuming, no doubt correctly, that she will agree. Most objectionable in this concluding stanza is the rhetorical manipulation that manages to foreground Swift's suffering and merit over the claims of a dying woman. A reader must be forcibly struck by a neediness so intense that it will displace the beloved, but such a reader might also believe that someone undergoing a prolonged and agonizing dying, as Stella evidently did, should be spared a performance that subtly diminishes her misery and inflates the speaker's own.

This same pattern of privileging his own grief can be seen in *On the Death of Mrs. Johnson*, begun on the night of Stella's death. Swift is writing in such emotional distress that his first thought is a kind of mechanical precision about time: 6 P.M. for her death, 8 P.M. for his learning of it, 11 P.M. for his taking up his pen to commemorate her life. He worked on the essay for several days, always indicating where he left off and describing his intruding health problems, which cause him to stop writing on January 29 and to absent himself from Stella's funeral on January 30. Julia Longe, who edited Lady Giffard's correspondence and appropriated that lady's hostility to Swift, interprets his illness as an excuse to avoid the funeral: "He was well enough to sit in his room and write, and one feels that had the positions been reversed, Stella would not have excused herself on this account."[21] Swift's chronic illness, so well known to those around him, may well have provided a convenient excuse to cover his fear of a possible emotional loss of control in public, an episode that would have been distasteful to his strong sense of reserve. Further, he always suspected hypocrisy in those who mourned extravagantly and disliked seeing others exhibiting grief, even when it was genuine. As he wrote to Stella, "There is something of farce in all these Mournings let them be ever so serious. People will pretend to grieve more than they really do, & that takes off from their true Grief" (*JS* 602).

To refer to Swift privileging his own grief, as I have done, is only part of the story. For one thing, we can know only our own emotional states firsthand: Swift's final poem for Stella speaks to her of his anguish over her dying, not her feelings about that looming event. And his anguish, both there and in the memorial essay, is terrible, however much he channels it into conventional forms. Swift cared for Stella, I conclude, as much as he was capable of caring, and he treated her as well as he was able to, according to his character and the circumstances of his life as he saw them.

Biographers and critics have primarily valued Stella for her long years of unswerving devotion to a famous man on his terms, terms that gave her very little latitude and him a great deal. However deeply Swift cared for Stella, he imposed strict rules on their association. She might have presided over his table when he entertained, but she had no official position there, nor, in keeping with his most stringent requirement, did she ever see him alone—a cruel barrier to intimacy. He was also secretly involved with another woman for fourteen of the twenty-seven years Stella spent in Ireland.

Commentators who accept that Stella was the love of Swift's life have nevertheless been divided in assessments of their relationship. Those who have condemned Swift's treatment of Stella have done so because he inflicted an irregular position on her, a condition that deprived her of autonomy without conferring status. Mark Twain annotated Thackeray on Swift with the comment, "That it was her fate to suffer 21 years of a love so trifling as Swift's ought to entitle her to the world's compassion for all time."[22] In 1894, Margaret Oliphant became the first writer to suggest that profuse sympathy of this sort might be both misguided and gender based: "Appearances of blighted life or unhappiness there are none in anything we know of [Stella]." She then offered in a long rhetorical question the thesis that male responses to Stella were influenced by gender attitudes: "Is it perhaps a certain mixture of masculine vanity and compassion for the gentle feminine creature who never succeeded in getting the man she loved to marry her, and thus failed to attain the highest end of woman, which has moved every biographer of Swift, each man more compassionate than his predecessor, thus to exhaust himself in pity for Stella?"[23] In 1913, Margaret Woods echoed Mrs. Oliphant's view that pity for Stella was unwarranted, although her rationale is the traditional view of many male writers without the compassion. Stella should not be considered "badly used," Woods asserted, because "she was the respected, the admired, the tenderly loved companion of a man who was not only a great genius but a great personality." As Swift's wife, Woods believed, Stella "would have found [his tiresome ways] still more tiresome, and complained as much as good wives do, which is often a good deal."[24]

Oliphant and Woods both illustrate a decidedly gender-based perspective, but neither is a feminist—or, for that matter, much of a researcher. Like their male counterparts of that era, they view the Swift-Stella relationship through a lens of sentimental idealization rather than historical recuperation. Except for unreliable stories, no evidence of unhappiness in Stella has survived, but since there is no firm evidence of any other sort, certainty about Stella's satisfaction with her life is unwarranted.

Even champions of Stella have generally failed to mention that her will set aside twenty pounds for a memorial tablet that was not raised during the seventeen years that Swift outlived her.[25] Yet the memorializing of the dead appears to have been a particular obsession of Swift's, in keeping with his observation that most people wish to be remembered after their deaths. "We observe, even among the Vulgar," he wrote, "how fond they are to have an Inscription over their Grave" (*PW* 4:244). As Dean of St Patrick's, Swift wrote to members of several prominent families to tell them that their family's funerary monuments in the cathedral were in need of repair. He was indignant if they failed to respond. When the heirs of the Duke of Schomberg ignored Swift's repeated overtures to set up a monument to the deceased duke, Swift had a memorial tablet engraved with a lengthy Latin inscription that pointedly concludes: "His reputation for virtue prevailed more among strangers than the kindredness of his blood prevailed among his own relations" (*W* 3:399n).[26] The intensity of Swift's feeling on the subject may be gauged by a letter to Lord Carteret in which he vows that if the duke's family tries to obtain the body to avoid paying for a monument, "I will take up the bones, and make of it a skeleton, and put it in my registry-office, to be a memorial of their baseness to all posterity" (W 3:302). Swift also took the initiative in erecting a monument to Lady Betty Germain's sister Penelope, who had died in Ireland some thirty years before at the age of twelve, a task no member of her family had undertaken or thought of undertaking until Swift broached it to Lady Betty. When taxed on the subject by the Dean, Lady Betty could remember only imperfectly when her sister had been born and when she had died (W 3:457).

Earlier in his life, Swift had proclaimed his intention of erecting a marble monument to Anne Long, Esther Vanhomrigh's beautiful cousin, whom Swift had known briefly and admired. Shortly after her death, he wrote to the Reverend Thomas Pyle, Anne Long's pastor, avowing his plan to place a monument over her grave "if no other of her friends will think fit to do it." He continued, with some fervor: "I had the honour of an intimate acquaintance with her, and was never so sensibly touched with any one's death as with hers.[27] Neither did I ever know a person of either sex with more virtues, or fewer infirmities" (W 1:406). In his account book for 1711–12, Swift devoted a page to Anne Long's death, in which he described her even more expansively: "She was the most beautifull Person of the Age, she lived in, of great Honor and Virtue, infinite Sweetness and Generosity of Temper, and true good Sense" (*JS* 445n).

Swift also placed a tablet in St. Patrick's in memory of his servant, Saunders (Alexander McGee). It reads in part: "His grateful Master caused this monument to be erected in Memory of his Discretion, Fidelity and Diligence in that humble station" (*C* 2:422–23n). According to Patrick Delany, Swift had intended to style himself more warmly as "friend and master," but was persuaded otherwise (*C* 2:423n). If McGee deserved such acknowledgment for his "Discretion, Fidelity, and Diligence," Stella surely merited at least the simple memorial she had requested, a tablet indicating that she had lived and died.[28]

Swift was no exception to his own observation that people wish to have a memorial. Brian A. Connery suggests that "the urge to memorialize himself . . . and be memorialized is, perhaps, the largest theme of Swift's work."[29] In addition to the memorializing of self apparent throughout his poetry, Swift composed his own epitaph and gave extremely precise instructions for the monument on which it would appear: "A Black Marble of   Feet square, and seven Feet from the Ground, fixed to the Wall, may be erected, with the following Inscription in large Letters, deeply cut, and strongly gilded" (*PW* 13:149). He was similarly precise about the time and place of his burial, specifying that his body should be interred "in the great Isle of the said Cathedral [St. Patrick's], on the South Side, under the Pillar next to the Monument of Primate *Narcissus Marsh*, three Days after my Decease, as privately as possible, and at Twelve o'Clock at Night" (*PW* 13:149).

Ehrenpreis, always protective of Swift in such matters, believes that his failure to implement Stella's instructions for a memorial was motivated by a desire to avoid scandal (E3:622–23). But this behavior is consonant with other omissions and withholdings. Stella is rarely called by name in Swift's writings. The *Journal to Stella* refers to her as MD, thought to be an abbreviation for "My Dear" or "My Dears," a term that would include Rebecca Dingley. The poems call her Stella. Above all, in Swift's correspondence and elsewhere in his writings, her designation is some permutation of *friend*—"our friend in Grafton Street," "my most valuable friend," and so forth—that appellation with which Swift thought to disarm public censure, private reproach, and his own psyche. When she was dead, he did refer to her by her actual name.

Swift protested too much that his feeling for Stella was friendship rather than love because this rubric freed him from the implications of a sexual relationship, which is, after all, a common distinction between the two. In his anguish over the dying Stella he wrote to James Stopford that "violent Friendship is much more lasting, and as much engaging, as violent Love" (W 2:660), an assertion that seems profoundly uninformed by human experience in its attempt to blur the distinction between the two states. Swift clearly intends to elevate friendship between a man and a woman to the status of love between them. He may have selected *violent* to oppose this special friendship to a superficial relationship—or to oppose it to what the world commonly thought of as friendship, that is, a less intense condition than love. Since violence has habitually been associated with passion, the choice of *violent* only emphasizes the difference that Swift seeks to erase.

In Swift's mind his friendship with Stella was superior in staying power and "as much engaging" as a relationship based on sexual love.[30] He would have regarded as exemplary the union of the saintly King Edward and his queen, Editha, who observed mutual chastity over the lifetime of their marriage: "There continued in them (sayth the Legend) a Conjugall love, without any Conjugall act; and favourable embrace, without any deflowring of Virginitie . . . she delighted him with love, but did not tempt him with lust; she pleased him with discourse and sweet societie, yet provoked him to no libidinous desire."[31] Swift's various celebrations of intellectual companionship in marriage, and corresponding denigration of unions lacking this quality, can be read biographically as justifications of his own practice. Here he seems to be asking Stopford, and perhaps society in general, to accept his own distinction.

It should also be pointed out that, for Swift, *friendship* is not only the name for all positive human relationships but a condition to which he attaches a number of important qualities: usefulness, gratitude, loyalty. James Woolley has observed that "*friend* and related words appear more frequently in Swift's verse than any other noun."[32] Given the importance of the idea of friendship for Swift, I cannot agree with Charles Peake that "to dispute whether such a profound and lasting attachment [to Stella] should be labelled 'love' or 'friendship' would be mere quibbling."[33] It wasn't so to Swift. He reserved the word *love* for "romantic love," entailing sex, and explicitly disavowed this kind of feeling for Stella:

> Thou, Stella, wert no longer young,
> When first for thee my harp I strung:
> Without one word of Cupid's darts,
> Of killing eyes, or bleeding hearts:
> With friendship and esteem possessed,
> I ne'er admitted love a guest. (*CP* 204)

Swift may have been misguided in defining love as a matter of romantic superficiality and transience, and exalting friendship as a matter of nonphysical qualities and enduring feeling, but he makes it clear that these are his definitions.

The endless stories about Swift and Stella prove that for most people the principle of a friendship equal or superior to sexual love has been unpersuasive. The putative secret marriage between Swift and Stella begged to be invented to explain what otherwise appears to the ordinary world to be inexplicable behavior: that is, a significant and long-lasting yet nonsexual relationship between two people who appear to have had no impediment to marriage. Evelyn Hardy thought that biographers accept or reject the marriage according to caprice;[34] it is, in point of fact, difficult to do otherwise, since whatever disproves this maddening biographical conjecture may just as easily prove it. Ehrenpreis, among others, rejects the idea because Stella signed her will "Esther Johnson, spinster" (3:405n). But if the marriage was secret, she was bound to have done or not done whatever was appropriate to an unmarried woman. She might have added the unrequired descriptive "spinster" to ally those persistent rumors of a secret marriage, either to keep it secret or because she was, in fact, a spinster. That Rebecca Dingley had no knowledge of such a union might also seem conclusive. On the other hand, secret is secret, and Dingley had the reputation of being a garrulous fool.[35] Swift's longtime housekeeper, Mrs. Brent, apparently dismissed the rumor with the assertion that the two had never spent a night together.[36] But no one has ever suggested that the marriage was consummated.

Swift's earliest biographers—Orrery, Delany, Deane Swift, and Sheridan[37]—all told a similar story: that in 1716 Swift and Stella were secretly married by St. George Ashe, the bishop of Clogher. Delany was a valued friend of both parties, while Orrery and Deane Swift knew Swift in his old age and were aided by Martha Whiteway, the cousin who was close to Swift in later years. Sheridan had the benefit of his father's long friendship with Swift. Finally, Monck Berkeley states that the bishop of Clogher "himself related the circumstance to Bishop Berkeley, by whose relict the story was communicated to *me*."[38] Although Berkeley's account agrees with the episode in the four major early biographers, no corroborating documentation has ever been found, nor does any informant assert that Swift admitted the marriage to him or to anyone else. It remains hearsay that many of Swift's contemporaries believed because, as Johnston writes, they "wanted to believe that he and Stella were man and wife. Apart from the question of secrecy, it dispensed with the need for some other explanation of his highly anomalous treatment of her."[39]

More recent male critics have sometimes failed to understand why Stella might want such a union. For Ricardo Quintana, if the ceremony took place, "the explanation must be sought not in the realm of reason but of nonsense."[40] He assumes that the particulars defined by these two terms will be self-evident without further discussion. For Ehrenpreis, Stella "had nothing to gain from an unacknowledged, invalid marriage that left both of them living as celibate friends" (E 3:405n). Sheridan, on the other hand, explains the marriage by saying that Stella pined because of the "indelible stain fixed on her character, and the loss of her own good name, which was dearer to her than life."[41] But a secret marriage would not have remedied this problem, since "good name" is a public rather than a private attribute.

If the issue were instead Swift's relationship to Vanessa, marriage—however invalid or covert—would have given Stella the satisfaction of "rendering such a union with her rival impracticable."[42] A private and unconsummated marriage might have had no legal status but great symbolic or psychological value. In this scenario, Swift was able to satisfy Stella's desire to be preferred over her rival without altering any part of their relationship.

Appealing as such a compromise might be, a secret marriage is unlikely for one brutal reason: Swift had exactly the life he wanted with Stella without marriage, and she did not have the leverage to override his wishes. This was made clear in 1704, when a man who did want to marry Stella presented himself. Since Swift did not marry her when faced with a suitor for her hand, it was unlikely that he ever would have.

Swift's snobbery further militates against the idea of marriage to Stella. *On the Death of Mrs. Johnson* contains the flat assertion, "She had little to boast of her birth" (*PW* 5:227). While Swift did not preserve the letters of the woman whose conversation alone made life tolerable,[43] he did save any number of trifling letters from aristocratic women. In 1735, he wrote to Lady Betty Germain that when he left England he had burned the letters he had received from ministers, "but as to the letters I receive from your Ladyship, I neither ever did or ever will burn any of them. . . . For I never burnt a letter that is entertaining, and consequently will give me new pleasure when it is forgotten" (*C* 4:344).

Many of those who reject the secret marriage have proffered explanations ranging from impotence to consanguinity in seeking to account for Swift's failure to marry Stella.[44] The writer who styled himself C.M.P.G.N.S.T.N.S. in the pages of *The Gentleman's and London Magazine* (1757) asserts that the decade after Queen Anne's death saw Swift's discovery that he and Stella were too closely related to marry: "The only woman in the world, who could make him happy as a wife, was the only woman in the world, who could not be that wife."[45] But Swift and Stella had already known each other for many years by that time, and

Swift had shown no inclination to make Stella his wife. Less dramatically, Richard Krafft-Ebing's idea of "sexual anesthesia," which "does not exclude nonsexual tenderness" or "require impotency," seems tailor-made for Swift, as does Krafft-Ebing's example of a man who wanted to marry "but only on rational grounds."[46] Such an explanation is even more suited to Swift apologists: in providing a scientific-sounding rubric for Swift's condition, it strips his behavior of oddity and disarms disapproval while at the same time preserving his manhood.

Given the initial puzzle of the Swift-Stella relationship, other details without sufficient context have tempted biographers into bizarre speculations. Swift wrote to Vanessa that a woman who did business for him had told him that she had heard that he visited Vanessa accompanied by "little master."[47] Ehrenpreis, eager to dampen any potentially lurid flames, assumes that this was a charity child from Stella's household. He has a curious footnote that this child must have been "like the girl mentioned in [Stella's] will," an inexplicable remark since the only child mentioned in Stella's will is Bryan M'Loghlin (E 3:94n).[48] Moreover, if Swift was as insistent on discretion as all his behavior suggests, he would hardly have taken a child from Stella's sphere into Vanessa's; this explanation is patently absurd. At the same time, it is hard to imagine what child might have accompanied Swift on such secret business.

Le Brocquy conjectures that this was an illegitimate child of Vanessa's fathered by Swift, who, after Vanessa's death, was taken in by Stella as an object of her charity.[49] This would be the Bryan M'Loghlin that Stella specifies in her will with what seems to be unusual generosity. LeBrocquy researched assiduously without finding the slightest shred of supporting evidence for this idea; although she did find a McLoghlin family that Vanessa probably knew, the entire speculative edifice rests on the assumption that "little master" is Swift's child. Were this to be merely a private way of referring to some common acquaintance, like Glass Heel for Charles Ford, the hypothesis of the child fathered by Swift falls. More plausibly, Victoria Glendinning believes that Little Master was a dog, an identification that would explain the casual nature of Swift's allusion.[50] Stella, having no children of her own, might well have become so attached to Bryan M'Loghlin that she provided for him in her will somewhat more generously than might have been expected.[51]

Wit in Swift's time was thought to be an exclusively male habit of mind: since women were regarded as intellectually inferior to men, they were expected to converse on a lower level that would automatically exclude the verbal felicity and nimbleness of mind associated with the exercise of wit. Moreover, wit requires a conversational assertiveness deemed inappropriate to women. "A Young Lady ought to beware of the Reputation of being Witty . . . as a Maid ought to speak but little, and that with Deference and Respect," John Essex writes in *The Young Ladies Conduct* (1722).[52] For Dr. John Gregory, addressing his daughters, "wit is the most dangerous talent you can possess."[53]

There is also a problem embedded in Essex's typical strictures; namely, the lack of a category for women like Stella who become mature adults without having married. For Stella's birth cohort, this figure was an all-time high of 16–18%.[54]

Although this statistically significant number of women remained single, they tended to be invisible to contemporary writers on women and perhaps to society itself: women were recognized as maidens, wives, and widows, with the erroneous assumption that the first group comprised only young women.

To praise a woman as a wit, then, required setting aside her typical feminine behavior and identifying her with masculine qualities. Swift commends the women he admires in exactly these terms: when he writes to Stella and Dingley that he does not like women as much as he did, he immediately adds, "MD you must know, are not women" (*JS* 90). In praising Stella's exceptional behavior as a conversationalist, Swift dismisses the "common topics of female chat; scandal, censure, and detraction" as unknown to her. Instead, he praises Stella for participating in a male discourse: "She understood the Platonic and Epicurean philosophy, and judged very well of the defects of the latter" (*PW* 5:230–31). Wit surpasses this kind of weighty conversation, however, by requiring the manipulation of language: Stella might have merely parroted Swift's opinion on Plato and Epicurus and a host of other topics, but to be witty, even if she followed Swiftian models, she had to be inventive on her own.

When Swift tasked himself to illustrate Stella's wit immediately after her death, he was limited by the anxiety of the occasion and his always unreliable memory.[55] One of the few "*Bons Mots de* Stella" that he is able to recall is a feeble joke at the expense of a grieving father:

> A Gentleman who had been very silly and pert in her Company, at last began to grieve at remembering the Loss of a Child lately dead. A Bishop sitting by comforted him that he should be easy, because the Child was gone to Heaven. No, my lord, says she, that is it which most grieves him, because he is sure never to see his Child there." (*PW* 5:238)[56]

In flourishing this evidence of Stella's wit Swift takes no notice of the discord between the bishop's serious attempt to comfort, an attempt endowed with particular authority because of his profession and his rank within it, and Stella's remark, nor does he appear to recognize the inappropriateness of Stella's response to a parent's grief for a dead child, a response within the hearing of the bereaved father.

Such a comment might be acceptable as a way of changing the tone and subject of the conversation from lugubrious to light: the gentleman's grief in company was a form of self-indulgence that a social gathering might find tiresome and Swift would certainly have found pretentious: he believed that even genuine grief should be restrained. Although he himself was grief-stricken at the death of Lady Ashburnham, who, perhaps because she reminded him of Stella, was his "greatest Favorite," he became impatient at seeing her mother and sister crying less than a month after her death (*JS* 602). Nevertheless, in commending Stella here, Swift approves the violation of what he had once described as "one of the best Rules in Conversation"; namely, "never to say a Thing which any of the Company can reasonably wish we had rather left unsaid" (*PW* 4:91).[57] For him, the middle of the anecdote seems to disappear, so that Stella's retort becomes a proper punishment for the gentleman's earlier "silly and pert" behavior.

Dr. Johnson accurately remarked of the *Bons Mots de* Stella that "the smart sayings which Swift himself has collected afford no splendid specimen."[58] His evaluation of Swift's praise of Stella concludes that "if Swift's idea of women were such as he generally exhibits, a very little sense in a lady would enrapture, and a very little virtue astonish him."[59] An early-twentieth-century critic, Alice Meynell, echoes this view when she asserts that the loss of Stella's letters to Swift is, after all, no great loss: "We have something of MD's letters in the Journal—this is the only form in which we desire them, to tell the truth; for when Swift gravely saves us some specimens of Stella's wit, after her death, as she spoke them, and not as he mimicked them, they make a sorry show."[60] Dr Johnson's statement that the *Bon Mots de* Stella were collected by Swift himself implies that Swift systematically chose the strongest or most representative examples of Stella's wit. No doubt he wanted to do this, but the assembled anecdotes are perhaps more revealing of his own predilections: drawn from more than a quarter century of social occasions in Ireland, they represent what made a lasting impression on him, not necessarily because of the quality of the remark but for idiosyncratic reasons. Nothing Swift was able to remember seems especially witty today, although Stella's comment on the making of matches, "I have heard Matches were made in Heaven, but by the Brimstone, one would think they were made in Hell," shows the kind of disposition that produces verbal cleverness. Some remarks were clearly enhanced by the situation, as when the Quaker apothecary sent her a bottle of medicine with "a broad Brim, and a Label of Paper about its Neck. What is that, said she, my Apothecary's Son? The ridiculous Resemblance, and the Suddenness of the Question, set us all a Laughing" (*PW* 5:238).

Perhaps the most recent anecdote in the *Bons Mots* was the exchange between Stella and one of her physicians when she was in danger of dying. Swift quotes the doctor as saying "Madam, you are near the Bottom of the Hill, but we will endeavour to get you up again." In answering "I fear, I shall be *out of Breath* before I get up to the Top," Stella merely replies according to the metaphor introduced by the doctor (*PW* 5:238). Yet to make any such rejoinder *in extremis* surely reveals a predisposition for verbal play. I cannot agree with Herbert Davis that the *Bons Mots* "add nothing to our knowledge of her,"[61] for Stella clearly had some flair, which she cultivated, knowing that it was pleasing to Swift: "Having seen some Letters writ by a King in a very large Hand . . . she said, it confirmed the old Saying, *That Kings had long Hands*" (*PW* 5:238). This shows a readiness of wit and verbal agility, although collections of proverbs indicate that it was a common saying.[62] Even so, Stella produced it aptly, which is one of the signal requirements for conversational wit.

In the movement from the occasion to the comment, her wit usually requires no remarkable leap of imagination. In one instance Swift recounts, "Dr. *Sheridan*, who squandered more than he could afford, took out his Purse as he sat by the Fire, and found it was very hot; she said, the Reason was, that his Money burnt in his Pocket" (*PW* 5:237). It is almost too neat, too obvious: Sheridan, notorious for his improvidence, literally illustrates the saying that money burns a hole in your pocket. (Today we would call him a straight-man.) Another anecdote that Swift produces involves more invention. Charles Jervas, the celebrated portrait painter, told someone who had inquired about his address that he lived "next Door to the King (for his House was near St. *James's*)." The questioner failed to understand, so Stella took control of the conversation by negating Jervas's mild joke and subversively rephrasing it: "You mistake Mr. *Jervas*, for he only means next Door to the *Sign* of a King" (*PW* 5:237)—in other words, a tavern.

Swift was not privileged to hear the wittiest of Stella's remarks to have survived, nor could it have been made in his presence: "When a stranger said that 'Vanessa must be an extraordinary woman that could inspire the Dean to write so finely upon her' Mrs Johnson smiled, and answered, that she thought that point not quite so clear; for it was well known, the Dean could write finely upon a broomstick."[63] The stranger of the anecdote is the most pronounced example of the naïf figure who serves as the occasion for several specimens of Stella's wit by asking a question or otherwise needing information. In other examples the naïf is at a loss which Stella's witty intervention addresses, at times with a certain amount of aggression, as when she mocks the bereaved father's grief. Here Stella's smile reveals her self-possession while responding within the frame of social discourse governing the unwitting stranger's remark. It communicates that the topic is a pleasant one, and that she will politely offer another point of view merely as a participant in the conversation rather than an interested party. She begins with a misleadingly tentative expression, which is then followed by a statement that undercuts the stranger's assertion almost completely. Stella claims no special knowledge of the Dean, only of his writing, but that knowledge she deploys like a weapon. Nothing in her demeanor or words betrays that the stranger has made a terrible gaffe by referring in company to what must have been a source of great distress to her—the humiliatingly public evidence that Swift had a close relationship with another woman. Stella's posture of control, coupled with the reply itself, merits admiration.

At the same time, comparing any example of Stella's wit to Swift's reveals how far short she fell of his standard, and how generous he was in writing that in an afternoon's or evening's conversation, the company unanimously agreed that she was always the person to say "the best thing" (*PW* 5:229). Swift could be brilliant in Latin: "When a woman's long train swept down and broke a fine fiddle, he produced: 'Mantua v[a]e miserae nimium vicina cremonae.'"[64] Swift both invokes the Virgilian original and enriches it. For Virgil, the line's only idea is the proximity of the cities, which causes land from both to be confiscated for war veterans.[65] The individual identity of the two cities is not relevant. Swift adds to this geographical proximity distinctive associations of Mantua and Cremona, the latter known for a long tradition of violin making, the former also the name of a woman's gown or mantle.

Elsewhere, Swift observed that punning "was a talent no man ever despised who excelled in it."[66] Stella could not pun, a deficiency Swift teases her about when he relates a typical instance of his own punning. After dinner, the company at Harley's was given fringed napkins:

My lord keeper spread one of them between him and Mr. Prior; I told him I was glad to see there was such a *Fringeship* . . . between Mr. Prior and his lordship. Prior swore it was the worst he ever heard: I said I thought so too; but at the same time I thought it was most like one of Stella's that ever I heard. (*JS* 249–50)

There is no sense of competition here: Swift writes with the knowledge that Stella will not dispute his preeminence. He was proud of her wit because she was his pupil and friend, not his rival, and his hyperbolic praise should be taken as evidence—in someone who loathed the inflated rhetoric of romance—of his deep affection for her.

Swift commended Stella to her prospective suitor by stating that he had never seen "that person whose conversation [he] entirely valued but hers," without specifying what made her conversation so valuable (*C* 1:146). In the remembrance he wrote after her death he does specify: "She never had the least absence of mind in conversation, nor [was] given to interruption, or appeared eager to put in her word by waiting impatiently till another had done." She never, he continued, "spoke much at a time" (*PW* 5:230). Unlike the characterization of Stella as a wit, these brief descriptions suggest that Stella was, above all, a good listener, following the model described in advice-book literature and unlike the so-called "learned ladies" whom Swift condemns for "impertinent talkativeness" (*PW* 9:92). The picture of approved behavior that emerges is one that sociolinguistics has often substantiated: the male holding forth to the attentive and generally silent female, the perfect listener.[67] As Mary Pendarves, the future Mrs. Delany, described Swift in a letter to her sister (1733), "He talks a great deal and does not require many answers."[68]

If advice books for seventeenth- and eighteenth-century women are any guide, the same male expectation of female behavior in conversation was virtually universal. Women who spoke too much not only annoyed men, they betrayed a dangerous tendency to reject their subordinate status in other respects. The tenor of a popular early-seventeenth-century text, *The Anatomy of a Woman's Tongue*, is revealed in its subtitle: *A Medicine, a Poison, a Serpent, Fire, and Thunder*.[69] A number of writers actually recommend silence to women as if it were simply one kind of speaking, and the best kind at that. Jacques Du Boscq approvingly noted of the Blessed Virgin that "the holy Scripture makes no mention, that ever she spake more than foure or five times in all her life."[70] Hannah More's essay *On Conversation* distinguishes between the silence of "lifeless ignorance" and the silence of "sparkling intelligence." The latter, she believes, "is the most flattering encouragement in the world to men of sense and letters to continue any topic of instruction or entertainment they happen to be engaged in."[71]

That Stella generally adapted herself to, or internalized, Swift's conversational requirements is understandable: he made no secret of the high esteem in which he held good conversation and what its requirements were.[72] To meet his expectations in this area was a passport into his society and an avenue to his approval.

Yet, Stella's conversation could be both assertive and transgressive. The poem *To Stella, Who Collected and Transcribed His Poems*, takes Stella to task for stubbornly refusing to admit that she is wrong and, worse, becoming angry when "a friend in kindness tries / To show you where your error lies" (*CP* 206). Delany reports another instance of Swift's displeasure when the Dean fell into "a furious resentment with Mrs. Johnson, for a very small failure of delicacy" in conversation.[73] It would be useful to know exactly what this "very small failure of delicacy" was, since one of Stella's bons mots that Swift quotes approvingly is open to this very charge: "A very dirty Clergyman of her Acquaintance, who affected Smartness and Repartee, was asked by some of the Company how his Nails came to be so dirty? He was at a Loss; but she solved the Difficulty, by saying, the Doctor's Nails grew dirty by scratching *himself*" (*PW* 5:238). This kind of remark directed toward a male body was generally not allowable to women, and the rules were stricter for single women.[74] Stella's genteel social circle was heavily weighted toward clergymen, who might have been expected to be less open to violations of conversational decorum.[75] At the same time, if the company in question consisted of minor clerics, subordinate to or dependent upon Swift's good graces, or merely overmatched by his powerful personality, they might well have followed his lead in approving Stella's witticisms. Swift most likely remembered this particular example because his own fastidiousness, coupled with his dislike of pretension, would have caused him to approve the satiric impulse. Stella exercises here the same kind of corrective that the satirist himself might, aggressively punishing a remediable bad habit that someone else has exposed. Still, her remark exemplifies a practice that Swift condemns in his *Hints towards an Essay on Conversation*: "To run a Man down in Discourse, to put him out of Countenance, and make him ridiculous, sometimes to expose the Defects of his Person, or Understanding; on all which Occasions he is obliged not to be angry, to avoid the Imputation of not being able to take a Jest" (*PW* 4:91). This is also the practice that draws Swift's greatest anger in his indictment of the "tribe of rattling, swaggering Ladies" whose acquaintance, he writes in his *Letter to a Young Lady on Her Marriage*, would be worse for the bride than that of a common prostitute (*PW* 9:93). The conclusion is inescapable that what Swift objects to is running down a man he approves of (especially himself); in other words, running down that seems unfair.

In the *Hints*, Swift observes that this conversational aggression now passes for raillery, whereas true raillery is a reproach that through "some Turn of Wit unexpected and surprising, ended always in a Compliment, and to the Advantage of the Person it was addressed to" (*PW* 4:91). The difference between theory and practice suggests that the confident assertion that begins Swift's brief essay—that it would be possible to avoid conversational errors—was mistaken. All of the "errors" Swift enumerates are simply too tempting to be resisted by a witty speaker.

In his memorialization of Stella, Swift remarks that risqué speech is "the highest affront to the modesty and understanding of the female sex" (*PW* 5:235). Yet in his own correspondence with Stella and Dingley, two maiden ladies, Swift himself flouts propriety by telling ribald jokes and making obvious allusions to sexual knowledge that in theory virginal women would not possess (or, if they did, would not admit to). In describing the strict hierarchy of such knowledge in the seventeenth century, Laura Gowing states that "gender made a difference, but so did age, and marital status: access to knowledge was supposed to be tightly limited."[76]

Swift's practice may be guided by a public/private distinction according to which he would not have made risqué jokes to the ladies in a face-to-face situation, or when other people were present, but felt free to do so within the privacy of his letters. Double entendre informs his comment on the ladies of Ireland, "who never walk at all, as if their legs were of no use, but to be *laid aside*" (*JS* 270). Swift also repeats in a letter to Stella and Dingley some verses made about Bolingbroke: "Gently I wait the call of Charon's boat, / Still drinking like a fish, and ——like a stoat" (*JS* 164). Of an Irish acquaintance Stella had evidently inquired about, Swift wrote: "I know nothing of his Wife being here. It may cost her a Clap (I don't care to write that Word plain)" (*JS* 519). The editor's note indicates that the word was "smudged by Swift from motives of delicacy" (*JS* 519n). But it was not smudged to the point of obliteration: this was no more than a gesture in the direction of delicacy and thus was humorously meant.

Referring to the phallic political poem he had written, *Sid Hamet's Rod*, Swift asks Stella if she likes it and if she understands it "all" (*JS* 110). And yet, in the same paragraph, he threatens "to break your head in good earnest, young woman, for your nasty jest about Mrs. Barton" (*JS* 109). Less than two weeks later he writes that a letter from Anne Long "has quite turned my stomach against her; no less than two nasty jests in it with dashes to suppose them. She is corrupted in that country town with vile conversation" (*JS* 118–19). The threatened violence against Stella for a "nasty jest" is part of the posture of comic railing that he sometimes assumes with her; a moment later she is asked to admit that she is "an impudent lying slut" (*JS* 109). But with the much admired Anne Long, Swift's dismay and his belief in the corrupting influence of bad conversation seem genuine. He may have wanted to choose those instances of transgression that were allowable to his close friend, instances like *Sid Hamet* that exhibit his own wit or, like the verses on Bolingbroke, give him the pleasure of sharing a "nasty jest" in private with his close friends. For Stella or Anne Long to take the initiative in retailing "nasty jests" to him was another matter, the difference between the passive role of listener and the active one of speaker.

When Swift wrote *On the Death of Mrs. Johnson*, he clearly wished to extol Stella as unusual, even unique—a pattern figure for her sex. How much this ideal corresponds to the real woman cannot be known: few later writers have wanted to interrogate the impassioned testament that Swift left to "the truest, most virtuous, and valuable friend, that I, or perhaps any other person ever was blessed with" (*PW* 5:227). Were Stella's arguments on the defects of Epicurus or Hobbes truly excellent, and, if so, were they simply arguments she had imbibed from Swift? Later generations have no basis for answering such questions, and those who knew Stella did not address them. But some notes made by Swift in an edition of Milton that he gave to the ladies in 1703 suggest that Stella lacked general information: "Palestine is explained to be the Holy-Land, Rhene and Danau, two German rivers, Pilasters are rendered pillars" and such figures as Alcides, Columbus, and Xerxes are identified. Scott, who claimed possession of "an exact transcript" of these notes, concludes that Swift would not have taken this trouble for Mrs. Dingley alone: "The inference plainly must be, that Stella was neither well informed nor well educated."[77] She was not, as we know, systematically educated and so may well have had gaps in her knowledge of exotic geography, mythical heroes, and historical figures, but it is entirely possible that Swift *would* have annotated with Mrs. Dingley in mind. In view of Stella's persistent eye trouble, he may have expected Dingley to read from the volume to Stella. That she did not share Stella's attainments seems more certain. In his good-natured poem about Dingley and the housekeeper, Mrs. Brent, he described someone so immersed in her own world of trivia that if Solomon were to appear, she (and Brent) would find his wit and wisdom irrelevant to their petty concerns. Swift must often have had the experience he recounts in the poem's final stanza:

> You tell a good jest,
> And please all the rest,
> Comes Dingley, and asks you, What was it?
> And curious to know,
> Away she will go
> To seek an old rag in the closet. (*CP* 267)

A similar portrait of Dingley is drawn in *Bec's Birthday* (*CP* 312).[78]

Much of Swift's appraisal of Stella's qualities is highly subjective, and much of it is abstract: "Her advice was always the best, and with the greatest freedom, mixt with the greatest decency" (*PW* 5:228). Swift thought of Stella as a paragon, but the mixture of freedom and decency is difficult to translate into actual advice, of which he gives no specific example. According to Swift, Stella was never interested in such common topics of conversation as "news, politics, censure, family-management, or town-talk," but the *Journal to Stella* is full of exactly those matters, and undoubtedly if Stella had objected to them, some trace of this objection would be visible on Swift's side of the correspondence.

Swift's poems for Stella are often taken to be evidence of his sensible determination to see women as human beings rather than goddesses or of a relationship so close that it could accommodate affectionate teasing and truthfulness. Although references in the birthday poems to Stella's gray locks, wrinkles, and obesity are only faint reflections of the criticism leveled against the female body elsewhere in Swift's writings, they seem to erupt into the poetic context from Swift's very loathing of female physicality, as if he cannot keep himself from taking notice of bodily decay, even within a context celebrating the nonphysical attributes of his closest companion.[79] It is surely a compliment for affection to transcend the effects of aging, but it is hardly complimentary to call attention to the process. Swift violates this intuitive rule because he is determined to promulgate a different standard, one that does not politely ignore aging but pointedly rises above it.

Regarding her birthday poems, had she been less of a devotee to Swift's way of thinking, Stella might have recoiled from the austerity of his vision, much as we may imagine Swift's early fiancée Jane Waring did upon hearing from her prospective bridegroom that beauty of person meant nothing to him, cleanliness everything.[80] Many years later, Laetitia Pilkington was to observe Swift singling out a dirty old woman in a crowd of beggars and saying, as he gave alms to everyone but her, "that though she was a Beggar, Water was not so scarce but she might have washed her Hands" (P 27).[81] The female body was always problematic for Swift, even when it belonged to the woman he valued supremely.

The fullest sense of Swift's relationship to Stella is found in *The Journal to Stella*, that collection of sixty-five letters Swift wrote to Stella and Rebecca Dingley when he was in England (1710–13).[82] In June of 1711, he wrote from Chelsea to the women he had left behind in Ireland: "I reckon you are now preparing for your Wexford expedition; and poor Dingley is full of carking and caring, scolding. How long will you stay? Shall I be in Dublin before you return? Don't fall and hurt yourselves, nor overturn the coach. Love one another, and be good girls; and drink Pdfr's health in water, Madam Stella; and in good ale, Madam Dingley" (*JS* 298).[83] The passage is characteristic of the *Journal* letters, chatty and teasing, mixing matter-of-fact questions such as "how long will you stay in Wexford?" with routine concerns for the women's health and safety and commonplace behavioral injunctions like "love one another and be good girls." The command not to fall and hurt themselves or overturn the coach reflects Swift's cautious concern: such accidents were a common part of early-eighteenth-century life. It is also his way of saying, as people still do today, "have a safe trip." The behavioral prescription adds, "have a *good* trip." Finally, by instructing the women to drink "Pdfr's health," Swift reveals his desire that they keep thinking of him, the great absent presence overshadowing their uneventful lives.

There is no exceptional wit or memorable turn of phrase in the passage, and the sentiments are those that anyone might express when good friends take a trip. Yet Swift's energetic language is infused with an intimacy that colors even the mundane questions and instructions. Swift wants to know where the women are at all times and what they are doing. He knows how Dingley acts when she prepares to go somewhere: "carking and caring, scolding." He knows what the women will be drinking: ale for Dingley and water for Stella.

It seems as if Swift conscientiously makes a certain number of references to Dingley in each of his letters, but we understand, as perhaps Dingley did not, that she exists there only as part of Stella's life and for this reason part of Swift's concern. In his grief over Stella's approaching death in 1727, he wrote bitterly to Thomas Sheridan that he had brought "both those Friends" to Ireland, "that we might be happy together as long as God should please; the Knot is broken, and the remaining Person, you know, has ill answered the End; and the other who is now to be lost, was all that is Valuable" (W 3:124).[84] He knew he was expressing what is usually unsaid, for he prompted Sheridan, "You agreed with me, or you are a great Hypocrite" (W 3:124). How much this outburst was inspired by Swift's emotional upheaval of the moment and how much it represented an underlying truth of Swift's feelings about Dingley cannot be determined. At times his greetings to her in letters to mutual friends seem affectionate, at other times merely perfunctory. On September 28, 1728, that is, the same year in which Stella had died, Swift wrote from Market Hill to John Worrall, "I beg Mrs Dingley's pardon for not remembering her debt sooner [sixteen pounds he instructs Worrall to pay her], and my humble service to her (W 3:199)." This seems correct but without the affection he goes on to display in his greeting of Mrs. Worrall. Swift's end-of-year letter to Dingley in 1734, however, appears warm: "Pray God bless you," he writes, "& restore your Health & give you many happy new years. I send you your usual Christmas Box. I will see you as soon as I can" (*C* 4:282). In keeping with his punctilious sense of obligation Swift maintained some relationship with Dingley until his own decline. She died in 1743.

Small wonder that Virginia Woolf's initial view of the *Journal* says nothing of Dingley but instead hails the perfect intimacy of the Swift-Stella relationship: "Without effort or concealment he could use those precious moments late at night or the first thing on waking to pour out upon her the whole story of his day, with its charities and meannesses, its affections and ambitions and despairs, as though he were thinking aloud."[85] This is an accurate description with one exception: certainly the effect Swift wished to create as he poured out the story of his day for Stella was the illusion of complete revelation, but there *was* effort and concealment, a sustained effort of concealment that accompanied the frank chronicling of the momentous and the commonplace, attentions received and slights endured. Early on, Swift offers a structure for his letters that promises openness and completeness: "Perhaps, little MD is pleased to know how Pdfr passes his time in her absence. I always begin my last the same day I ended my former" (*JS* 35). The effect is one of total and continuous revelation: "When I write to MD ... it is just as if methinks you were here and I prating to you, and telling you where I have been: Well, says you, Pdfr, come, where have you been today? come, let's hear now. And so then I answer" (*JS* 167). Swift also disarmed those occasions that might have been suspect by skillfully surrounding them with innocuous matter. He has, for example, a whole range of reassuring circumstances to explain his frequent dining with Mrs. Vanhomrigh—including the habit of expressing this particular in terms of dining with *her*, as if to suggest that other members of the Vanhomrigh family were inconsequential.

The times when he did indeed discuss his life "as though he were thinking aloud" could convey the impression that he was always so forthright. He was, in fact, quite clever in creating an aura of innocent activity truthfully recounted: "Pdfr's at home, God help him, every night from six till bed-time, and has as little enjoyment or pleasure in life at present as any body in the world" (*JS* 167). The absurdity of this statement indicates that it was meant to be read by Stella as transparently false. She knew that he was enjoying his busy life, playing a part in the world of power: the extravagance of his declaration—*every night, any body in the world*—was contradicted by other activities reported in his letters. Like the excessive expressions of affectionate concern found elsewhere, this is simply language intended to communicate heart truth: because they are apart, Swift tells Stella, even if he does not literally give up every pleasure, he does not truly enjoy life.

The metanarrative of the letters themselves also reinforces the implausible idea that Swift privileged the letters to MD over his work for the government or other activities. To mail his twenty-ninth letter to them, he made the coachman stop at the post office at two o'clock, on his way to dine with the most important government figure in England, the lord treasurer. He sometimes reports that he was out late, yet wrote to MD nevertheless, or even left a social gathering early in order to do his nightly letter writing.

Given Swift's compulsive and methodical nature, the terms he established for communicating with Stella and Dingley, such as writing at the end of every day, quickly became unbreakable conventions. In his twenty-third letter he remarks, "Is it not plaguy insipid to tell you every day where I dine; yet now I have got into the way of it, I cannot forbear it neither" (*JS* 267). This particular habit became a source of prevarication when Swift felt the need to conceal how often he dined at the Vanhomrighs.

Even before this became an aspect of his life that he kept from Stella, Swift might well have felt some guilt at the difference between his present life and that of the ladies he had urged to settle near him in Ireland. In his first year in London, he writes of a night when he "was dreaming the most melancholy things in the world of poor Stella, and was grieving and crying all night" (*JS* 110–11). He has, the dream suggests, abandoned Stella, and without him she will suffer "melancholy things." His grief at such a prospect affirms his deep feeling for Stella; at the same time, he could never sacrifice his ambition on her account, no matter how many times he protests to the contrary. Later, he had a recurring dream that he found himself in Ireland, "and that I have left my cloaths and things behind me, and have not taken leave of any body; and that the ministry expect me tomorrow, and such nonsense" (*JS* 221). Finding himself in Ireland is a nightmare: everything he values, possessions and job, remains in England. Significantly, the ladies do not have a role in this frequent dream: it is a simple expression of his conscious feelings of wanting to live in England and not in Ireland. By interpreting this dream to mean that "Swift is needed everywhere," Michael V. DePorte blurs the distinction I find to be critical between where Swift wants to be (London) and where he finds himself in his dream (Ireland).[86]

Swift's curiosity about Stella and Dingley corresponds to, but doesn't equal, theirs about him. His letters describe his own doings and comment on theirs as, presumably, their letters described their doings and commented on his. But this is a false parity. Swift was now in London, the center of the world as he and his correspondents knew it, and he was close to the seat of power, associating with aristocrats and ministers every day. Socially, he was much in demand: his letters coruscate with references to noblemen with whom he mingled and dined on a regular basis. How could the modest circumstances of Stella and Dingley's Irish life compare in any respect? It was a life that Swift had already lived and taken the full measure of. And while it was unlikely that in her limited circle Stella could (or would) undertake an intrigue that would be kept from Swift, or needed to be kept from him, he was hiding from her an aspect of his life that she would have regarded as of the greatest importance: his attraction to a much younger woman, Esther Vanhomrigh, whom he had dubbed Vanessa.

The knowing reader is bound to invest the so often repeated "I dined with Mrs. Vanhomrigh" with deeper meaning than it could have had for the unknowing Stella, although Stella may have had her suspicions. In response to a direct query from her about someone "that boards near me, that I dine with now and then"—probably an allusion to Vanessa's mother, Swift turns aside the effort to obtain more information, first with a flat denial—"I know no such person: I do not dine with boarders"—and then mock indignation: "What the pox! You know whom I have dined with every day since I left you, better than I do" (*JS* 87). This bluster was part of the facade of transparency.

And Swift, as if to arm himself against an unlikely discovery, always gives some reason other than his own inclination for dining at Mrs. Vanhomrigh's. On July 6, 1711, he writes: "An ugly rainy day; I was to visit Mrs. Barton, then called at Mrs. Vanhomrigh's, where Sir Andrew Fountaine and the rain kept me to dinner; and there did I loiter all the afternoon, like a fool, out of perfect laziness, and the weather not permitting me to walk; but I'll do so no more" (*JS* 309). Nevertheless, the very next day he reports having dined again at Mrs. Vanhomrigh's and passing the evening there. To disarm this admission he adds, "very dull and insipid" (*JS* 310). The weather was often the reason given for Swift's choosing the Vanhomrigh table: "I dined with Mrs. Van; for the weather is so bad, and I am so busy that I cannot dine with great folks"—a comforting reminder that "Mrs. Van" is not socially prominent (*JS* 395).

Swift usually wants to convey that he dined with Mrs. Vanhomrigh out of convenience, since she lived nearby, or as a last resort when he "could get no invitation to dinner at court." On August 14, he tells Stella and Dingley that he was "mortified . . . not knowing where in the world to dine, the town is so empty; I met H. Coote, and thought he would invite me, but he did not: Sir John Stanley did not come into my head; so I took up with Mrs. Van, and dined with her and her damned landlady" (*JS* 360). So, it turns out, Swift did dine with boarders, after all. At other times he insinuates that he was without volition in the matter of dining. On one occasion he was "going to dine with Dr. Cockburn, but Sir Andrew Fountaine met me, and carried me to Mrs. Van's" (*JS* 383). Stella might have noticed that between the ninth and the twenty-third of the month Swift had admitted to going to Mrs. Vanhomrigh's five times.[87]

Swift often attributed agency in this matter to Sir Andrew, who on another day is described as having made Swift "dine again with Mrs. Van." Swift represents himself as leaving soon in order to answer a letter of MD's. And again, he writes that he accompanied Sir Andrew and remained after dinner, this time because of his health: "My cold made me loiter all the evening" (*JS* 309).

In another letter Swift deftly turns the subject from his own dining to sympathetically imagining Stella's: "I dined with my neighbour Vanhomrigh, and MD, poor MD, at home on a loin of mutton and half a pint of wine, and the mutton was raw; poor Stella could not eat, poor dear rogue, and Dingley was so vexed" (*JS* 231). Swift is often humorous in his dramatic renditions of Stella and Dingley's life in Ireland, but these fantasies are also controlling, prescribing their activities, putting words, as well as meat, in their mouths.[88]

A thoughtful person might have observed how much at home Swift was at the Vanhomrighs'. On more than one occasion he mentions that he keeps or changes his gown and periwig there. When he had debilitating pain in his neck and collar bone, he went to Mrs. Vanhomrigh's, where he could be "easy." When business at the Secretary's office caused him to miss the dinner hour, he nevertheless went to Mrs. Vanhomrigh's late in the afternoon and "made them get me three herrings."

Her lodgings were located "but five doors off," so all of this is represented as mere convenience.

In spite of Swift's care to always furnish a plausible reason other than his own desire to account for his frequenting the Vanhomrigh dinner table, or to indicate that it was not pleasurable to be there, Stella might have gathered otherwise from his entry of October 21, 1711: "Mrs. Van would have me dine with her again to-day, and so I did, though Lady Mountjoy has sent two or three times to have me see and dine with her, and she is a little body I love very well" (*JS* 390). Contradictory impulses inform this statement: Swift's weakness for aristocratic acquaintances leads him to brag about Lady Mountjoy's eagerness to see him and his failure to respond, while his habit of telling Stella where he dined causes him to incautiously confess to still another dinner at the Vanhomrighs. Stella might have wondered why the attraction of Mrs. Vanhomrigh's table trumped the urgings of a titled personage he loved "very well."

If on one level Swift wished to keep Stella from speculating about his frequent appearance at Mrs. Vanhomrigh's, on another he enjoyed referring to these occasions in ways that were meaningful to him but would not be understood by Stella. "I sat the evening with Mrs. Vanhomrigh, and drank coffee, and ate an egg," he writes (*JS* 380), enumerating these innocent-seeming and unremarkable activities as if, once again, he had had a dull time of it. His letters to Vanessa, however, invoke their drinking coffee as an intimate ritual, one probably infused with sexual excitement. For the reader of Swift's correspondence with Vanessa, the unexceptional journal entry marks a meeting between the two, just as the many references to dining with Mrs. Vanhomrigh are more accurately read as opportunities to see her elder daughter.

At times Swiftian concealment goes further. On February 23, 1713, he wrote that he did not attend a meeting of the society he belonged to because "I had Business that calld me anothr way, so I sent my Excuses, and dind privately with a Friend" (*JS* 628). Ehrenpreis's research in Swift's account books reveals that he was at the Vanhomrighs that night. In fact, according to Ehrenpreis, "time and again, when his account book tells us he visited the [Vanhomrighs] . . . a letter to Ireland mentions either nothing or simply 'a friend'" (E 2:641). This practice suggests that Swift wanted to avoid too many mentions of the Vanhomrigh household, no matter how innocuously presented.

In his letter entry for December 18, 1711, Swift states, "I have been writing letters all this evening till I am weary," but he naturally fails to specify that one of these letters is a short note to Vanessa, which concludes, "Adieu til we meet over a Pott of Coffee, or an Orange and Sugar in the Sluttery, which I have so often found to be the most agreeable Chamber in the World" (*JS* 441; W 1:399). Had Stella been privy to this communication, she might have reflected on the frequency of meetings alluded to and the likelihood that another would soon take place since Swift found the chamber in which he met Vanessa to be the "most agreeable in the world." This might be contrasted with his many epistolary protestations of coming to Ireland, trips that were invariably postponed with extravagant regrets about missing MD.

Given his precautions, it is arresting that, although Swift never mentions the other Vanhomrigh children, he writes to Stella on August 11, 1711, that Mrs. Vanhomrigh's "eldest daughter is come of age, and going to Ireland to look after her fortune, and get it in her own hand" (*JS* 333).[89] It seems an utterly gratuitous comment since he does not convey this news with the idea of making the two women acquainted, as he elsewhere does in announcing the journey to Ireland of someone he knows. Swift might have reasoned that Stella would have no cause to react to a mention of Mrs. Vanhomrigh's elder daughter; from her perspective the widowed mother would have been the more logical recipient of Swift's interest. But it is also possible that rationality had nothing to do with this comment, that Vanessa was in Swift's thoughts to such a degree that he could not help but exhibit her in a letter to Stella, albeit in disguise.

Certainly Swift cared deeply about Stella and also, to a much lesser extent, about her companion. Nevertheless, the expressions regarding their well being, the "God blesses" that are lavishly sprinkled throughout the letters, especially the early letters, seem exactly that—sprinkled. They also seem to be loosely correlated with time spent at the Vanhomrighs, as if to make up to Stella, at least rhetorically, for Swift's defections with Vanessa, or more generally, to make up for the absence that placed Swift not only at a physical remove from her, but in another sphere altogether. Late in the *Journal*, as affairs of state weigh on Swift more and more and the Oxford ministry approaches crisis, these expressions all but disappear. Williams notes by the end of 1711 a weakening in "the spontaneity and unaffected naturalness of the expressions of affection" for the ladies (*JS* xxxix). From here on, he finds that such expressions become perfunctory, as Swift becomes increasingly preoccupied with the difficulties of the ministry. A typical example of this tendency is Swift's May 1711 closing adjuration: "Believe that MD's felicity is the great end I aim at in my pursuits" (*JS* 276). Treating this exhortation as a serious statement of the purpose of Swift's activities would be ludicrous. He was, in fact, hopeful at that time of an English preferment that would have removed him from Ireland permanently. Stella, Williams believes, would have read such declarations as allusions to a time when the two could marry (*JS* xxxviii). At the least she would have interpreted them as exemplifications of the underlying premise of Swift's letters: that she remained at the center of his thoughts in spite of his busy life away from her.

Swift's excessive protestations occasionally read like boilerplate, filling up the page when he can think of nothing further in the way of news. He writes extravagantly, for instance, "Farewell, my dearest lives, and delights, I love you better than ever, if possible, as hope saved, I do, and ever will. God Almighty bless you ever, and make us happy together; I pray for this twice every day; and I hope God will hear my poor hearty prayers" (*JS* 302–3). Could Swift have genuinely been praying to abandon the dazzling life he was then leading for a return to Stella and Ireland? No doubt part of Swift could reflect nostalgically on the pleasures he revisits here, but the greater part of his will at the moment of this fervent prayer was bent on other scenarios—as he inadvertently tells Stella directly after his pious and prayerful farewell: "I . . . have every day numbers of considerable men teazing me to solicit for them. And the ministry all use me perfectly well, and all that know them, say they love me" (*JS* 303). How flattering to the man who hungered for recognition and felt its lack all his life, and how painful to compare Swift's boasting with the portrait drawn by Bishop White Kennett in 1713 of a self-important Swift bustling about:

> He stopped Francis Gwyn, Esq., going in with the red bag to the queen, and told him aloud he had something to say to him from my lord treasurer. . . . He turned to the fire, and took out his gold watch, and telling him [Dr. Davenant's son] the time of day, complained that it was very late. A gentleman said he was too fast. "How can I help it," says the Doctor, "if the courtiers give me a watch that won't go right?"[90]

Ministers being what they are, and Swift's sense of insecurity being what it was, he also avows to the ladies that the only love and kindness he can count on is that of MD. The letter concludes with a coda that sounds like a benediction, one that must have pleased Stella above all others: "Stella, Dingley, Pdfr, all together, now and forever all together" (*JS* 303).

The "little language," a kind of baby talk, is part of this texture of affectionate reference as is a panoply of names for the two women that have an infantilizing effect, in part because they are often diminutives: *little MD, little dear sirrahs, little monkies mine.* Swift will refer to himself as Pdfr in connection with MD, but when he writes about a serious issue it is always in the first person. Pdfr is the name for intimacy, but also for triviality. Revealingly, he tells his correspondents: "Pdfr is going to be very busy; not Pdfr, but t'other I" (*JS* 344). Writing about himself in even a small personal matter, such as his habit of exercise, he will prefer to say "I": "oo walk plodigiousry I suppose, oo make nothing of walking to too to to ay, to Donibrook: I walk too as much as I can: because sweating is good; but I'll walk more if I go to Kensington" (*JS* 537). The first part of the sentence uses the little language to make gentle fun of the ladies' walking—they were not the enthusiasts for exercise that Swift was. But once the topic shifts to Swift's walking, the prose is direct and clear: this is serious walking under discussion, not the comic walking—to where? wherever Swift can imagine—associated with Stella and Dingley.

The letters often exhibit a serious utterance followed by a comment indicating Swift's awareness that he may have lost his audience. The tone will change abruptly, and standard English will give way to the little language. On one occasion Swift unburdens himself at length about Tom Leigh, a clergyman whose "formal ways annoyed Swift," according to Williams (*JS* 10n). The complaint goes on and on through several exchanges of he said/I said, while Swift becomes more incensed:

> Don't you see how curiously he contrives to vex me, for the dog knows that with half a word I could do more than all of them together. Butt he onely does it from the Pride & envy of his own heart, and not out of a humorous design of teazing, he is one of those, that would rather a Service should not be done, than done by a private man and of his own Country. (*JS* 587)

Then, he states or questions: "You take all this, don't you[.] Nite dee sollahs, I'll go seep a dazey" (*JS* 587). The adult conversation is over with what seems to be a sudden illumination that he has gone on too long, beyond his friends' interest or ability to comprehend his argument: he may have simply been unburdening himself to the only audience he could address so frankly. The little language restores intimacy and effects closure.

As his London life was drawing to an end, Swift similarly shared with his friends his attempts to save the ministry from internal dissension. "Tis impossible to save People against their own will; and I have been too much engaged in Patchwork already," he muses in December of 1712. Then he cuts short this train of thought with a question, "Do you understand all this Stuff?" and provides his own answer: "No—well zen you are now returnd to Ombre & the Dean, & Christmas, I wish oo a very merry one." The rest of the entry is in the little language, concluding with "Nite deelest Md" (*JS* 580–81). Swift seems to realize in the midst of his musings that philosophical conjectures about human nature are inappropriate to the ladies: social occasions, such as card-playing and holidays, are more their concern, so he switches to a reassuring babble. In spite of Swift's retrospective portrait of Stella as a nonparticipant in a female culture that he holds in contempt, it seems likely that much of her life with Dingley was lived in that very culture.[91]

The coupling of Swift's allusion to the ministers loving him with his assertion that only the love of MD can be counted on yokes together his great desire to be fully appreciated and the attendant fear that these politicians are simply using him as they do others, a fear that modern research has confirmed.[92] He could reveal his fears in the intimacy of the *Journal*, recounting how he had been repeatedly promised a place by the Lord Treasurer and then put off. It was intensely frustrating to Swift in 1712 to be passed over for several desirable deaneries in England. The negotiation that finally made him Dean of St. Patrick's was agonizingly and humiliatingly prolonged, causing him to complain that "this Suspense vexes me worse than any thing else" (*JS* 663). His comment on the outcome seems from the heart: "Neither can I feel joy at passing my days in Ireland; and I confess I thought the ministry would not let me go" (*JS* 662). The first assertion must have wounded Stella, although its intent is directed elsewhere; the second, Swift's admission that ultimately he was not as important as he had imagined, was a hard admission for him—but he could share it, and other similar revelations, with Stella, perhaps with her alone of his friends.

Referring to his efforts to keep Bolingbroke and the Lord Treasurer together, he tells her, "I act an honest part; that will bring me neither profit or praise. MD must think the better of me for it: nobody else shall ever know it" (*JS* 389). Swift can also count on Stella's sympathy with his successful but unrewarded efforts to secure the First Fruits for the Irish clergy: "I thought the clergy in convocation in Ireland would have given me thanks for being their solicitor, but I hear of no such thing," he writes (*JS* 334). He further enlists her to play an active part in finding out what is being said in Ireland: "Pray talk occasionally on that subject, and let me know what you hear" (*JS* 334). On the matter of how his writings were received in Ireland, he was equally assiduous, surprised that she has not commented on his recently published *Description of a City Shower*. He writes: "How chance you did not see that before your last letter went; but I suppose you in Ireland did not think it worth mentioning" (*JS* 86). This complaint invites a reassuring denial from Stella.

Swift's own sensitivity to Stella's possible disappointments and difficulties is much less well developed. He can voice sincere concern for her physical state, recommending exercise and jaunts to curative waters, but just as his own preoccupation prevents him from realizing how Stella may feel about his disappointment in receiving a deanery in Ireland and how it conflicts with his many protestations of happiness with her there, so he has no idea that the saying he passes on to her that "*in men, desire begets love; and in women love begets desire*" (*JS* 570) could give Stella any discomfort—as if the topic of love and desire is so removed from their relationship that it can be forthrightly discussed as a motivating factor in the affairs of men and women in general but not applicable to themselves. All of Swift's energies of subterfuge seem to have been concentrated on protecting the secrecy of his attraction to Vanessa. In other respects, Stella could be taken for granted.

We can do nothing but speculate about Stella's state of mind at this time. She may still have entertained hopes that Swift would marry her, as Williams thinks, since the disinclination to marry that Swift had expressed in 1704 was confided to her suitor, William Tisdall, rather than to Stella herself. Her supposed unhappiness, if apocryphal, was bound to be invented, since the logic of the situation seemed to demand it.

If Vanessa was the true rival who had to be concealed in the *Journal*, Swift nevertheless writes about many valued women friends with whom he had a range of relationships. But in every case where he openly admired a woman in his letters, circumstances were such that Stella would not be fearful of a rival. Most were aristocrats, most were married, some were elderly, some were described as ugly. Lady Orkney, for example, was portrayed as kind and maternal towards Swift although she "squints like a dragon" (*JS* 379). In keeping with her nurturing role she provided Swift with various practical items, including medicine for his various ailments, as did another good friend, Lady Kerrey.

The subterfuge, evasion, and denial of responsibility that characterized Swift's self-presentation as a published writer also informed his personal life. Whatever the original recipients of the letters thought, to my knowledge no later reader has accepted the controlling fiction that Swift is addressing Esther Johnson and Rebecca Dingley equally.[93] And in spite of the calculated and long-term deception that the *Journal to Stella* embodies, no reader can fail to register the profound intimacy of the letters. If Swift held back the crucial information that he was involved with another woman, he nevertheless revealed a great deal about other areas of his life. It is impossible to imagine him speaking frankly of his disappointments to Vanessa, who clearly idolized and idealized him, but to Stella he confides the ambitions, hopes, and defeats that he most likely voiced to no one else in such a naked form.

Even this self-exposure had to be shared with Rebecca Dingley. The anomaly of the relationship enshrined in the *Journal to Stella* is this inclusion of a third party: somewhat akin to having sex with a Siamese twin, the intimacy had to embrace someone extraneous to it but difficult to ignore. Swift presumably wanted the respectability conferred by Dingley's presence: no doubt this is why almost all the letters are addressed to her rather than to Stella. The price he paid was making Dingley as privy to his secrets as was Stella. This was simply the condition of things, but Swift's true feeling may be glimpsed when he records a dream he had that Stella has come to England alone: "I asked her after Dingley, and she said, she had left her in Ireland, because she designed her stay to be short" (*JS* 404). The dream query acknowledges that Stella without Dingley is unusual and must be accounted for. It is explained in the way of ordinary rather than dream logic, but no doubt this answer expresses Swift's desire to see Stella without Dingley, coupled with the understanding that this can only be for a brief time, a time that can occur only in the dream world.

3

*V*anessa

The Questions

I agree with that Gentleman (whoever he is) that said to answer letters was a part of good breeding, but he would agree with me, that nothing requires more caution, from the ill uses that have been often made of them, especially of letters without common business. They are a standing witness against a man, which is confirmed by a Latin saying—for words pass but Letters remain.

—Swift to Knightley Chetwode, May 8, 1731

I have worne out my days in sighing and my nights with watching and thinking of –, –, –, – – – – who thinks not of me how many letters must I send you before I shall receive an answer?

—Vanessa to Swift, CelBridge [November/December] 1720

Swift's observation to Knightley Chetwode reflects both his caution and his fear, qualities that eminently inform his correspondence with Vanessa. She, in contrast, is associated with the passionate importuning and despair of the 1720 letter cited above, a characterization that distorts the Swift-Vanessa correspondence and by extension their long involvement.

Because of the tempestuous and secret nature of the relationship Swift carried on with Vanessa, his efforts to marginalize and erase her are understandable. That, unlike Stella, she eluded his control was due as much to the difference in socioeconomic condition between the two women as to their dissimilarity of temperament. Vanessa's personal fortune, and the absence of older family members with authority over her, allowed her to indulge her feelings and to make demands that would not have been possible to the differently circumstanced Stella, encumbered with a constant chaperone in the person of Rebecca Dingley and burdened with the strict propriety that made possible her inclusion in Swift's public life, however meager that inclusion was compared to the role of an acknowledged wife.

Vanessa not only preserved and numbered Swift's letters to her, she made copies of her own letters to him, all that has survived of her side of their correspondence. In the many instances where no reply of Swift's exists to one of these drafts, we cannot be certain that she actually sent the letter, or conversely, that Swift's reply has not been lost. She knew that Swift was impatient with her complaints and may on occasion have found it enough to vent them by writing, diary fashion, without sending the letter on. Commentators, understandably exasperated by the paucity of hard evidence about the Swift-Vanessa relationship, have tended to make no distinction between the drafts and sent letters.

Swift's influence was such that Vanessa's instructions to her executors to publish this correspondence after her death in 1723 were not carried out during Swift's lifetime:[1] the younger Thomas Sheridan states that soon after Vanessa's death the letters were on the verge of being published when his father, "getting intelligence of it . . . applied so effectually to the executors that the printed copy was cancelled."[2] The surviving letters are twenty-eight from Swift to Vanessa and seventeen draft replies (W 1:399n). They fall into two groups, separated by a hiatus of five years: letters of 1712, 1713, and 1714; then letters of 1720, 1721, and 1722 (W 1:433n). This odd clustering would indicate gaps in the correspondence even without the evidence of Vanessa's system of numbering, which suggests that many letters are missing: A. Martin Freeman, the first collector of the entire surviving correspondence, thinks "it would be rash to assume that we now have more than half the original number which were exchanged."[3] Nor do we know how censored the correspondence that survives may have been. In spite of the pressure brought to bear on the first attempt to publish the correspondence, Freeman sees no motive for anyone to have destroyed the letters. He believes that "the present incomplete state of the collection is the result of hurried pilfering, committed at a time when the letters were not bound together or chronologically arranged."[4] Pilfering may have occurred, but we should not discount the motive of protecting Swift's reputation as an explanation for missing letters.

Vanessa herself would not have destroyed any of Swift's letters, although she must have destroyed letters he wrote to her sister that he sometimes alluded to. Early on she had kept back a letter to Anne Long that Swift had expected her to forward, and she seems never to have gotten over a jealous reaction when Swift wrote to her sister. She told him that she took "very ill" his addressing a letter to her mother: "you promised the letter should be Directed to me" (W 1:508). At her instigation she and her mother counted the number of references to Moll and Hessy in this letter and found them to be equal. Vanessa was still not satisfied: "You talke to Moll, and only say now hessy grumbles" (W 1:508). This possessive impulse would persist: in July of 1720 she is offended that Swift has written what he jokingly called a "love letter" to her sister: "When I opened yo' letter I thought you had wrote me two as you said perhaps you might but instead of that to find 'twas a letter to another and that a love letter how do you think I could support it" (W 2:339). Vanessa was thirty-two at the time and Moll was fatally ill.

What letters survive are sufficiently remarkable, especially in light of the common view that Vanessa ceaselessly pursued a reluctant Swift. This is the opinion of the most recent male biographers of Swift, Irvin Ehrenpreis (E 3:380–83) and David Nokes (N 259–62). Ehrenpreis refers to Vanessa's "emotional blackmail" (E 3:94), while Nokes depicts a Swift altruistically attempting to cheer up a woman given to "morbid self-pity"(N 259). In this widely accepted interpretation, while Swift tried to disengage himself for fourteen years, Vanessa preyed upon his compassion by parading her griefs before him. As le Brocquy observes, those who dismiss the relationship in this fashion "have chosen to ignore Swift's own statement that they met regularly, once a week, over a long period."[5]

Dr. George Berkeley, one of Vanessa's executors, assured Dr. Delany several times that the correspondence contained "nothing which would dishonor the character or bring the least reflection upon Cadenus."[6] In light of the sentiments Swift expresses in the letters and the record of long intimacy they document, the comment is puzzling. It could mean that Berkeley, a busy and important man, had read, or remembered, cursorily or incompletely. Possibly, so long after Swift's death, he merely wanted to speak tactfully of him to one of the Dean's closest friends. It must have appeared to Berkeley in 1767 that the correspondence would never be published.

Biographers have generally sided with Berkeley's view—that is, with Swift and against Vanessa. For Bernard Acworth, writing in 1947, Swift "was plagued very much with her wild and passionate letters. His replies, when he made them, were reserved, patient, weary, sometimes irritable, very rarely angry, and always paternal as befitted the Dean of the Cathedral."[7] Modern commentators have struggled to rationalize Swift's statements in the letters and thus save him from bad faith. David Masson characterizes Swift's side of the correspondence as "kindly letters,"[8] while Howard Williams invents a complicated rationale to explain Swift's use of French in his letter of May 12, 1719, to Vanessa: "The style of this French letter . . . is so hyperbolical, and so different from the somewhat cavalier manner of his English letters, that we must suppose that the politeness of the language inspired the extravagance of the compliments."[9] A more persuasive explanation might be found in the letter's context, which we can only imagine from the letter itself, the first of the correspondence after a hiatus of more than two years. It must be in response to one that Vanessa wrote in French, containing the misinformation that Swift had left Dublin for three months without telling her, a circumstance that would have aroused all of her feelings of rejection and perhaps led to violent statements of the sort found elsewhere in her letters. Swift's primary purpose, then, would have been to restore the uneasy equilibrium of their relationship by soothing Vanessa about his trip and repeating his usual praise. But however hyperbolic, these compliments were not mere words: it was part of Swift's great gift for friendship that he exaggerated the merits of all his friends, indulging Charles Ford, whom Pilkington found pretentious and affected, and describing Stella as a female paragon. But French was not a language that Swift knew well, so his lavish compliments, elevating Vanessa higher than the rest of humanity, are suspect.

Nokes, wanting to deflate some of these compliments, suggests that writing in French was "like a promise with fingers crossed. Somehow it doesn't quite count. Otherwise, what he says here is frankly dishonest" (N 261). This is clearly unacceptable to Nokes, who wants to invalidate these statements in keeping with his own view that Swift's "esteem and honour for Stella were always greater than for Vanessa" (N 261). He seems to find it inconceivable that a man might simultaneously tell two different women that each was paramount in his affections.

A similar reading can be found in Ehrenpreis, with some admission that Swift was partially responsible for encouraging Vanessa, or at least for allowing "compassion" to overcome his desire to stay away. In short, the thesis advanced by Bishop Berkeley has remained intact in the hands of Swift's most prominent late-twentieth-century biographers. Of the dashes that Swift suggested to Vanessa as a way of conveying tender epithets in their letters without writing the actual words, an invention attributable to Swift's constant fear that others would read the letters, Nokes says that Vanessa "seized on his idea ... with great enthusiasm, and strewed her letters with these cryptic symbols of affection" (N 257). Swift's announcement that he was coming to see her at Celbridge "called forth a whole battery of strokes" (N 258). True enough, but when Swift responded with his own set of dashes, Nokes remarks dismissively that this "hail of strokes [is] too profuse to be intense" (N 259).

Ehrenpreis says that he will "pass over the many piquant or touching sentences from Swift's letters to Vanessa because they would misrepresent the general effect of a man straining to transform a romantic obsession into a placid, playful intimacy" (E 3:395). Such passages should not be overlooked, however, for they are unparalleled in Swift's writing. They are, in fact, so arresting that Ehrenpreis could legitimately fear their effect on his hypothesis of Swift's striving for a "placid, playful intimacy," the sort that characterizes the *Journal to Stella*. At the same time, Ehrenpreis's acknowledgment that there are "many" such sentences is surely an argument for engaging rather than ignoring them.

In contrast to such attempts on the part of men to minimize Swift's feelings in the correspondence, women have been more skeptical of the supposed desire to disengage. Margaret Woods described the letters to Vanessa as "far indeed from bearing out the view, improbable in itself, that for some twelve years Vanessa besieged Swift with a love which he consistently discouraged."[10] Reviewing the Swift-Vanessa correspondence in 1933, Alyse Gregory commented on Swift: "He who understood society as a thief understands his jemmy, with the same grim stealth, or as a hangman knows his knots, did not comprehend so much about the heart of a girl."[11] Passing over Gregory's sinister comparisons, her observation is sensible. If Swift did indeed want only Ehrenpreis's "placid, playful intimacy" with Vanessa, he was, at the age of fifty-four, extraordinarily naive in writing to her on 5 July, 1721: "Cad- assures me he continues to esteem and love and value you above all things, and so will do to the End of his Life; but at the same time entreats that you would not make your self or him unhappy by Imaginations" (W 2:385). He may have expected the second clause to cancel the first, but since the first statement is an emphatic and absolute declaration, and the second a vague and weakly couched plea, there is little likelihood that the final effect of the sentence would be to moderate the passionate feelings that Vanessa expressed to Swift so often. Her letters are often out of control, pleading with him to write or visit, by turns angry and conciliatory, one letter complaining of his neglect while the next attempts to placate because she knows that her complaints irritate him. Swift was not so much trying to extricate himself as to calm Vanessa into something resembling Stella's state of docile acceptance of a status quo that was unalterable. Vanessa's "Imaginations" were all about overcoming that stasis.

Some critics have assumed that Swift's third-person references were a means of dissociating himself from the sentiments attributed to "Cad." They may have been, but they are also commonplaces of Swift's writing in general. After all, in the *Journal to Stella* he calls himself *Pdfr*. It seems more likely that this was a habit of self-presentation based originally on Swift's fear of his letters falling into unfriendly hands.[12] He must have known that for Vanessa the use of his special name, one that evoked the poem written for her, would simply reinforce a tender intimacy rather than project distance.[13]

The letter of July 5th does contain some of the material that Ehrenpreis is most comfortable with: precepts about exercise of the sort that Swift was apt to inflict on everyone he cared for and an account of his own ordinary activities, which was also meant to be instructive. But these passages are outweighed and enveloped by those that Ehrenpreis would pass over as "piquant" or "touching." The peremptory "Settle your Affairs and quit this scoundrel Island" would surely have disheartened Vanessa had it not been followed by the seductive phrase, "and things will be as you desire" (W 2:386). What Swift might have meant by this contradictory statement has predictably eluded those commentators who do not want to find his posture questionable: the sentence seems to embody Swift's wish to be free of Vanessa coupled with his desire to please her. The idea is a fantasy: if only Vanessa were to disappear from Swift's life, but at the same time do so happily, a worrisome problem would be resolved without Swift's agency. He would not be guilty in any way.

The irreconcilable suggestions also replicate the backing and forthing of *Cadenus and Vanessa*, where the poet produces numerous arguments against the love of pupil for tutor but can never bring himself to close off completely the possibility of a romantic denouement. In the poem, the outcome of Vanessa's pursuit of Cadenus must be kept secret, only because it had to be so in the reality that prompted the poem. Swift's motives for keeping the relationship going were probably a compound of genuine affection, his pleasure in her adoration, and his fear of an abandoned Vanessa creating a scandal, with the proportion of each feeling to the others changing over time and impossible for us to recover today.

Whatever Swift meant by ordering Vanessa to leave Ireland and yet asserting that she would be happy doing so, what Vanessa would have thought upon reading it is more certain. She had written to Swift in unmistakable terms about his meaning for her: "t'is not in the power of arte time or accedent to lessen the unexpressable passion which I have for —— nor is the love I beare you only seated in my soul for there is not a single atome of my frame that is not blended with it" (W 2:351). What might have been intended by Swift merely as comforting rhetoric would have fed those feelings over which, she repeatedly wrote to Swift, she had no control.

The letter continues with Swift reiterating his sentiments in French: "Rest assured that no one in the world has been more loved, honored, esteemed, adored by your friend than you."[14] If all close friends may be loved, honored, and esteemed, the word *adored* conveys something beyond the ordinary descriptions of friendship. Perhaps Swift was crossing his fingers, figuratively speaking, as he penned his sweeping and absolute declaration, but Vanessa, who wanted to believe, would not have known this. More important to a biographical investigation of Swift, he surely understood how she would interpret these words. To Vanessa, French must have seemed to be a token of their intimacy, the language associated not with prevarication but with love.

Swift concluded in English, "I drank no Coffee since I left you, nor intend till I see you again. There is none worth drinking but yours, if *my self* may be the judge" (W 2:386). The meaning of "drinking coffee," repeated so often in Swift's letters to Vanessa, is not necessarily stable. When it occurs in the earliest letters it appears to refer only to the pleasant experience of drinking coffee together in a room in Mrs. Vanhomrigh's house. In the first extant letter, December 18, 1711, Swift concludes: "Adieu till we meet over a Pott of Coffee, or an Orange and Sugar in the Sluttery; which I have so often found to be the most agreeable Chamber in the World" (W 1:399). He reinforces this image in a playful letter of August 15, 1712, in which he writes, "I long to drink a dish of Coffee in the Sluttery, and hear you dun me for Secrets, and—drink your Coffee—Why don't You drink your Coffee" (W 1:437). The latter part of the sentence seems to be what Vanessa would intersperse with her efforts to find out government gossip.

When Swift is away from London in June, 1713, Vanessa echoes his earlier allusion to food and drink: "It is impossible to tell you how often I have wished you a cupe of coffee and an orange at your Inn" (W 1:502). Drinking coffee, then, has become a shared ritual which Vanessa invokes as if to encourage Swift to think of her while they are apart. Her earnestness here, in the single reference to drinking coffee in her letters to Swift, is in keeping with the intensity of her feeling, while his early references are lighter. The assertion that begins Swift's hasty note from Windsor, "I did not forget the Coffee; for I thought you should not be robbed of it" (W 1:443), seems to be a straightforward reference to coffee intended as a gift from Swift to Vanessa. His letter of June 6, 1713, to her mother, by referring humorously to Mrs. Vanhomrigh's coffee as "rats-bane," and alluding to the coffee Vanessa spilled at Dunstable, makes coffee an example of "harmless levity shared with mother and daughter" (W 1:505n). Nevertheless, it should be added that Vanessa and her mother were unlikely to interpret anything about Dr. Swift in the same way. For Vanessa, even a humorous reference to coffee would conjure up the time she spent alone with him in the sluttery, that location he had pronounced the most agreeable in the world.

Later references to coffee drinking are hardly plausible as literal utterances: they articulate and underscore an intimacy that can easily be read as erotic. In a letter written less than a year before Vanessa's death, Swift's claim that he is "not chearfull enough to write, for I believe Coffee once a week is necessary to that" resonates against an earlier assertion: "there is none worth drinking but yours" (W 2:425, 386). In this private way Swift conveys to Vanessa her importance to him not simply as a woman he praises for her many (gender-blind) virtues, but as a woman who attracts him sexually. I doubt that this attraction culminated in intercourse because nothing on Vanessa's side of the correspondence can be read as even a veiled reference to it.[15] Had it happened, Vanessa could not have refrained from using such a powerful fact as part of her campaign to bind Swift to her. Instead, her letters reveal frustration that has a sexual dimension.[16]

Swift also wrote what Vanessa would have been less likely to appreciate, that if he could not have their special ritual, he could get along without it: "The best Maxim I know in this life is, to drink your Coffee when you can, and when You cannot, to be easy without it" (W 2:425). This marks the difference between them: Vanessa defined her life singlemindedly in terms of Swift, while he had a much larger sphere in which she was confined to a small and secret corner.

Early on in their correspondence there is something of the tone of the *Journal to Stella* in Swift's brief letters. One concludes, "Pray be merry and eat and walk; and be good, and send me your Commands. . . . Pray God preserve you, and make You happy and easy.—and so adieu bratt—" (W 1:498). She, in turn, can joke about not hearing from him in a manner that becomes impossible later. "Had I a correspondant in China I might have had an anwer by this time," she writes in 1712 (W 1:438). After the Vanhomrigh family's visit to Windsor that same year, the editors of Swift's account books suggest that "the tone of their relationship changes," so that Vanessa's name is deliberately suppressed from his accounts.[17]

Certainly there were times when Swift wrote lightheartedly to Vanessa, and times when he wrote of mundane matters without those "piquant" or "touching" passages that Ehrenpreis refuses to cite. But the nonplayful sort of intimacy—that is, intimacy as the world understands it—is rarely absent, because these were two people who knew each other well: Vanessa had private meetings with Swift, a pleasure he withheld from Stella. Swift had the added satisfaction of seeing in Vanessa, as he also saw in Stella, a woman whose taste he had shaped. He was pleased with the dissatisfactions Vanessa expressed with an assembly she attended, an attitude that mirrored his own. One of the saddest aspects of Swift's influence on Vanessa is the isolation her attempts to emulate him brought about in her life. Unlike Stella, she was barred from entering Swift's social sphere, where the quality of the company, since it had been chosen by Swift, would have met with her approval. Attempting to follow his advice to seek out company, but irrevocably molded by Swift to regard the society available with contempt, she had written to him of her experience:

> One day this week I was to visite a great lady . . . where I found a very great Assembly of Ladys and Beaus (dressed as I suppose to a nicety) . . . I heartily wished you a spectator for I very much question if in your life you ever saw the like scene or one more Extraordinary the lady's behaviour was blended with so many different character's I can not possibly describe it with out tireing your patience but the Audience seemed to me a creation of her owne they were so very Obsequious their form's and gestures were very like those of Babboons and monky's . . . one of these animals snatched my fan and was so pleased with me that it seased me with such a panick that I apprehended nothing less then being carried up to the top of the House and served as a friend of yours was but in this one of their owne species came in upon which they all began to make their grimace's which oppertunity I took and made my escape. (W 2:423)

In her attempt to, as she imagines, see things through Swift's eyes, Vanessa consciously identifies with a Swiftian fiction, the misanthropic Gulliver, and rejects her social cohort.

In response to Vanessa's satiric description of this occasion, Swift wrote to her that they were both "too hard to please." To say that he might have confessed the same shared attitude to someone else, a good friend or a relative, is beside the point. He was writing to a woman who had declared her love for him to be the overwhelming event of her life, and he had used the same word, "love," in his letters to her, a word he explicitly withheld from his feelings for Stella. However Swift meant it, love would have been the unspoken subtext in Vanessa's reading of this declaration of affinity.

Margaret Anne Doody thinks that Swift's circle of women writers "might perhaps be seen as a group of Vanessas," suggesting that Swift wanted to know more women as intelligent and spirited as the heroine of his poem *Cadenus and Vanessa*.[18] This shift from the poetic context that Swift controlled to a more complicated historical situation is fraught with real life difficulty. The fictive Vanessa could be contained in poetry, abandoned in the text with a coy nonconclusion. Unlike the real Vanessa, she did not combine her intelligence and spirit with any troubling usurpations.

Far from wanting more Vanessas, Swift came to regard the one Vanessa in his life as an intractable problem. *Cadenus and Vanessa* is, after all, an elaborate compliment with the underlying design of reconciling the too assertive Vanessa to her mentor's refusal to draw closer. It is openly contradictory, torn between opposed exigencies of valorizing Vanessa's unusual abilities and returning her to an existence that could make little use of them, a situation Swift seemed unable to appreciate, let alone resolve. And far from being pacified by Swift's flattering portrait of her in poetry, in life Vanessa remained demanding: the relationship of real life Cadenus and Vanessa may well have ended in acrimonious rupture.[19] Even without a climactic parting, Vanessa's letters demonstrate a serious unhappiness. Her instructions to publish their correspondence after her death evidences a desire to claim public recognition for having had a place in Swift's life, that acknowledgment that he had always denied her. More existentially, this defiant initiative was an assertion of identity. It is sobering to reflect that if the letters had been destroyed, Swift's explanation of *Cadenus and Vanessa* might have prevailed and Vanessa been denied any significance in his biography.

When *Cadenus and Vanessa* was published, Swift was both bitter and dismissive. To Knightley Chetwode he wrote that the poem was "a Task performed on a Frolick among some Ladyes," surely an untruth. It was, in turn, "onely a cavalier Business," a "Private humorsome thing," and "a Trifle" which he could barely remember. He twice proclaims indifference to the opinion of people who will "like me less" for this, and twice refers to the publication as attributable to human baseness (W 2:639). The considerable space Swift devotes to presenting a carefully controlled reaction suggests that he was extremely upset. Almost three months later, when he refers in a letter to Thomas Tickell to "the Thing you mention which no Friend could publish,"[20] he feels no need for a long exculpatory passage like the one in his letter to Chetwode. Now the publication serves as an indication that his policy of secrecy with Vanessa had been woefully incomplete. He tells Tickell that it "shews how indiscreet it is to leave any one Master of what cannot without the least Consequence be shewn to the World. Folly malice, Negligence, and the

Incontinence in Keeping Secrets . . . ought to caution men to Keep the Key of their Cabinets" (W 2:649). Thirty years earlier, he had written in anger to Varina, "Philosophy advises to keep our desires and prospects of happiness as much as we can in our own breasts, and independent of anything without" (W 1:124). It was the misfortune of first Stella and then Vanessa that after his experience with Varina Swift did indeed keep his happiness, if not all of his writings, within his control.

Although Ehrenpreis dismisses the idea that Vanessa lived in misery because of Swift, the great theme of her correspondence, her image in Scott's *Life of Swift* has a romantic appeal. An aged man, the son of Vanessa's gardener, told Scott's correspondent that he remembered her well: "He said she went seldom abroad, and saw little company; her constant amusement was reading, or walking in the garden. . . . She avoided company, and was always melancholy save when Dean Swift was there."[21] This gentle image configures Vanessa as the abandoned woman pining for her absent lover with the refined sadness of a Tennysonian heroine, a Marianna of the Moated Grange or Lady of Shalott. Although there might have been moments of gentle melancholy, this image is a nineteenth-century distortion: the letters reveal passionate assertion rather than quiet desperation. "I do assure you I have to[o] much spirrite to sitt down contented with this treatment," she warns Swift (W 2:318). Certainly her letters never suggest the resignation that Swift, the indefatigable teacher, constantly tried to instill in his pupil. Instead, they are full of stratagems for bringing him to her, appeals to which she devoted a furious energy.

She knows what will annoy him and attempts to disarm him in advance: "I have done all that was possible to hinder my self from writeing to you till I heard you were better for fear of breaking my promise but t'was all in vain for had [I] voued nither to touch pen Inck or paper I ceartanly should have had some other invention therefore I beg you wont be angery with me for doing what is not in my power to avoide" (W 1:510). Similar statements occur repeatedly in her letters: whatever limits Swift imposes, Vanessa is always testing them and always reminding him that she cannot help herself. For Swift, the attraction of Vanessa, compounded of her sexual appeal, her absolute devotion, and her replication of his ideas, was tempered by the potential danger of her impetuous nature creating a scandal. In the early years of their relationship in England, this danger must have been exciting, but it was also more remote. Settled into the comfortable routine of his life in Ireland as Dean of St. Patrick's, Swift had achieved through his own efforts respectability, financial security, and a literary reputation. Vanessa, on the other hand, had little to lose. The lack of self-control she constantly proclaimed in her letters posed a threat of disruption to Swift's life and public image, one that at times she seems to have employed calculatedly to bring Swift to her.

The "questions" that are alluded to in several of Swift's letters are first introduced as the conclusion of a long series of negatives in an early letter (1714): after Swift upbraids Vanessa for visiting him in Wantage and dilates at length on the need for keeping their association within strict bounds, he writes, "I would not answer your Questions for a Million; nor can I think of them with any Ease of

Mind. adieu" (W 2:72). The questions were probably posed by Vanessa to Swift in person at Wantage; they are not asked in any extant letter. His reluctance and disquiet make these questions seem both direct and personal. They could only, given Swift's reaction, be uncomfortable questions about their relationship: his commitment to Vanessa and their future. Six years later, "the Questions wch you were used to ask me, you may suppose to be all answered; just as they used to be after half an hour debate, entendez vous cela" (W 2:337). Answered, perhaps, but Vanessa responds two weeks later that they have not been answered to her satisfaction, and Swift then writes with exasperation that it was never possible "to answer any thing to your satisfaction" (W 2:340). We can conjecture that Swift's answers were his usual protestations of admiration, often extravagant, but that these words, unsupported by more tangible signs of affection, were not enough for Vanessa.

In his second-to-last letter to her, dated June 1, 1722, when Swift was traveling, he paints an idyllic picture of their meetings at Kendall's, a bookseller near Vanessa's Dublin residence. As part of this scene he writes, "I answer all the Questions you can [ask] me in the affirmative" (W 2:421). In other words, with a comfortable distance separating Swift from Vanessa and her importunings, he can give her the affirmations she wants in this elliptical way.[22] An appropriate retrospective on the questions occurs in Swift's last recovered letter to Vanessa, dated August 7, when he was still traveling:

> I see you this moment as you are visible at ten in the morning, and now you are asking y^r Questions round and I am answering them with a great deal of affected delays, and the same scene has passed fourty times as well as the other from 2 till 7; longer than the first by 2 hours, yet each has ses agremens particuliers. (W 2:430)

The enigmatic "other" scene is not identified in Swift's cryptic allusion to their time together: it is the only reference in the letters, other than the repeated allusions to drinking coffee, that may be interpreted sexually. I take the passage to mean that of their two activities, one involving some sort of physical intimacy, the other conversation, both are pleasing—even though conversation with Vanessa includes her badgering Swift with questions he is unwilling to answer fully.

As is usual in his correspondence with Vanessa, Swift in this letter wants to redirect her fixation into other activities, such as riding or reading "diverting or amusing books," yet at the same time he negates this advice, as he almost invariably does, by feeding her passion with repeated invocations of a shared past, not only the "fourty times" but the litany of named episodes: "the Scenes of Windsor, Cleveland row Rider Street" and so on (W 2:430). By admitting he often thinks of these times, he keeps Vanessa's desperate hopes alive. Yet he also chronicles the very lack of movement in their relationship that has created Vanessa's desperation. However many times the same scene has been played, it has led to nothing more than Swift's extravagant compliments. And this letter also contains several familiar criticisms of Vanessa, a dollop of tender solicitation—"I wish little Heskinage could do as much"—and no compliments (W 2:430). He commends old memories to her, but his listing of them is perfunctory. For Swift, merely thinking about the past and about Vanessa is satisfaction enough, and he would like her to emulate him in this as well as in taking exercise and using her mind.

Vanessa often expressed her love for Swift in terms that were as much threats as protestations of constancy. At the end of 1720, she concluded a long passage in this vein with the injunction, "don't flatter your self that separation will ever change my sentiments" (W 2:351). By then, since they had known each other for ten years, Swift had every reason to believe this declaration. When he did not answer, Vanessa wrote again, even more recklessly, "Was I an Enthusiast still you'd be the Deity I should worship . . . is it not more reasonable to adore a radiant forme one has seen than one only discribed" (W 2:352–53). Swift did not respond to Vanessa's cluster of three letters avowing her passion and pleading to see him, although he did visit the two sisters a few days before Mary Vanhomrigh's death.

At other times he replied to her effusions with attempts to disarm them. When Vanessa professed her determination "to try all maner of humain artes to reclaime you and if all those fail I am resolved to have recorse to the black one" (W 2:319), Swift turned aside her intensity with a lightly expressed threat of his own: "If you write as You do, I shall come the seldomer on purpose to be pleased with Your Letters, which I never look into without wondring how a Brat who cannot read, can possibly write so well." He continues in this vein, "You need make use of no other Black Art besides your Ink" (W 2:319–20). Vanessa had followed her reference to seeking black magic by admitting that Swift could transform "all this furry in to good humer" (W 2:319). He may be responding to this when he tells her that she is "a white Witch, and can do no Mischief" (W 2:320). Stripped of the trappings of magic, Vanessa acknowledges that Swift makes her personal world what it is, and he admits that she has no similar power over him. What earns her his approbation is her power of expression, but like other roads to his approval, this is, for Vanessa's love, a dead end.

Vanessa had at least two suitors, Dean Winter and Dr. Price, later archbishop of Cashel,[23] but she must have been too emotionally involved with Swift and too financially independent to be tempted by marriage to either of these clergymen. However worthy, they could not compete with Swift's brilliance.[24] As Ehrenpreis observes, "The hoard of shared and secret memories which Swift kept polishing in his letters obviously gave their conversations a resonance that nobody else's could match" (E 3:384). Further, in an ironic parallel to his description of Stella's conversation, Vanessa had written to Swift in 1713, "I find no conversation upon earth comparable but yours" (W 1:508).[25]

More insidiously, the pattern of Swift's letters to Vanessa, like that of *Cadenus and Vanessa*, always reinforced their intimacy. Less than a year before her death, Swift included some verses he had written for her. They begin:

> Nymph, would you learn the onely Art
> To keep a worthy Lover's heart.

And they end with a comforting affirmation of their relationship:

> For who could such a Nymph forsake
> Except a Blockhead or a Rake
> Or how could she her Heart bestow
> Except where Wit and Virtue grow. (W 2:337)

Vanessa, the poem asserts, is the very nymph to keep a lover, and the lover she chooses will be "worthy." As Vanessa had plainly told Swift a number of times, he was her choice and this would never change (nor did it). Swift's tone is light in the surrounding letter, but his verses gave her reason to think that they were profoundly suited to each other.

Our obsession with understanding through classification would place Vanessa today in that recently identified category of "women who love too much." The decision she made to construct her life around a love that was so cramped and unfulfilling, relegated to mere scraps of affection doled out, when convenient, by a fitfully attentive beloved, would be almost incomprehensible today except as masochistic aberration. In the early eighteenth century, when women had far fewer options, Vanessa's course is more understandable as it progressed over time rather than, as we can see it, as a whole. But the gaps in our knowledge of Swift and Vanessa are apt to be significant. Those hours spent together at Kendall's on a regular basis must have been deeply pleasurable to both parties, alternating between "two scenes," each of which had its particular agreeableness. Swift left such encounters satisfied: he had no wish to expand them or deepen his commitment to Vanessa. She, on the other hand, going back to her life of lawsuits and a dying sister, was seduced by those happy hours to want, to demand, more. Whether out of regard for her feelings or to spare himself more scenes, Swift would never tell her forthrightly that there could be no more; he made excuses of pressing business and frequent illnesses that she suspected were excuses but ultimately preferred to accept to the alternative of a permanent rupture.

The contrast between Stella's death and Vanessa's points up the difference between the place each held in Swift's life, one publicly acknowledged, one carefully clothed in secrecy. Swift confessed to others his suffering at the approaching loss of Stella; he prayed over her sickbed; immediately upon her death he wrote a record of her life that confirmed his deep affection for her. All these testimonials were denied to Vanessa, as was, for the most part, the sympathy of history. Sophie Shilleto Smith, the first woman to write an entire book about Swift, had this to say about Vanessa:

> Her death in the year 1723 removed from his path the woman who, by the mischief of which she was capable, was a constant source of danger to his happiness and that of Stella. It is impossible to lament her death. Let those sentimentalists grieve who see in every man an artful villain with designs on a woman's honour and happiness, and in every sentimental woman an injured saint. We cannot.[26]

The magisterial first-person plural has the effect of enhancing this judgment, as if it were handed down from an authority figure of greater magnitude than a critic. Smith's crude polarities, artful villain versus injured saint, require her to deprive

Vanessa of any justification in order to acquit Swift of illicit designs. She accordingly reads her, as so many have, as no more than a source of danger and mischief, the potential spoiler whom Swift was well rid of.

Evelyn Hardy sees Swift and Vanessa in another set of stereotypical gender terms: Swift as "the stronger of the two ... was bound to crush a weaker nature."[27] It would be more accurate to situate Swift within a gender dynamic that gave him the power to define the relationship and the mobility to control it. Vanessa could not seek him out; she had to wait for him to come to her. Like Stella, Vanessa could only choose to accept Swift's terms or to reject them: her powers to alter these terms were severely limited. In many of her overtures to Swift Vanessa displayed considerable daring; in her refusal to renounce her passion she displayed unswerving purpose. She failed, not because Swift was stronger than she but because, not wanting what she did, he needed no strength to resist it.

4

cAfter Stella

The Constant Seraglio

Swift got along with women across the social spectrum during his adult life, including the poor street vendors he patronized with his charity and encouragement, his long-time housekeeper, the wives and sisters of his chapter clergy, and the middle-class and aristocratic ladies of the London and Dublin circles he frequented. He was so successful in attracting the admiration of gentlewomen that two writers of the time displayed a marked envy of this ability. Lord Orrery, after relating an anecdote of Swift and a worshipful female admirer, assimilates Swift to a Turkish potentate, a comparison designed to describe Swift's power accurately and at the same time make fun of it:

> You see the command which Swift had over all his females; and you would have smiled to have found his house a constant seraglio of very virtuous women, who attended him from morning till night, with an obedience, an awe, and an assiduity, that are seldom paid to the richest, or the most powerful lovers; no, not even to the Grand Seignior himself.[1]

Lady Mary Wortley Montagu, writing privately in her commonplace book, gave the same image a nastier twist. Orrery's allusion implied a lack of sexuality at odds with the idea of a harem of women but nevertheless equated Swift with its ruler; Lady Mary not only renders the lack of sexuality explicit, she radically reduces Swift's status from potent master to emasculated servant: "Dr. S[wift] in the midst of his Women, like a master E[unuch] in a seraglio."[2] After reading Orrery's biography of Swift with great pleasure, Lady Mary wrote to her daughter,

Lady Bute, that "Dr. Swift, who set at defiance all Decency, Truth, or Reason, had a croud of Admirers . . . with a number of Ladies of fine Taste and unblemish'd Characters."[3]

Both Orrery and Lady Mary were writers who would not attain Swift's greatness and who had problematic relationships with ambition, Orrery because the father he worshipped thought little of his talents, Lady Mary because she was conflicted, as an aristocratic woman, about the desirability of literary fame.[4] As a man, Orrery could doggedly strive to prove his father wrong, while such a straightforward posture was unavailable to Lady Mary: "For a time she became almost a Scriblerian, and when we remember how the members of that circle looked back on the period of its meetings as a golden age we may see further into the bitterness of her later insistence that Pope, Swift, Gay and Arbuthnot were both socially and artistically contemptible."[5] Lady Mary would advise her granddaughter to "conceal whatever learning she attains, with as much solicitude as she would hide crookedness or lameness."[6]

Swift may have been no more class-conscious than anyone else in an age in which distinctions of birth and fortune were inescapable, but as a man who had had to make his own way and constantly felt undervalued, he always took pleasure in the attention of the rich and powerful. The *Journal to Stella* is full of his encounters with titled women, and his correspondents include a number of these figures. His most enduring such friend was Lady Betty Germain, a daughter of Lord Berkeley who was nineteen when Swift joined the earl's household as its chaplain in 1699. Although Ehrenpreis maintains that Swift resumed a correspondence with Lady Betty in 1730 only because he wanted favors, and ceased to write when he no longer had this motive (E 3:700), this judgment is based on only five surviving letters.[7] Her twenty-seven letters to Swift, letters he diligently saved, reveal that she valued his friendship and was happy to accommodate his requests. But women like Lady Betty, however admiring, were in a position to condescend to Swift, whose position was that of a favor-seeker.

In choosing his friends in Ireland, where he assembled the "constant seraglio" after Stella's death, Swift was governed by a shrewd principle of practicality, one he elucidated in a letter to Pope. Those who are "subject like us to bodily infirmities," he wrote, should seek out "great people" only occasionally and instead choose companions of

> a middle kind both for understanding and fortune, who are perfectly easy, never impertinent, complying in every thing, ready to do a hundred little offices that you & I may often want, who dine and sit with me five times for once that I go to them, and whom I can tell without offence, that I am otherwise engaged at present. This you cannot expect from any of those that either you or I or both are acquainted with on your side; who are only fit for our healthy seasons, and have much business of their own. (W 3:180)

Such a calculating approach to friendship is in keeping with the realistic thought expressed in Swift's letter to James Stopford, written when Stella was dying, that at his age it would be "too late to engage in a new Friendship" (W 2:660). Swift's fears of dragging on "a wretched Life till it shall please God to call me away" were proved unfounded by the steady appearance of pliant and deferential young women paying court to the Dean and welcoming his instruction (W 2:656).[8]

In the late-twentieth-century movement to rehabilitate Swift's attitude toward women, Margaret Anne Doody's "Swift Among the Women" makes a persuasive case for Swift as a man and writer who, in spite of certain notorious poems, received a great deal of favorable attention from his female contemporaries.[9] Doody remarks as unwittingly contradictory Orrery's charge that Swift regarded women as only partial rather than whole beings and his description of the group of female admirers he referred to as "a constant seraglio." There does seem to be a contradiction somewhere, for at times Swift's writings in his own voice are highly critical of women, and many negative representations of them occur in his literary texts. Yet, as a matter of record, he did have many staunch women friends and admirers, and—as Doody documents—a number of eighteenth-century women writers were influenced by his work.

The situation is not as strange as it might first appear; on the contrary, in terms of traditional gender relations, it is all too familiar. As modern studies of speech suggest, "discourse in contexts where there exists an asymmetric power relation will orient to and reflect the assumptions and world view of the more powerful participant."[10] Testimonials to Swift from admiring women need to be read sociolinguistically according to this model, which is that of the asymmetrical relationship between a powerful male speaker, whose approbation was highly desirable, and a relatively powerless woman, who had many reasons to want to please the illustrious Dean.

The Swift who had many women admirers was a well known writer and a patriot of such renown that the prime minister of England was told that it would take an army to arrest him (*PS* 2:629n). Such a man had, in Pierre Bourdieu's useful term, a large "capital of authority" with women who themselves wrote or who appreciated literary merits.[11] Moreover, Swift was considerably older than the women who constituted his "seraglio," and this could only have increased his authority. He was also a man of the cloth, another enhancement of status, and a natural pedagogue who took particular delight in instructing young women, women who, as he himself deplored, were virtually uneducated and therefore at a further disadvantage. It hardly seems accidental that he was drawn to the company of women much younger than himself, who would most certainly be impressed by his formidable intellect and wit, not to mention his renown.[12] Such women were an adoring and noncritical audience for Swift's own work. His good friend Patrick Delany noted that "the most effectual way of paying court to him, was to listen with attention," a quality that had been inculcated into women of his era and class.[13]

Women also composed a group Swift could criticize with impunity, both in life and in art.[14] Orrery has provided a telling example of this. He was introduced to a young woman at the Dean's whose reading aloud of *Death and Daphne* was accompanied by the Dean's constant correction. She "assured me smilingly, that the portrait of Daphne was drawn for herself." Orrery demurs at the unflattering character, but Swift tells him, "'That Lady had rather be a Daphne drawn by me than a Sacharissa by any other pencil.' She confirmed what he had said, with great earnestness."[15]

Surely it was easy for Swift to be expansive in the company of those gentlewomen who gave him the attention and admiration he often missed conspicuously in other venues, an audience that constantly clamored for his latest work and no doubt always received it with praise. Women were also most apt to fit the requirements Swift enumerated in his letter to Pope.

Swift could take liberties even with the wellborn in the interest of self-assertion, as he does with the rather cruel trick that he plays on Lady Burlington (according to Laetitia Pilkington, one instance among a thousand others that might be related). Apparently, Swift and the newly married Earl of Burlington colluded in allowing Lady Burlington to imagine that the unpretentiously appearing Dean was someone of no consequence:

> After Dinner, said the Dean, "Lady *Burlington*, I hear you can sing; sing me a Song." The Lady looked on this unceremonious manner of asking a Favour with Distaste, and positively refus'd him; he said, she should sing, or he would make her. "Why, Madam, I suppose you take me for one of your poor paultry *English* Hedge Parsons; sing when I bid you." As the Earl did nothing but laugh at this Freedom; the Lady was so vext that she burst into Tears, and retired.
>
> His first Compliment to her when he saw her again, was, "Pray Madam, are you as proud and as ill natur'd now, as when I saw you last?" to which she answered with great good Humour,—"No, Mr. Dean, I'll sing for you, if you please."— From which time he conceived great Esteem for her. (P 38)

Even an earl's wife could be shown that Dean Swift was a man of consequence, who was free to contrive rude behavior as a joke on her ladyship.

Lady Burlington's good-natured reaction passed Swift's test, a test we see him administering to many women in one form or another. The test is explicitly described in a revealing letter to Mary Pendarves, written by Swift after she had ended her visit to Ireland:

> With all my disposition to find faults, I was never once able to fix upon anything that I could find amiss, although I watched you narrowly; for when I found we were to lose you soon, I kept my eyes and ears always upon you, in hopes that you would make some *boutade*. . . . this hath been my case with several ladies whom I chose for friends: in a week, a month, or a year, hardly one of them failed to give me a *boutade*. (*C* 4:259)

Swift defines a *boutade* as a horse's unexpected misstep and then applies it to disappointments in the ladies he mentions.[16] That few failed to produce the watched-for *boutade* gave Swift the pleasure of having his beliefs about most women confirmed. The idea is turned into a compliment when Swift tells Pendarves that he hoped she would make a *boutade* so that he would be reconciled to losing her company.

Other anecdotes show the same principle at work: Swift reproaches a woman for some failure; if she responds properly, he forgives her. When Swift dined at a farmhouse near Quilca, Sheridan's residence, his hostess thought to honor her distinguished guest by dressing in finery. Swift pretended not to recognize her:

> "*I always heard Mrs. Riley was a prudent woman;* she would never dress herself out in silks and ornaments only fit for ladies of fortune and fashion. No! Mrs. Riley, the farmer's wife, would never wear anything beyond plain stuffs and *other things suitable.*" Mrs. Riley, who really was a woman of sense, took the hint, went out, changed her dress to an apparel proper for a farmer's wife, & returned; the Dean then took her by the hand, & said in the most friendly manner, "Your husband wanted to pass off a fine lady upon me, dressed up in silk in the pink of the mode, for his wife, but I was not to be taken in."[7]

Swift enjoyed the company of those rare women who did not commit *boutades*: one of his persistent themes is the pleasure of their conversation. In *Hints towards an Essay on Conversation* he complains that conversation has degenerated, "owing, among other Causes, to the Custom arisen, for some Years past, of excluding Women from any Share in our Society" (*PW* 4:94). Including women "would lay a Restraint upon those odious Topicks of Immodesty and Indecencies, into which the Rudeness of our Northern Genius is so apt to fall" (*PW* 4:95). Swift departed from custom by advocating that women remain at the dinner table when the meal was ended rather than be exiled to the drawing room, but this idea, advanced in the *Letter to a Young Lady, on Her Marriage,* leads him to remark to the woman addressed that he has little respect for "the Generality of your Sex." He does not agree with what he proffers as the accepted view that "Women are incapable of all Conversation," but the word *conversation,* such an important Swiftian value, reminds him of the trivial talk of women, who, as a sex, employ "more Thought, Memory, and Application to be Fools, than would serve to make them wise and useful" (*PW* 9:90–91). And from there it's a short step to preferring monkeys.

Swift also wanted women to hold the interest of their husbands through good sense and intellectual companionship rather than physical charms, a program that required the cooperation of husbands as well as wives (*PW* 9:89–90). Like other men of his time, including Defoe, he gave no thought to possibilities beyond this limited and traditional role.

Complexities of the sort that characterized Swift's relations with Stella and Vanessa did not enter into the friendships that Swift formed with younger women after first Vanessa and then Stella passed from the scene, but these later admirers might well have been made uncomfortable by some of Swift's poems about their sex. While they would not have seen themselves mirrored in the horrors of the decaying prostitutes in *The Progress of Love* and *A Beautiful Young Nymph Going to Bed,* they might have paused over poems like *The Journal of a Modern Lady* that, however comic in tone, indict gentlewomen as frivolous, empty-headed, and extravagant. But Orrery's anecdote about Lady Acheson is instructive in this respect. When a woman was singled out for Swift's friendship, she had been favored by a famous man who made no secret of his high standards.

When Swift knew that he would lose Stella, his most valuable friend, he recognized the approaching event as a catastrophe from which he could never fully recover. His correspondence to intimates frankly states that he could not replace Stella—not that she was technically irreplaceable, although her loss was "unspeakable" and inspired both grief and terror, but that he was too old to embark upon another such intimacy. Little more than nine months after Stella's death, he wrote to the Reverend Thomas Wallis about Wallis's recent loss of his wife: "Such misfortunes seem to break the whole scheme of man's life; and although time may lessen sorrow, yet it cannot hinder a man from feeling the want of so near a companion, nor hardly supply it with another" (W 3:203).[18] Swift's feeling words to Wallis were surely informed by his own process of loss, in which time would transform the raw specific grief into the absence of a companion.

The difficulty of bearing the loss of friends continued to be on Swift's mind. Apropos of Congreve's sudden death, he wrote to Pope, "Years have not yet hardened me"; he wished "almost, that I never had a friend" (W 3:210). Swift clearly envied Dr. Helsham, a man of exemplary qualities who loved his many friends but wasn't bothered by losing one of them. "Is not this the true happy man?" Swift asked Pope, and then asserted that he would give half his fortune "for the same temper" (W 3:210). Nokes observes that "even in his ideals, Swift retained a sense of financial prudence" (N 350). Since Swift follows the wish for such a temper with the qualifying "yet I cannot say I love it" (W 3:210), his rhetorical gesture should be read differently from Nokes's interpretation: although Swift envies the absence of suffering in Helsham, who mourns a friend no more "than at the loss of his cat," Swift's remark is a measure of his suffering rather than an expression of an "ideal." He cannot in actuality change his own temper, which was to feel such losses profoundly.

When Stella's death was imminent, Swift several times expressed the anxiety that he was now too old to create an intimate friendship with a woman. With his typical habit of assuming the worst, he did not consider that his now well-established fame would draw into his orbit young women who had literary aspirations or, like Mary Pendarves, were happy to have their intelligence recognized by such an imposing literary figure. All of the women discussed in this chapter, like Stella and Vanessa before them, were eager to have Swift's approbation—to be good enough to please a man like Dean Swift, whose standards for company were known to be high. If he sometimes chided them, it was in the context of a relationship in which he took them seriously, and they felt complimented. In the constant seraglio, Swift did not replicate his earlier relationships with Stella and Vanessa, but he did repeat certain aspects of those experiences: it was simply his nature to instruct, and these women—with the possible exception of Lady Acheson—were amenable to instruction. They had the further charms of youth, and wit enough to hold Swift's interest in the years that elapsed between Stella's death and his own decline.

The first woman to absorb at least some of Swift's need for a new companion after the death of Stella was Lady Acheson, a young woman whose parents were longtime friends of Swift. She was married to Sir Arthur Acheson and was, at the time of making Swift's acquaintance, the mother of four living children (having given birth to seven). Swift paid his first visit to the family at their estate, Market Hill, only some four months after Stella's death. When the prolonged visit ended, he summed up his satisfaction to Pope:

> Sir A. is a man of sense, and a scholar, has a good voice, and my Lady a better; she is perfectly well bred, and desirous to improve her understanding, which is very good, but cultivated too much like a fine Lady. She was my pupil there, and severely chid when she read wrong; with that . . . and writing family verses of mirth by way of libels on my Lady, my time past very well and in very great order. (W 3:209)

Swift had a positive regard for his host at Market Hill, but the much lengthier description of Lady Acheson and his relationship with her establishes the focal point of his interest. In short, as Ehrenpreis observes, "It was Moor Park and Hetty Johnson all over again" (E 3:602), but with the reassuring difference that Lady Acheson was married and Swift was now almost sixty years old. Not only did Lady Acheson not mind being satirized by Swift, she demanded it: several months into his first visit with the Achesons, Swift wrote to Sheridan that he was so taken up with lampoons on her "that I have no time for any Thing else, and if I do not produce one every now and then of about two Hundred Lines, I am chid for my Idleness" (W 3:194). There appears to have been some parity of chiding, then, as well as an openly expressed desire on Lady Acheson's part to be the subject of Swift's verses, however unflattering. But as Orrery's anecdote and Swift's references in his letters demonstrate, the critique of Lady Acheson was intended to be humorous and inoffensive and was so taken by her. Even her description in *Death and Daphne*, which Orrery found so uncomplimentary, was proudly claimed by Lady Acheson, who, according to Swift, "shews every Creature the Libels I have writ against her" (W 3:194).

During this period Swift's letters about Market Hill reflect contentment. He must have felt, after the recent anguish of loss, that he had found a safe haven: a comfortable refuge and doting friends, one of whom was a young woman in need of his instruction and welcoming his friendship. There was little likelihood of her romantic entanglement or dependence: like the other women who gladly sat at his feet after Stella's death and accepted his "severe chiding," she presented no complications that Swift would need to evade. Explaining his extended stay, Swift wrote to Sheridan: "I am well here, and hate Removals. . . . I hate Dublin, and love the Retirement here, and the Civility of my Hosts" (W 3:192). Pope perceptively saw that Market Hill was attractive to Swift not only for the "planting and building" he undertook there but for "the society of a valuable Lady. I conclude . . . that you quarrel with her, and abuse her every day, if she is so" (W 3:201). The quarreling and abuse, the severe chiding, were mock-actions, part of the role Swift played as schoolmaster to a woman who was not a schoolgirl, who was in fact his hostess. Had he not found her "valuable," as Pope intimates, he would not have bothered.

The comic rendering of Lady Acheson's faults must have been mitigated for her by Swift's own self-portrait, one which characterizes him as a foolish extremist:

He loves to be bitter at
a lady illiterate;
If he sees her but once,
He'll swear she's a dunce;
Can tell by her looks
A hater of books:
Through each line of her face
Her folly can trace;
Which spoils every feature
Bestowed her by nature,
But sense gives a grace
To the homeliest face. (*CP* 350)

If the portrait of the teacher–love interest in *Cadenus and Vanessa* is redolent of bad faith, the construction of an admirable and finally blameless figure,[19] the character of Swift here is accurate self-parody. These are Swift's pet precepts about women exaggerated to the ridiculous. And yet there is face-saving, although not the evasive kind of *Cadenus and Vanessa*. The distortions of Swift's sensible ideas and well-meaning interventions can be attributed to the speaker, Lady Acheson. As he does in so many poems of self-representation, Swift calibrates his own image with a perfect ear for how he might sound to an unsympathetic Lady Acheson while exercising his virtuoso talent for creating other, authentic voices and numerous extravagant rhymes, all designed to entertain his doting hosts. This same portrait of the unwelcome and foolish Dean, the antitype of the Achesons' valued guest, recurs in the other Market Hill poems, on one occasion not only spoken by the voice of Sir Arthur Acheson but presented as actually written by him.[20] Swift must play all parts and in this way control them, using his own foibles as material for comic turns given to voices that on their own could never be so dazzling.[21]

After Lady Acheson and Sir Arthur separated, Swift remained friendly with her and her mother, with whom she lived.[22] The Achesons had hoped that their elder son, a student at Trinity College Dublin, would benefit from occasional visits to Swift, but evidently the Dean formed a poor impression of him. In 1735 he expressed himself decisively in a letter to another clergyman:

> How, a wonder, came young Acheson to be among you? I believe neither his father nor mother know any thing of him; his mother is at Grange with Mrs. Acheson, her mother, and, I hear, is very ill of her asthma and other disorders, got by cards, and laziness, and keeping ill hours. Ten thousand sackfuls of such knights and such sons are, in my mind, niether worth rearing nor preserving. I count upon it that the boy is good for nothing. (*C* 4:375)

From this it appears that Swift had detailed knowledge of Lady Acheson, who, in spite of her enumerated faults, is excluded from his sweeping condemnation of father and son—"such knights and such sons." We do not know what Sir Arthur did to merit Swift's dismissal, but the poem *The Dean's Reasons For Not Building at Drapier's Hill* dilates upon their incompatibility. A subtext of this theme is Sir Arthur's failure to pay attention when Swift talks:

> Who, while I talk, a song will hum,
> Or, with his fingers, beat the drum. (*CP* 428)

Real conversation, in which the parties freely exchange ideas, was essential to Swift's idea of male friendship, but talking to Sir Arthur was nothing more than "prating to a bust" (*CP* 429). Little wonder that Swift turned away from the husband but maintained his friendship with the wife.

Yet Lady Acheson, like Stella before her, was stubbornly wedded to her own opinions. Swift's opposing impulses toward her are probably embodied in his poem *Daphne*, in which the protagonist "knows, with equal ease, / How to vex and how to please" (*CP* 433). The poem's shifting address suggests Swift's difficulty in finding the proper relationship between his exasperation and affection:

> Send me hence ten thousand miles,
> From a face that always smiles:
> None could ever act that part,
> But a Fury in her heart.
> Ye who hate such inconsistence,
> To be easy keep your distance. (*CP* 433)

The speaker, referring to the Dean in the third person, concludes by addressing Daphne:

> Heaven forbid he should despise thee;
> But will never more advise thee. (*CP* 434)

The remove of third-person is curious. Swift might as easily have written *I* instead of *he*, for the identification of speaker and *he* is tacit. Perhaps that would have been too bald an assertion for these closing lines, when Swift's affection for Lady Acheson is clearly at war with his annoyance that she would not adopt his opinions as her own.

Swift felt so strongly about their disagreements that he also wrote *Twelve Articles*, a verse record of his plan to limit his disappointment. It, too, concludes with an effort to preserve their friendship by containing Swift's aggravation:

> Never will I give advice
> Till you please to ask me thrice;
> Which, if you in scorn reject,
> 'Twill be just as I expect.
>
> Thus we both shall have our ends,
> And continue special friends. (*CP* 435)

This poem leaves the door to Swift's advice open a crack: instead of "never," he now writes that "never" may be abrogated by asking three times—in effect, begging. His sense of being completely in the right can only be appeased by a kind of humiliation, similar to the bind he put Stella in when he dared her to transcribe the poem that criticized her.

Swift's continuing friendship with Lady Acheson after his break with Sir Arthur and her removal to the environs of Dublin suggests that he did remain fond of her in spite of her transgressions. On the other hand, the intimacy of a long sojourn in the same household was over in 1730. What continued until her death in 1737, an event not reflected in Swift's correspondence, would perforce have been more distant.

There is a curious aspect of Swift's interest in Lady Acheson. She was a woman with four children at the time of their meeting, yet his poetry never refers to this part of her life, one which must have been, if not prominent, at least noticeable during Swift's long visits. *Death and Daphne* is subtitled "TO AN AGREEABLE YOUNG LADY, BUT EXTREMELY LEAN," a description that suggests a nubile virgin rather than a married woman with children.[23] The poem's narrative has Death seeking a wife and considering Daphne for the role, just as if she were free to wed. Nora Crow Jaffe's ingenious reading of the poem casts Swift in the role of death, approaching Daphne/Lady Acheson in a disguise that captures his sense of his age and unattractiveness to someone roughly half his age.[24] Daphne's extreme leanness becomes the negative counterweight to her suitor's deficiencies: at the poem's conclusion she is even found wanting by Death, who recoils from her cold touch. In this way, Jaffe thinks, Swift protected himself from Lady Acheson "because he found her young, agreeable, and married."[25]

The most significant poem relating to Lady Acheson, the epistle *To a Lady*, has some of the elements that characterize the Market Hill group, although its ambitious scope and satiric apologia transcend the "family verses of mirth" that Swift produced to please his hostess.[26] This time the lady has set her sights higher than a lampoon: she "desired the author to write some verses upon her in the heroic style" (*CP* 514). In terms of the Swift/Lady relationship, the poem breaks into two parts: the first, reminiscent of the other Market Hill poems, is a spirited exchange between the Dean and the Lady about the Lady's qualities, while the second, beginning at line 133, shifts the subject to the dominant speaker, who both offers an apologia for his satire and turns it against the "nation's representers."[27] His speech embodies a glaring contradiction between the smiling satire he advocates and the punitive satire he practices. Now the Lady makes a brief intervention to protest the Dean's intemperate storming, so at odds with the satiric principles he affirms. The conclusion returns to the original subject of treating the Lady in a heroic style, but whereas the first part of the poem gives the complaining Lady a significant part, here the focus has shifted to the justifying writer. He defends his practice as both suited to his temperament and effective:

> From the planet of my birth,
> I encounter vice with mirth.
>
> .   .   .   .

> Thus, I find it by experiment,
> Scolding moves you less than merriment. (*CP* 518, 520)

But Swift has shifted the terms of the argument between the two speakers from praise versus blame to the efficacy of different kinds of criticism, comic or serious. He has, he states, given the lady the same laughing and lashing that he has brought to bear on public figures. He can do no more—or less.

The elaborate image of the muse as a malfunctioning rocket that bursts before reaching its destination is intended to convince the Lady that Swift's muse is unsuited to lofty numbers:

> Thus, should I attempt to climb,
> Treat you in a style sublime,
> Such a rocket is my muse;
> Should I lofty numbers choose,
> E'er I reached Parnassus' top,
> I should burst, and bursting drop. (*CP* 521)

Judith Mueller has pointed out the sexual implications of the imagery, with its connotations of premature ejaculation.[28] Yet the fizzling rocket, unlike premature ejaculation, is an image of success rather than failure, since it proves capable of affecting the lady's brain:

> Make you able upon sight
> To decide of wrong and right;
> Talk with sense whate'er you please on;
> Learn to relish truth and reason.
>
> Thus we both should gain our prize:
> I to laugh, and you grow wise. (*CP* 521–22)

In Mueller's words, "Ultimately, Swift's failure becomes success, his impotence power, and his unmanliness a recuperation of the gender hierarchy it would seem to undermine."[29]

Throughout the poem the speaker-satirist, like Swift himself, has to be right, not only about his own practice but about what the lady wants: not to have her praises sung "in strain sublime," but to be chastised effectively—as he best knows how to do—so that she will deserve praise for growing wise. Her appeal to be treated differently in his poetry becomes still another occasion to demonstrate that he knows best.

Laetitia Pilkington was the most prominent of Swift's late-life women protégées as well as the first and often the best of the biographers who had known the Dean personally.[30] The accommodating Dr. Delany presented to Swift her flattering poem "*To the Rev. Dr. Swift, On His* Birth-day," with such irresistible lines as "Behold in Him with new Delight, / The Patriot, Bard and Sage unite"

(P 26). Pilkington came as part of a couple, with her husband Matthew, an ambitious clergyman. One imagines that this less interesting personage was tolerated because of his talented wife, but possibly this is the effect of her having written the account of their marriage after its acrimonious breakup. Swift seems to have been charmed not only by the couple's deference, but by their diminutive size, a characteristic that made it more natural for him to think of her as much younger than her age. At their first meeting he expressed surprise that "this poor little Child" was married. He took her alone into his study to show her "all the money he got working for the Ministry," but warned her not to steal it. There was no money, but Swift then showed her a "Drawer filled with Medals" and bid her to choose two for herself: "But he could not help smiling, when I began to poize them in my Hands, chusing them by Weight rather than Antiquity, of which indeed I was not then a Judge" (P 27).

During dinner, Swift called his servants to task in a dramatic fashion. When the roast was found to be overcooked, he summoned the cook and asked her to bring it back less well done. She naturally protested that this was impossible, whereupon Swift exclaimed, "Why, what Sort of a Creature are you to commit a Fault which cannot be amended?" (P 27). He charged his male servants to use force if necessary in the future to ensure that the meat was not overcooked. Then he caught the butler helping himself to a glass from a bottle of ale and docked his pay severely, "for I scorn to be out-done in any thing, even in Cheating" (P 28).

Not surprisingly, as an unfamiliar guest in the presence of a celebrated figure like Dean Swift, Pilkington was exhausted by these contentious interruptions of the meal. After dinner, she became the object of Swift's attention with an unexpected request: "Pray Mrs. *Pilkington* tell me your Faults" (P 28). She was able to neatly evade the question, and Swift went on to imitate a prudish lady making coffee. When Pilkington had followed his instructions in helping with the coffee, Swift told her husband, "I have found her out to be a damn'd insolent proud, unmannerly Slut" (P 29). He elaborated that "a Lady of modern good Breeding" would have insisted on making the coffee herself and led to an accident. The perceptive Pilkington concluded that the Dean's practice was to preface "a Compliment with an Affront" (P 29).

I have repeated at some length Pilkington's account of her first meeting with Swift because it contains multiple instances of Swiftian behavior that might well be characterized as showing off. Swift reminds Pilkington of his former greatness by referring to the money he had been given by the Ministry: that there is no money is to their discredit, not his. Next, he displayed his medals, creating an opportunity to impress Pilkington with his indifference to such worldly marks of recognition. During dinner Swift engineers two separate scenes in which he directs the action and demonstrates his wit. The second instance might even have been staged, since it strains credulity that, given his master's well-known policy of severity in such cases, one of Swift's servants would tipple before his very eyes and that of the company.

Swift continues to perform for the couple by imitating a prudish lady, and he both holds Pilkington's attention and keeps her off balance by asking her an unexpected question and then answering it himself in an outrageous way. The entire performance has the dazzle and surprise of a fireworks display: a new acquaintance like Pilkington could not predict what form the Dean's wit would assume next, nor did she understand that the spectacle was intended to further impress the admiring newcomers that Swift was auditioning. Swift, too, must have been invigorated by staging such a scene for his approving yet somewhat intimidated audience.

Pilkington passed the test:[31] she became an accepted member of Swift's social circle and a quondam pupil of the Dean, inspired to write her poem *The Statues* as a rebuttal to his "eternally satirizing and ridiculing the *Female* Sex" (P 39). Doody accordingly lauds Swift's role in encouraging a woman to write, yet were we to give Swift credit here, we might also credit the man who batters a woman with inspiring her to take a course in self-defense.[32] This is only part of the story, however, for Pilkington goes on to avow, "If I have any Merit, as a Writer, I must gratefully acknowledge it due to the Pains he took to teach me to think and speak with Propriety" (P 45).

Her own satiric poetry lacks Swift's energy and power; unlike Mary Barber, Swift's most talented woman protégée, Pilkington did not easily write in the vein of her mentor, although she sometimes attempted his subjects. Describing the omnipresence of lying, she produces aphorisms that never move beyond the poem's initial assertion:

> Study this superior Science
>   Would you rise in Church or State;
> Bid to Truth a bold Defiance;
>   'Tis the Practice of the Great.[33]

The poem's jingly rhythm works against the seriousness of its content. Swift's "epigram," *Advice to a Parson*, has a similar theme, but the gravity of the poetic ideas is supported by the longer anapestic lines, and it is alive with specifics. An explicit picture of the negative qualities required for advancement is contrasted with the assumed façade of proper behavior:

> Would you rise in the church, be stupid and dull,
> Be empty of learning, of insolence full;
> Though lewd and immoral, be formal and grave,
> In flattery an artist, in fawning a slave.
>
> .   .   .   .
>
> Would you wish to be wrapped in a rochet—in short,
> Be as proud and profane as fanatical Hort. (*CP* 501)

The concluding example of unmerited success climactically assembles three strong negatives—proud, profane, and fanatical—to drive home its point.

The metrically regular rhymed quatrain that Pilkington favors, alternating tetrameter and trimeter, is effective in a ballad narrative but ill suited to the kind of weight she often makes it bear:

> O God! since all thy Ways are just,
>   Why does thy heavy Hand
> So sore afflict the wretched Dust
>   Thou didst to Life command! (*Expostulation*, 86)

The combination of metrical regularity and abstraction tends to diminish even a heartfelt expression of suffering like *Expostulation*, as it does a poem that seems to be merely an exercise in responding to Swift's satirizing of women:

> *Strephon*, your Breach of Faith and Trust
>   Affords me no Surprize;
> A Man who grateful was, or just,
>   Might make my Wonder rise. (*Song*, 57)

Early in her career, when Pilkington wrote her lines on Strephon's perfidy, she had not yet experienced the perfidy of her own husband. Her verbal facility did not produce memorable poetry: it would be her *Memoirs*, infused with the bitterness of her difficult life, that would endure.

Swift's influence is everywhere apparent in the *Memoirs* in a way that would have chagrined him: Pilkington learned from Swift those self-representations of innocence in the face of slander or unfeeling indifference. She often quotes such passages, especially from *Verses on the Death of Dr. Swift*.

As numerous anecdotes in the *Memoirs* illustrate, their relationship was that of the paternalistic teacher and great man to a much younger woman regarded indulgently as a little girl. On one occasion Swift asked Pilkington's help in pasting letters in a book: "I intended to do it myself, but that I thought it might be a pretty Amusement for a Child, so I sent for you," she reported him saying. And her reply: "I told him I was extreamly proud to be honoured with his Commands" (P 33). Such instances in the *Memoirs* could be multiplied. Virginia Woolf was struck by the absolute nature of Swift's power over Pilkington: "He could beat her and bully her, make her shout when he was deaf. . . . She had to pull off her stockings if he told her to."[34]

Pilkington became a subject of scandal when her husband was awarded a divorce on grounds of adultery, and Swift, with his fetish for respectability, promptly and definitively renounced her. His letter of March 9, 1737/38, to John Barber names Delany as the "unlucky Recommender" who foisted the couple on Swift, but it seems more an occasion for satirical exaggeration than real anger: "He forced me to countenance Pilkington; introduced him to me, and praised the Witt, Virtue and humour of him and his Wife. Whereas he proved the falsest Rogue, and she the most profligate whore in either Kingdom" (C 5:95). Swift remarks that Pilkington was seeking a maintenance from her husband, who had none to give her; then he turns to another topic, and, as far as the record shows, thought no more about the young woman who now had to support herself and two young children, a woman who had been a favored member of his circle. Class probably entered into Swift's repudiation: he had been friendly with several king's mistresses without feeling himself morally tainted.

Like Swift, Pilkington's society condemned her: the *Gentleman's Magazine* found a grim and ironic moral in the desperate struggle of her post-divorce years: "To those who read her life she cannot surely have lived in vain since she has scarce related a single incident which does not concur to prove that no natural excellence can attone for moral defects nor any power of pleasing others secure an equivalent for the chearful independence of honest industry."[35] Had Pilkington only had the opportunity to gain a cheerful independence through "honest" industry, presenting her writings as her own rather than under James Worsdale's name, she would undoubtedly have preferred that road—one that would have allowed her to take credit for her own work. Instead, she became for her time merely another fallen woman who illustrated the expected inability of women to combine wit and chastity.[36] Eventually the elderly Colly Cibber gave Pilkington the idea of writing her memoirs.[37] After listening to her "Account of Doctor *Swift*" for three hours, he urged her to "write it out, just as you relate it, and I'll engage it will sell" (P 160). She followed his advice and, in Woolf's words, became part of "the great tradition of English women of letters."[38]

In writing about her struggles and her vulnerability, Pilkington achieves, as well as a place in literary history, a feminist consciousness,[39] the product of a terrible if familiar feminine story of struggle and hand-to-mouth living, of children taken away, of debtor's prison, illness, and early death—and, perhaps the most essential ingredient, her sense of herself as a woman who deserved a better fate.[40] The ultimate tragedy of Pilkington's life, as Walter and Clare Jerrold write, was her marriage to a man who courted renown in an area where his wife had the greater talent. Pilkington, most anxious to present an image of blamelessness in her *Memoirs*, describes herself as acknowledging her husband's superiority: "He not only surpassed me in natural Talents, but also had the Advantage of having those Talents improved by Learning" (P 49). This is what she wrote after the fact. At the time, it must have been irresistible to show what she could do, especially when the audience was the great Dean: "Matthew desired to be thought a wit, but his wife's tongue was quicker and sharper than his; he wished to set up as a poet and published one little volume, but Laetitia could produce better verse than his on any and every occasion; he was patronized by Dean Swift, and then Laetita crept in, under his arm as it were, and became a constant companion to the Dean."[41]

Matthew Pilkington never forgot or forgave, and neither did his wife: her autobiography is obsessed with his persecutions, for which she imagines the only revenge open to her:

> *That I, like the Classics, shall be read*
> *When Time, and all the World are dead.* (P 87)

Swift lent his prestige to another woman poet, Mary Barber, in the form of a preface to her collection of poems in which he praises Barber while simultaneously qualifying her achievement:

She seemeth to have a true poetical Genius, better cultivated than could well be expected, either from her Sex, or the Scene she hath acted in, as the Wife of a Citizen.

> Yet I am assured that no Woman was ever more useful to her Husband in the Way of his Business. Poetry hath only been her favourite Amusement; for which she hath one Qualification, that I wish all good Poets possess'd a Share of, I mean, that she is ready to take Advice, and submit to have her Verses corrected, by those who are generally allow'd to be the best Judges.[42]

Swift's comment, intended to be complimentary to Barber, is not as forceful as Dr. Johnson's memorable remark comparing a woman preaching to a dog walking on its hind legs: "It is not done well; but you are surprised to find it done at all."[43] Still, there is some similarity. Both Barber's gender and her modest station in life as the wife of a woolen-draper presuppose that she will not have cultivated her "natural endowment," just as the conditions of Dr. Johnson's world as he saw it presupposed that women would not preach. Barber's talent was, in Swift's estimation, "better cultivated than could well be expected"—but given that very little could be expected, this does not mean that it was well cultivated by male standards. It would never have occurred to Swift to assess Barber's poetry without special pleading: she is not a poet as this role was understood in his time, that is, as an exclusively male role, but a woman who writes poetry when she is able to take time from her real occupation of keeping house.

According to Swift, Barber "never writes on a Subject with general unconnected Topicks, but always with a Scheme and Method driving to some particular End" (*BP* 42). This much might be expected of any conscientious writer: as evidence of "poetical Genius" it is less than compelling. In other respects the picture is all too predictable. Barber did not neglect her role in order to write: poetry was only "her favourite Amusement." This was a time in which "versifying wives were by most husbands deemed *fantastical*,"[44] but such excuses for women writing continue into the early twentieth century, demonstrating that married women at least needed to justify writing for publication and to style themselves as less serious writers than men. As Pilkington commented in her *Memoirs*, "[I] was sensible the Compliments I received were rather paid to me as a Woman, in whom any thing a Degree above Ignorance appears surprizing, than to any Merit I really possess'd" (P 49). Given this reality, it is impossible to tell how much of Swift's presentation of Barber to a reading public is calculated to disarm the common idea that women, especially wives, should not write poetry, and how much reflects his own view of women as poets.

Docile female pupil that she was, Barber was ready to take advice on correcting her poems from her (male) betters, most notably, of course, Dean Swift himself. In her own preface, Barber, too, acknowledges "the Goodness of some Men of Genius, who with great Condescension undertook to correct what I had written" (*BP* 48). As Pilkington remarked of Swift and women, "When he found them docile, he took great Pleasure to instruct them" (P 45).[45] Pilkington tends to be contemptuous of Barber, possibly because Swift regarded Barber as the most talented of the women poets in his circle.[46] It is easy to see why he did: Barber could write competent satiric verse in Swift's comic manner and with some of his vernacular ease. As one of many such examples, her poem *An Unanswerable Apology for the Rich* creates a Swiftian portrait of the self-deceived Castalio, a rich man who imagines that he would help the poor, if only he had the means: "Alas! to ease their woes he wishes, / But cannot live without ten dishes" (*BP* 75).

Barber's *Written for My Son, and Spoken by Him at His First Putting on Breeches* is another poem in Swift's meter and manner, a history of the foolishness of fashionable clothing:

> Our wiser ancestors wore brogues,
> Before the surgeons bribed these rogues,
> With narrow toes, and heels like pegs,
> To help to make us break our legs. (*BP* 73)

Swift would have avoided the infelicity of *toes* following hard upon *rogues*, and his last line would have been smoother, but he was bound to have approved the theme and taken pleasure in a skill that resembled his own.

That Swift was a congenial influence appears everywhere in Barber's poetry. *Stella and Flavia*, for instance, is a direct descendant of Swift's birthday poems for Stella in its comparison of a woman with a "lovely mind" to a woman whose only positive attribute is her face:

> Then boast, fair Flavia, boast your face,
> Your beauty's only store:
> Your charms will every day decrease,
> Each day give Stella more. (*BP* 138–39)

The imprimatur of a well known writer like Swift could indeed open doors for a protégée. His friend Lady Elisabeth Germain wrote that Barber had presented herself, and, "since you desire it you may be very sure she shall not fail of my entreaties to his Grace of Dorset for her" (W 3:325). Swift's intention to help Barker extended to recommending her husband as a source of livery: the obliging Lady Betty had accordingly given the name of the woolen merchant to Lord Dorset, who discovered that he asked "a greater price than any body else" and could not guarantee that the liveries ordered would be ready in time (W 3:433). Swift, like Dr. Delany, could be an overly enthusiastic recommender.

The promotion of Mary Barber was to have more serious consequences for Swift than the unsatisfactory service of her husband. Swift's attitude toward a woman poet who he believed had some genuine talent was remarkably generous, for the too presumptuous use of Swift's name to further Barber's poetic career caused him considerable embarrassment. As he recounted to the Countess of Suffolk, he had not known Mrs. Barber "till she was recommended to me by a worthy friend [Patrick Delany] to help her to subscribers, which by her writings, I thought she deserved" (W 3:416).

Swift's wholehearted endorsement emboldened Barber to ask Pope to correct her verses, which Pope delicately complained of to Swift. Swift's letter of response to Pope repudiated Barber's behavior but offered a sympathetic understanding of it: "I believe there was a great Combat between her modesty and her Ambition" (W 3:383). Worse was to follow. Three letters extravagantly praising Barber were sent to the Queen, two under Swift's signature and the third unsigned but attributed to Swift—to his mortification when it became generally known. It was unthinkable that Swift, who for a number of years had nursed, and not silently, a deep-seated grievance against Queen Caroline, should address such a communication to her. His initial reaction, expressed to Pope, bordered on frenzy:

> I can onely say, that the apprehensions one may be apt to have of a friend doing a foolish thing, is an effect of Kindness, and G^d knows who is free from playing the fool sometime or oth^r: but, in such degree as to write to the Qu— who hath used me ill without any cause, and to write in such a manner as the lett you sent me, and in such a Style, and to have so much zeal for one almost a Stranger, and to make such a description of a woman as to prefer her before all man kind, and to instance it as one of the greatest grievances of Irel^d, that Her M— hath not encouraged M^{rs} B— a woollen-drapers wife, declined in the world, because she hath a knack at versifying, was to suppose or fear a folly so transcendent that no man could be guilty of who was not fit for Bedlam. (W 3:411–12)

Swift protests that circumstances make it absurd that he should write such letters as are attributed to him, but amazingly, his impassioned denial of responsibility for the letters does not reveal any anger at Barber or assign culpability to her. He does allow himself to deprecate her position in life (a woolen-draper's wife, declined in the world), but not gratuitously: for a writer of Swift's reputation to send extravagant letters to the Queen about a stranger who is also a nobody *would* suggest that he had taken leave of his senses.

In more restrained terms he repeated this denial to the Countess of Suffolk, who he knew would carry it to the Queen. The need to defend himself to the Countess must have been distasteful to Swift since he had reached the harsh conclusion that she was merely a courtier, incapable of the friendship he had once imagined possible.[47] Her reply, although clearly joking, could only have made Swift more uncomfortable—and was intended to do so. Swift, the Countess wrote, had disparaged her as "a Woman, and a Courtier." It was therefore pleasing to her to hear of Swift suspected of folly: "the Man of Wit, The Dignified Divine, The Irish Drapier . . . this Monitor of Princes, This Irish Patriot, This Excelent Man at Speech and Pen . . . under Suspecions of having a violent Passion for Mrs Barber" (W 3:434). Swift must then in his next letter defend himself against the allegation of some illicit motive: "She [Mrs. Barber] seems to be a Woman of piety, and a poeticall Genius; and though I never visited her in my life, yet was I disposed to do her good offices on the Doctor's account; and her own good character" (W 3:437). Under extreme provocation Swift remained fair to Barber and supportive of her project to publish her poems.

The account of this affair by a partisan of the Queen, Charlotte Clayton, Viscountess Sundon, vindicates Swift as the author of the letters but assumes that Barber wrote them as "a creature of that unscrupulous man [Swift]." She comments that the Barber affair "brought a great deal of odium upon him," although it seems likely that it merely confirmed views already held by the political party in power.[48] Lady Russell wrote to Mrs. Clayton from Bath, on October 18, 1731, that she had met Mrs. Barber there and found her to be "a strange, bold, disagreeable woman."[49] Such a comment made by a woman of title about someone like Barber might mean only that Lady Russell found Barber's assertiveness in seeking to publish her poetry strange, bold, and disagreeable.

During this time Dr. Delany remained passionately convinced of his protégée's innocence, and it appears that eventually everyone else accepted it, too, including Swift.[50] Mary Pendarves, who heard all about the episode when she visited Ireland, became a staunch supporter of Barber and continued to have warm relations with her until Barber died.[51] This was more than the friendly condescension to a social inferior that probably characterized many such relationships. From Bath, Pendarves wrote to Swift to express her dissatisfaction with most of the people she had encountered there and to tell him "my solace is Mrs. *Barber*, whose spirit and good countenance cheers me whenever I hear or see her" (*C* 4:451).[52]

Swift confirmed his forgiveness by aiding Barber when she was in financial difficulties and even assigning to her benefit his *Polite Conversation*. Hearing from Pendarves that she was enjoying Barber's company at Bath, he replied with genuine concern: "I am very glad to find that poor Mrs. Barber hath the honor to be in your favour. . . . I think she hath every kind virtue, and only one defect, which is too much bashfullness" (*C* 4:456). Swift seems to have forgotten Barber's forwardness in approaching Pope and her aggressive solicitation of help to publish her poetry. She, in turn, was always mindful of what she owed her most distinguished patron. Using an excuse Swift often gave for not answering a letter promptly, illness, she then wrote, "I humbly beseech you to pardon me nor think me ungratefull or in the least insensible of the infinite obligations I lie under to you which, Heaven knows, are never out of my Mind" (*C* 4:538–39). When Swift evaluated his friends according to the rubrics *grateful, ungrateful, indifferent,* and *doubtful,* she received the accolade of *grateful* (*C* 5:271).[53]

Barber's own self-presentation begins with the following apologia:

> I am sensible that a Woman steps out of her Province whenever she presumes to write for the Press, and therefore think it necessary to inform my Readers, that my Verses were written with a very different View from any of those which other Attempters in Poetry have proposed to themselves: My Aim being chiefly to form the Minds of my Children. (*BP* 45)

Barber counters her departure from the expected female sphere with a noble maternal purpose that she hopes will justify her presumption. As her poems demonstrate, she was well aware of prevailing male attitudes about the role of women:

> What good's in a dame that will pore on a book?
> No—give me the wife that shall save me a cook. (*BP* 101)

Women, too, could be expected to be hostile to violations of conventional feminine behavior. In Barber's account of soliciting subscriptions for her book of poems, a series of women ridicule her:

> Servilla cries, "*I hate a wit*;
> Women should to their fate submit,
> Should in the needle take delight;
> 'Tis out of *character* to write." (*BP* 200)

Fulvia remarks categorically that "Verses are only writ by Men"(*BP* 201). Barber's critics here have some of the petty malice of the disembodied voices in *Verses on the Death of Dr. Swift*:

> "Her sickness is a feint, no doubt,
> To keep her book from coming out."
> "Of wit," says *Celia*, "I'll acquit her,"
> Then archly fell into a *Titter*. (*BP* 202)

Barber's poem works as *Verses* does, presenting negative versions of the poet ascribed to others but within a poem that validates the poet. It is, in keeping with the distance between Barber and Swift as poets, less subtle: each character who criticizes Barber or women writers is methodically discredited. Sylvia is haughty, Olivia loses money gambling and so will not pay for a subscription, Belinda "loves to blame." But Barber manages to mention that Swift and Lord Dorset each subscribed for ten copies of her book while "many, truly good and great," also looked upon her project with favor. However much rejection might have stung, Barber was able to turn it into comic verse.

As Barber's most recent editor remarks, her work constantly bears witness to "the position of women in [her] society and her obligation to placate a succession of patrons and wealthy friends."[54] In the eighteenth century such cultivation may not have been perceived to be a degrading experience, but it was certainly a deforming one. Male writers also had to please patrons, but it was a more straightforward job, one that did not require any apology for their neglect of "real duties" in order to write.

Mary Barber, grateful and humble, is a textbook example of what has been true down through the centuries: women have habitually denied, defended, or ignored negative male attitudes toward their sex, and for the best of reasons: their own need to survive within a male-dominated hierarchy. Arnold Krupat writes about another marginalized group: "Native Americans have had to make a variety of accommodations to the dominant culture's forms, capitulating to them, assimilating them, sometimes dramatically transforming them, but never able to proceed independent of them."[55] The same could be said for those eighteenth-century women poets who, like Barber, tried to insert themselves into a male literary establishment in opposition to societal hostility and rejection. They used what they could and discarded the rest, at what cost to their self-respect and art we can only speculate.

Pilkington and Barber struggled with financial difficulties most of their lives, but the young widow Mary Pendarves, later Mrs. Delany, began her life as a member of a prominent aristocratic family, the Granvilles, and ended it as a favored friend of King George III and his queen. The royal couple enjoyed Mrs. Delany's company so much that she was "installed as a life tenant in a house near Queen's Lodge which the King had made over to her and fitted up for her, personally supervising the workmen. . . . He was there to welcome her when she moved in."[56] Swift appreciated the lively intelligence and general attractiveness of the thirty-one-year-old Mary, although, when they first met, she wrote to her sister that another young woman had engrossed his attention: "Miss Kelly's beauty and good-humour have gained an entire conquest over him, and I come in only *a little by the by*."[57] Miss Kelly was to be a short-lived favorite: in spite of Swift's assiduous attendance at her bedside, she died. Pendarves, however, only improved upon the first impression she made on the Dean during her year-and-a-half visit to Ireland. Like the other young women who were both friends and pupils of the aging Swift, she was happy to be instructed. She wrote to her sister, "The Dean of St. Patrick's . . . calls himself *"my master,"* & corrects me when I speak bad English, or do not pronounce my words distinctly. I wish he lived in England, I should not only have a great deal of entertainment from him, but improvement." She does not explain why she writes to her sister that, in comparison with Swift, "Dr. Delany will make a *more desirable friend*, for he has all the qualities requisite for friendship." No doubt the younger and less prepossessing Dr. Delany was more approachable to a young woman than the Dean of St. Patrick's. Pendarves's first mention of Swift describes him as "so extraordinary a genius" but also as "a very *odd companion*."[58] He was bound to be intimidating to a woman half his age.

Of the women singled out for Swift's special favor, Mrs. Delany, as she became known to posterity, would go on to the greatest success in her lifetime. Late in life she was often called "Dr. Swift's Mrs. Delany,"[59] but unlike Pilkington and Barber she achieved a personal and artistic success that had nothing to do with him. One section of George Ballard's book *Memoirs of Several Ladies of Great Britain* (1752) was dedicated to Mrs. Delany, "the Truest Judge and Brightest Pattern of all the Accomplishments which adorn her Sex," just one of many such tributes she received during her lifetime.[60] For Fanny Burney, she was "the most revered of friends, and, perhaps, the most perfect of women."[61]

Although Mary Granville had evinced a flair for paper cutting at the age of eight, her only creative outlet during her early adulthood was embroidery—at which she excelled. Her artistic nature found greater expression only after her late marriage to Patrick Delany, an indulgent husband who encouraged her multiform talents. And so in middle age she decorated mantelpieces and ceilings in seashell or stucco designs that are still valued today.[62] She took drawing lessons from Hogarth, did portraits and sketches, and finally, as an elderly widow, invented the form of the flower collage, a representation of a flower "composed of hundreds of finely cut snippets of colored paper," some of which she dyed herself.[63]

Burney has left an appreciative description of the artform Mrs. Delany invented: "It is staining paper of all possible colors, and then cutting it out, so finely and delicately, that when it is pasted on paper or vellum, it has the appearance of being pencilled, except that, by being raised, it has still a richer and more natural look."[64] Erasmus Darwin, in canto 2 of his long poem *The Botanic Garden*, described Mrs. Delany's flower art with the appreciation of a trained botanist *and* an artistic sensibility:

> So now Delany forms her mimic bowers,
> Her paper foliage, and her silken flowers;
> Her virgin train the tender scissars ply,
> Vein the green leaf, the purple petal dye:
> Round wiry stems the flaxen tendril bends,
> Moss creeps below, and waxen fruit impends.
> Cold Winter views amid his realms of snow
> Delany's vegetable statues blow;
> Smooths his stern brow, delays his hoary wing,
> And eyes with wonder all the blooms of spring.[65]

In an explanatory note he stated that "Mrs. Delany has finished nine hundred and seventy accurate and elegant representations of different vegetables with the parts of their flowers . . . in what she terms paper mosaic." He believed that her work, now known as the *Flora Delanica*, probably contained "a greater number of plants than were ever before drawn from the life by any one person." The effect of her method was "wonderful," and he thought the accuracy of her collages superior to that of drawings."[66] The prominent botanist Sir Joseph Banks echoed this admiration. He was known to say that Mrs. Delany's representations of flowers "were the *only* imitations of nature he had ever seen from which he could venture to describe botanically any plant without the least fear of committing an error."[67]

This was all in the future when the young widow met Swift. After Pendarves returned to England, Swift initiated a correspondence with her. In addition to telling her that she had gained his good graces by not making any *boutades*, he rather incautiously applied his own standard of womanly excellence to her: "I much question whether you *understand a fan*, or have so good a fancy *at silks* as others" (*C* 4:258). Had Swift been privy to the lively correspondence between Pendarves and her sister Ann Granville, he would have discovered that she could assess and satirize fashionable dress very well and without the heat of a Swiftian indictment. Of a countess in a petticoat with a huge embroidery, she wrote: "It was a most laboured piece of finery, the pattern much properer for a stucco staircase than the apparel of a lady,—a mere shadow that tottered under every step she took under the load."[68]

Pendarves reserved her anger for social issues, particularly those concerning gender. It might have taken Swift aback to learn that a year before meeting him she had written an intemperate denunciation of men, although her sense of their general unacceptability parallels his position that most women were severely flawed:

> Would it were so, that I went ravaging and slaying all odious men, and that would go near to clear the world of that sort of animal; you know I never had a good opinion of them, and every day my *dislike strengthens*; some *few* I will except, but *very few*, they have so despicable an opinion of women, and treat them by their words and actions so ungenerously and inhumanly.[69]

The violent fantasy of ridding the world of "that sort of animal" is reminiscent of Gulliver's contemplating the destruction of the Yahoos in Houyhnhnmland.

Having been forced at seventeen to marry a repulsive old man, Pendarves remained unattached for twenty years after her husband's death ended their seven-year marriage. Writing to Ann about one of the many attempts to persuade her to wed again, she described matrimony in entirely negative terms: "Matrimony! I marry! Yes, there's a blessed scene before my eyes of the comforts of that state. —A sick husband, squalling brats, a cross mother-in-law, and a thousand unavoidable impertinences . . . but stop my rage! be not too fierce."[70] This was a side of Pendarves that found expression to Ann when she thought about gender relations but which she concealed from Swift.

What often inspires Pendarves's indignation is the unfairness of the double standard: "The minutest indiscretion in a woman (though occasioned by themselves [that is, by men]), never fails of being enlarged into a notorious crime; but men are to sin on without limitation or blame."[71] Nevertheless, she is not arguing for greater freedom for women; she shared Swift's conservative morality and would only have liked to see it enforced on men as well as women. Pendarves perceived this same unfairness in other social practices, such as a man's failing to leave his daughters or wife well provided for while concentrating his wealth on a male descendant. As she wrote to her sister,

> There is one *error* which most fathers run into, and that is providing *too little* for daughters; young men have a thousand ways of improving a little fortune, by professions and employments, if they have good friends, but young gentlewomen have no way, the fortune settled on them is all they are to expect—they are incapable of making an addition.[72]

This sensitivity to the financial disadvantage of women may have caused her to befriend such impecunious writers as Mary Barber and Elizabeth Elstob, the gifted Anglo-Saxon scholar. Like Swift, Pendarves was a good friend to such women, ceaselessly recommending her protégées to her own friends as well as patronizing them herself.[73]

Pendarves evidently found nothing in Swift's behavior or opinions to arouse her protofeminist ire, since her letters to him are full of ingratiation, sometimes more than even Swift could bear. In response to her statement, "I know you pay me a great compliment in writing," he retorted: "You have made me half angry with so many lines in your letter which look like a kind of apology for writing to me" (*C* 4:416, 455-56). Beneath the protestations each saw the other as a rare exception in a sex full of faults.

Swift's first surviving letter to Pendarves (October 7, 1734) asserts their hierarchical relationship by reminding her, through the business of the *boutade*, that he chooses women friends, rather than vice versa, according to his exacting standards. That established, the letter is long and complimentary. In Pendarves, Swift had found a woman friend who met all his requirements: in addition to good sense and willingness to be instructed, she satisfied his weakness for connection to the great (the great themselves having been ruled out in his letter to

Pope as too unavailable). As Mary Granville, Pendarves was the niece of Lord Lansdown, a kinswoman of Lord Carteret, a lifelong close friend of the Duchess of Portland—whose parents were friends of Swift—and someone who moved easily in aristocratic circles. So Swift can write "Are you acquainted with the Duke of Chandos?"—and go on to relate a story that culminates in asking her to intercede with her uncle to find out from Chandos why he has not responded to a letter of Swift's (*C* 4:259–60). Although Lord Lansdown proved unhelpful, Pendarves placed the matter "into hands that will pursue it diligently . . . for whatever lies in my power to serve you, is of too much consequence for me to neglect" (*C* 4:271).

Swift's friendship with Pendarves was mostly epistolary, but it is difficult to avoid some parallels between her and Stella, as if, so late in life, Swift faintly retraced the pattern of that supreme friendship. Like Stella, Pendarves had intermittent eye trouble, which provoked Swift's solicitude, and, as he had said about Stella in his poem *Stella at Woodpark*, Swift told Pendarves that apropos of her visit to a country house called Paradise, wherever she resided "must needs be a *paradise*" (*C* 4:455). Repeating the advice he had given to Stella more than thirty years earlier, he often advised Pendarves to move to Ireland where her income would go twice as far. Some of this urging is raillery, but it was so persistent that Pendarves felt called upon to respond seriously, "My lot is thrown on *English* ground" (*C* 4:415). In spite of this clear signal, Swift could not resist another jocular allusion. If, as he has heard, the place where Pendarves is staying is known simply as a good watering place for a horse, "we have ten thousand such paradises in this kingdom, of which you may have your choice" (*C* 4:455). The aging Dean, feeling neglected by Irish friends and increasingly prey to his chronic ailments, seems to have idealized the young English widow whom he met in social gatherings a handful of times. Like his description of Stella's conversation, in which everyone in the company always agreed that she had said the best thing, Swift imagines himself in Pendarves's company, a "silent hearer and looker-on," simply enjoying that company in which "he could never be weary" (*C* 4:456).

If Stella, according to Swift, was acclaimed and admired by all who knew her, this was true of the elderly Mary Delany in a much wider social circle. Hannah More addressed laudatory verses to her, and Fanny Burney wrote in 1783: "She is remarkably upright. . . . Benevolence, softness, piety and gentleness are all resident in her face."[74] As a young widow Pendarves never lacked for suitors, but her letters to Swift usually included a special greeting to Dr. Delany. When the fifty-nine-year-old widower proposed, the forty-three-year-old widow accepted in spite of her brother's strenuous opposition to Delany's lowly origin. Fourteen years later, Delany composed an eloquent tribute to his wife, remarking "a most lovely face of great sweetness, set off with a head of fair hair, shining and naturally curled; with a complexion which nothing could out-do or equal, in which, to speak in the language of poets, 'the lilies and the roses contended for the mastery.'"[75]

Swift also gave evidence of a genuine appreciation of Pendarves. When it became clear that he could not persuade her to return to Ireland, Horace facing a long separation from Galatea came to mind, prompting Swift to quote the Latin original of *Odes* 3.27.13. These lines may be freely translated as "I grant that you be happy wherever you prefer to be / And, Galatea, that you live mindful of me" (*C* 4:299).[76] The passage captures the spirit of the long-ago *Journal to Stella*, so full of good wishes for MD and admonitions to think of Pdfr.

Part II

*T*HE FAIR SEX

Written for the Honour of the Fair Sex
—Epigraph to *A Beautiful Young Nymph Going to Bed*

Swift never used "the fair sex" unironically: it affronted him as a linguistic dishonesty promulgated by a distorted romantic conception of women. By applying the term to "old Beggar-women, and Cinder-Pickers" (P 178) he reminded his society of the foolishness of such an all-inclusive description and the reality that its romantic fantasy ignores. In the same vein, the brides-to-be who must have their virginity affirmed by an encounter with a lion, a test that few can pass, are referred to collectively as the "Fair Sex." With similar irony Swift dedicates his poem about a bedraggled streetwalker "to the Honour of the Fair Sex."

In the *Journal to Stella*, Swift wrote that he would not "meddle with the Spectator, let him fair-sex it to the world's end" (*JS* 482). "Fair-sexing it" suggested to Swift a flattery of women that characterized them as goddesses or perfect beauties rather than the flawed human beings they were. This facade of appearance needed to be penetrated to reveal the imperfections it cleverly but dishonestly concealed. Swift renders the prostitute Corinna's hard life comically not so much to make fun of her—this would be gratuitous, since society had already labeled and condemned her—but to satirize the idea that a prostitute tricked out in so many artificial parts can be included under the sign of the "fair sex." If no one would think to use the epithet seriously for a woman of the streets, Swift knows that the male gaze, intent on seeing women as objects of sexual and romantic fantasies, might regard young ladies of the middle class, like the Celias and Chloes of his poetry, as appropriately represented by it—although these women, too, in Swift's view, conceal disgusting habits. Pilkington says that she first thought that Swift was trying to "affront the Fair Sex" (P 178) when he wrote *The Lady's Dressing Room*; her experience with

100

a dirty landlady later in life convinced her that there was some realistic basis for the poem. An early and enduring way of reading that text and *Strephon and Chloe* has been as a libel upon women. More current interpretations have fixed Swift's satiric attention on the Strephons who err so badly in their idealization of Celia or Chloe.[1] The stance of these poems is typically not either/or, since Swift rarely presents an ideal to counterbalance a satiric target; rather, men are taken to task for their foolish attitude toward women, while women are critiqued for lack of cleanliness, excretion, and deception.

Swift seems to have regarded this aspect of his writing as lighthearted, joking with Pilkington, Lady Acheson, and Pendarves about the failings of their sex and not expecting them to take serious offense. In *The Journal to a Modern Lady* he addresses Lady Acheson with mock innocence:

> It was a most unfriendly part
> In you, who ought to know my heart,
> Are well acquainted with my zeal
> For all the female commonweal:
> How could it come into your mind,
> To pitch on me, of all mankind,
> Against the sex to write a satire,
> And brand me for a woman-hater? (*CP* 365)

After more lavish protestation, Swift turns to the satirizing of a "modern lady." In 1735, after the notorious "excremental poems" had all been written and published, Swift jokingly told Pendarves that "even my vein of satire upon ladies is lost."[2]

5

$\mathcal{M}$aternity

Mothers, both collectively and individually, are strikingly absent from Swift's poems and prose fictions, his correspondence, and what we know of his conversation. Even the *Letter to a Young Lady, on Her Marriage* is entirely about the young lady's role as a companion to her husband and makes no mention of children.[1] We see women in many guises in Swift's writing, from the flayed woman of *A Tale of a Tub* to the decaying whores of *The Progress of Beauty* and *A Beautiful Young Nymph Going to Bed*, from the gentlewomen engaged in frivolous social pastimes to the same class of women caught by Swift's harsh spotlight in their boudoirs. There are also poems praising the childless women Swift called Stella and Vanessa. And *Gulliver's Travels* shows Gulliver suggesting to his Houyhnhnm master the castration of Yahoos as a way of humanely ending that inferior species by preventing reproduction, and thus maternity, among them. There is some evidence that Swift and many of his countrymen would not have minded a similar measure for Irish beggars.[2] Claude Rawson writes that "only ten years before *A Modest Proposal* and seven before *Gulliver's Travels*, a statute was mooted for castrating them."[3]

Comparing Swift to other writers of his time reveals more differences than similarities on the topic of maternity. Daniel Defoe, a man of Swift's generation, includes and often foregrounds motherhood in his extensive consideration of women in fiction and nonfiction: "For a Man or Woman to marry, and then to say they desire to have no Children," he wrote, "That is a Piece of preposterous Nonsense, next to Lunacy." He also belonged to the minority who believed that it was morally wrong for a woman past the age of childbearing to marry because "such a Conjunction . . . loses to the World the Produce of one Man."[4] As Carol

Houlihan Flynn remarks of his fiction, "Implicit in the sexual action is the sexual reaction, the childbearing and the children that follow."[5] Swift clearly disagreed. His unfinished essay *Of the Education of Ladies* brings up this commonly held principle as one of many that need reformation: "It is argued, That the great end of marriage is propagation: That, consequently, the principal business of a wife is to breed children, and to take care of them in their infancy" (*PW* 4:226). In challenging this role Swift would even be at odds with Mary Wollstonecraft, who would assert later in the century that the woman who "neither suckles nor educates her children scarcely deserves the name of a wife, and has no right to that of a citizen."[6] More pertinently, he differed from the majority of writers on women of both the seventeenth and the eighteenth century. As "a Physician" tersely commented on the role of a woman, "She is only to Conceive, to give Suck, and to breed up Children."[7]

Alexander Pope, almost twenty years younger than Swift and thus much more a product of early-eighteenth-century culture, is almost equally uninterested in writing about maternity.[8] Like Swift, he was a bachelor, although probably more because of his deformity and illness than a desire to remain celibate, and, like Swift, he kept company with a particular woman friend who never married.[9] The intense friendship and mutual admiration of Pope and Swift has tended to obscure their differences: Pope was a product of Roman Catholic culture and the close-knit community it engendered in an age of persecution and political uncertainty. More germane to this discussion, he was the cherished son of parents with whom he lived for most of his adult life. Pope may not have chosen motherhood as a frequent subject, but when he does write about it, he casts himself in the role of the devoted son who exercises the maternal office for his own aging mother:

> Me, let the tender Office long engage
> To rock the Cradle of reposing Age,
> With lenient arts extend a Mother's breath,
> Make Languor smile, and smooth the Bed of Death,
> Explore the Thought, explain the asking Eye,
> And keep a while one Parent from the Sky![10]

Pope gave every indication of extreme grief upon the death of his ninety-year-old mother. Two years later his garden boasted an obelisk raised in her memory and inscribed in Latin, "Ah Edith! / Best of Mothers / Most Loving of Women. / Farewell."[11] There is no record of any public pronouncement on Swift's part when his mother died, nor, although his passion for memorializing is amply evidenced elsewhere, is there any mention of raising a monument to Abigail Erick Swift.[12]

Margaret Anne Doody has compared Swift's representation of women excreting to Pope's portrait of the goddess Dulness in *The Dunciad*, arguing that "to a woman reader the fact that 'Celia shits' is probably less upsetting or annoying" than Pope's representation of horrific maternity.[13] At first glance, it would not seem profitable to compare representations of real women within a realistic context performing a bodily function that is not sex-specific and an imaginary monster symbolizing the proliferation of bad literature in an epic setting. Moreover, it is not the fact of female excretion in Swift's poetry that might annoy a woman reader so much as the male attitudes that inflect the fact. One may read the negative ascription of maternal power in Pope somewhat differently from Doody: its "uncreating word" implies the existence of genuine creativity. The poet asserts the importance of maternity as an activity and as a trope, an attitude markedly absent from Swift's consideration of women.[14]

An exception to Swift's practice of ignoring maternity or treating it negatively is the little-known poem *The First of April*, inscribed to Mrs. E. C., Elizabeth Cope, the second wife of Swift's good friend Robert Cope (*CP* 258–60). Apollo dispatches the nine muses to the Cope country seat to care for the children within; they assume that the mother is neglectful, but when they observe her unseen, they discover a model of wifely and maternal concern, which leads them to realize that the mission was an April Fool's joke. Slight as it is, *The First of April* does at least affirm that Swift understood what the world regarded as admirable maternal performance: "To kitchen, parlour, nursery flies, / And seems all feet, and hands, and eyes" (*CP* 259). Although the poem is a graceful compliment, its presentation of maternity lacks the telling detail and verbal flair so characteristic of Swift's style elsewhere, as if—for all of his affection for the Cope household—he is not truly engaged by the subject of ideal motherhood. Another April Fool's joke, in a letter to Lady Acheson, links maternity to the grotesque: "Mrs. —— was brought to bed yesterday morning at five o'clock of a half child, just as if it were divided in two equal parts. It had one eye, half a nose and mouth, one leg, and so from top to bottom" (W 3:465). This perverse maternity calls forth Swift's more characteristic style of precise detail to create verisimilitude. No one in the poem *The First of April* is visualized so completely as this newborn half-person. Swift even adds, slyly, "They could see it was a boy, or rather half a boy" (W 3:465), suggesting a visual image that he does not elaborate.

For most people the experience of maternity that will powerfully shape later attitudes is that of a child relating to his or her mother. But Swift had little association with his mother in infancy and childhood. A fluke of circumstance resulted in the two being separated for the first critical years of life, when Swift's nurse took the year-old infant with her to Whitehaven, England, and then did not bring him back to Ireland for three years, supposedly because his mother preferred not to chance another sea voyage before that time. Swift described his nurse as being "so carefull of him that before he returnd he had learnt to spell, and by the time that he was three years old he could read any chapter in the Bible" (*PW* 5:192).[15]

It is unclear whether Abigail Swift left Ireland to settle in England before or after Swift's return:[16] in any case, she kept her older child, Jane, with her, but her son—whose father had died before his birth—became part of the large household of his uncle Godwin Swift. In adulthood Swift regarded his uncle's charity as grudging and insufficient; just as he had had no chance to form a bond with his mother, he formed no relationship with a parental figure in Godwin's household. For practical purposes the penniless boy passed his childhood years as an orphan, not destined to see his mother again until, at the age of twenty-one, he was a refugee from upheavals in Ireland. When he appeared at her door in Leicester early in 1689, "Swift cannot have remembered ever having seen his mother before."[17] The seven months that he then lived in her house would be the only such period in his life, although John Nichols maintains that she "sometimes came to Ireland, to visit him after his settlement at Laracor," and Patrick Delany refers to Swift's "frequent visits to England to visit his mother,"[18] trips that are substantiated by Swift's account books to the extent that he stopped in Leicester when he went to or from London in 1703 and 1704.[19] On one occasion recorded in his account book for the years 1709 and 1710, Swift spent a month "in the neighborhood" on his way back to Ireland, suggesting that there may have been other attractions than Abigail Swift in the Leicester area.[20]

The lack of contact in childhood may have contributed to the cold-blooded attitude expressed in the autobiographical fragment entitled "Family of Swift." Here Swift admits to an enduring resentment because his father married a woman undistinguished in family and fortune. He affirms that he had felt the consequences of that marriage "not only through the whole course of his education, but during the greatest part of his life" (*PW* 5:192). In the world Swift saw himself a part of, such a statement reflects an unsentimental but accurate appraisal of the effects of a marriage that could produce no advantages of familial connection or fortune. Even at the early age of twenty-four, Swift wrote to the Reverend John Kendall, his friend and cousin, that he had observed many instances of such marital disaster among his own acquaintance:

> Among all the young gentlemen that I have known to have ruined them selves by marrying (which I assure you is a great number) I have made this general Rule that they are either young, raw & ignorant Scholars, who for want of knowing company, believe every silk petticoat includes an *angell*, or else they have been a sort of honest young men, who perhaps are too litteral in rather marrying than burning & so entail miseries on them selves & posterity. (W 1:105)

Later, Thomas Sheridan, his closest friend in Ireland, would impress Swift as a prime example of this poor policy: "He acted like too many clergymen, who are in haste to be married when very young; and from hence proceeded all the miseries of his life" (*PW* 5:217). Swift assured Kendall that he was determined not to make this costly mistake himself.

The one distinctive detail about Swift's mother that we learn from his correspondence is her concern during that seven-month visit that he might have fallen in love inappropriately. Along with Swift's assessment of his own parents' marriage, this maternal warning may have inspired the emphatic statement of his letter.

In keeping with Dr. Delany's attribution of "filial piety" to him,[21] Swift's treatment of his mother during her lifetime exemplified his tendency to follow moral prescriptions punctiliously. He voiced no personal animus against her, but by the same token there is little evidence of an affectionate attachment.[22] Biographers who have posited such an attachment either offer no evidence for it or endow Swift's words on his mother's death with more weight than they can bear. If Swift had a meaningful relationship with his mother, it has not left traces in the form of documents or contemporary observation. Nevertheless, earlier biographers automatically assumed a close bond. More realistically, Doody writes that Swift's mother "never tried to live near him or seemed greatly concerned for his welfare . . . emotionally she seemed self-sufficient, apparently finding her son superfluous."[23]

In his brief reflection on her death, Swift does refer to Abigail Swift as his "dear mother," which may be a conventional epithet more appropriate to the occasion than a token of deep feeling. His tribute to her, jotted in an account book intended for no eyes but his own, should be taken as a sincere assessment: "If the way to Heaven be through piety, truth, justice, and charity, she is there" (*PW* 5:196). At the same time, it is completely impersonal. Swift felt no need to go beyond an enumeration of abstract virtues, not even to provide a telling illustration of them. Nor is there any sense of his own particular experience of the person who was his mother. Instead, he describes the relation of her death to himself: "I have now lost my barrier between me and death: God grant I may live to be as well prepared for it, as I confidently believe her to have been!" (*PW* 5:196).

Swift's focus on self is understandable, especially in a private passage, but it hardly suggests, as Ehrenpreis maintains, that Abigail Swift's death "shook and depressed him profoundly."[24] On the contrary, the particulars that she died "after a long sickness, being ill all winter, and lame, and extremely ill a month or six weeks before her death" might indicate that her death was anticipated and even regarded with a measure of resignation.[25] Nichols's analysis of the passage seems accurate in noting Swift's expression of "filial piety, and the religious use *which he thought it his duty to make* of that melancholy event"[26] (my emphasis). Extracting a religious meaning or message from this death would be a predictable response for a cleric, but the somewhat awkward clause that I have italicized interposes a recognizably Swiftian quality of calculation between the event and the reaction.

Ehrenpreis begins his monumental biography with the statement that "for a man who claimed that his family were 'of all mortals what I despise and hate,' Swift surely had much to do with them" (E 1:1), going on to cite numerous instances of his financial generosity to family members. The two positions are not mutually exclusive: Swift thought his relatives were undistinguished and had little desire to admit them to his life, but he was always sensitive to propriety and to the requirements of religion. He honored the obligations of blood kinship by extending help to his sister and others, although he described himself to Pope as "utterly void of what the World calls natural Affection" (*C* 5:150). He went on to characterize his relations in belittling terms. In a letter to William Richardson, he mentioned Deane Swift, then glossed: "Mrs Whiteway says he is my Cousin; which will not be to his Advantage, for I hate all Relations" (*C* 5:145). Mrs. Whiteway herself he described as "one whom I should more value if she were not a Cousin and the onely one (except her Daughter) whom I can endure in my Sight" (*C* 5:89). In his autobiographical fragment Swift characterized the Ericks, his mother's people, as deriving "their Lineage from Erick the Forester, a great Commander, who raised an army to oppose the Invasion of William the Conqueror." From this high point the family declined in every age until at the present time they were "in the condition of very private Gentlemen" (*PW* 5:191).

Stripping the parent-child bond of affection or special status is a frequent Swiftian project that accords with a man who had experienced childhood as parental absence. Although ingratitude is a capital crime among the Lilliputians, they exempt children's behavior toward their parents from this commandment. According to Gulliver, they held that a child was under no obligation to his mother "for bringing him into the World; which, considering the Miseries of human Life, was neither a Benefit in itself, nor intended so by his Parents" (*PW* 11:60). In Lilliput sex and nurturance are reduced to the same principle of animal nature: they are neither rational nor altruistic and therefore deserve no commendation. Nor, Swift has the Lilliputians conclude, does producing children of itself fit either sex to educate them.

One of the resolutions for old age that Swift made as a young man is a strange warning: "Not to be fond of children, or let them come near me hardly" (*PW* 1: xxxvii). Such an attitude can be linked to another early formulation of self-protective conduct. In an outpouring of bitter feeling to Jane Waring, the only woman to whom he proposed marriage, Swift wrote that "Philosophy advises to keep our desires and prospects of happiness as much as we can in our own breasts, and independent of anything without" (W 1:124). In this sentiment he was akin to Sir Francis Bacon, who asserted that "He that hath *Wife* and *Children*, hath given Hostages to Fortune; For they are Impediments, to great Enterprises. . . . Certainly, the best Workes, and of greatest Merit for the Publike, have proceeded from the *unmarried*, or *Childlesse Men*."[27]

While marriage suggested to Swift the possibilities of poor connections and insufficient fortunes,[28] common concerns of his time, he is unusual for the early eighteenth century in linking offspring inextricably with degeneracy. Reproduction for eighteenth-century women was "their main task and the activity that most clearly established their gendered identities and social value."[29] Swift's religion valued women as mothers almost exclusively, to the point that one current of opinion maintained that women past the age of childbearing should not marry:[30] "Protestant theologians taught that a woman was created for maternity, and that in caring for her children she was serving the Lord."[31] As Alexander Niccholes writes in his *Discourse on Marriage and Wiving*, "The end of Marriage is *proles*, i.e., *Issue*; it was the Primal Blessing, *Increase and multiply*."[32] Niccholes, whose pamphlet is directed to male readers, vividly invokes the commonplace truism that by means of woman a man lives on in his children: "Thou continuest thy Name, thy Likeness, and thy Generation walks upon Earth, and so livest in thy Similitude, in Despight of Death, when thou thyself art dead, and raked up in Dust, and otherwise without Remembrance, unless by some ruinous Stone, or ragged Epitaph."[33] Another popular clergyman, Thomas Gataker, reminds that the want of children is "*now more uncomfortable*, when men are subject to mortalitie, than it had then beene [before the Fall], when Man was himselfe, to have lived alwayes." Since it provides a kind of immortality, propagation is God's blessing: "And indeed," Gataker asks rhetorically, "what greater *blessing* could God bestow upon Men"?[34]

According to the book of Timothy, women could even be rehabilitated from Eve's transgression in the Garden through motherhood: "She shall be saved in childbearing, if they continue in faith and charity and holiness with sobriety."[35] In seventeenth- and early-eighteenth-century texts the character of a good woman was defined chiefly by maternity: "With what diligence does she discharge the duty of a *Mother?*" Timothy Rogers asks. "With what marvellous industry does she rear up the little Plants when she looks on her dear and lovely Children?"[36]

For Swift, however, maternity seemed to be yoked with decline. He disliked his kin, he told Pope, because they were "a numerous Race, degenerating from their Ancestors" (*C* 5:150). Gulliver expresses views congruent with those Swift utters in his own voice: according to Gulliver, the degeneration Swift attributes to his own family is true of Englishmen as a whole. In the extreme view of generational decline in book 4 of *Gulliver's Travels*, dissipated noblemen marry women of "mean Birth, disagreeable Person, and unsound Constitution, merely for the sake of Money. . . . The Productions of such Marriages are generally scrophulous, rickety, or deformed Children, by which Means the Family seldom continues above three Generations" (*PW* 11:256). Gulliver concludes that "a weak diseased Body, a meager Countenance, and sallow Complexion, are the true Marks of *noble Blood*" (*PW* 11:257). After seeing the spirits of ancient heroes in Laputa, he observes "how much the Race of human Kind was degenerate among us, within these Hundred Years past" (*PW* 11:201). The similarity between Swift's directly expressed views on this subject and those of Gulliver can be seen in the early *Argument Against Abolishing Christianity* (1708):

> Pray, what would become of the Race of Men in the next Age, if we had nothing to trust to, besides the scrophulous consumptive Productions furnished by our Men of Wit and Pleasure; when having squandered away their Vigour, Health, and Estates; they are forced, by some disagreeable Marriage, to piece up their broken Fortunes, and entail Rottenness and Politeness on their Posterity? (*PW* 2:30)

Swift's ideas on this subject remained consistent. In an issue of the *Intelligencer* devoted to education (1728), he concludes his scathing indictment of upper-class educational failure with the grim satisfaction that this ignorant nobility will bring about its own destruction, "so many great Families coming to an End by the Sloth, Luxury, and abandoned Lusts, which enervated their Breed through every Succession, producing gradually a more effeminate Race, wholly unfit for Propagation" (*PW* 12:53).

The class explanation of degeneracy, men marrying inferior women, is supplemented by Gulliver's explanation of the pox, which also blames women, in this case prostitutes, whose malady "bred Rotteness in the Bones of those who fell into their Embraces . . . this and many other Diseases, were propagated from Father to Son" (*PW* 11:253). The pox, Gulliver maintained, "had altered every Lineament of an *English* Countenance; shortened the Size of Bodies, unbraced the Nerves, relaxed the Sinews and Muscles, introduced a sallow Complexion, and rendered the Flesh loose and *rancid*" (*PW* 11: 201).[37]

Even the abstract offspring Swift attributed to matrimony in *Thoughts on Various Subjects* are entirely negative: "Repentance, Discord, Poverty, Jealousy, Sickness,

Spleen, Loathing, etc." (*PW* 4:243). Such progeny are akin to those of the Goddess Criticism in *The Battle of the Books* (1704): Ignorance, Pride, Opinion, Noise, Impudence, Dullness, Vanity, Positiveness, Pedantry, and Ill-Manners. The Goddess is both horrendous and conscientiously maternal, with "excrescencies in form of Teats, at which a Crew of ugly Monsters were greedily sucking" (*PW* 1:154).[38] In addition to suckling her offspring with spleen, she flies to the aid of William Wotton, her favorite child, dispatching two of her "beloved Children, *Dulness* and *Ill-Manners*," to aid him.

Swift's portrait of Liberty and her last daughter, Faction, in *The Examiner* is a similar personification of reprehensible maternity. Liberty indulges Faction to the extent that the daughter becomes unendurable, an outcome that Swift often advised real-life parents to avoid: "*Above all, she* [Faction] *frequented* Publick Assemblies, *where she sate in the Shape of an* obscene, ominous Bird, *ready to prompt her* Friends *as they spoke*" (*PW* 2:103). The "Fable of Faction," as Swift styles it, is clear enough: to represent faction, a woman who has not been properly restrained comes to mind.

Gulliver is often the object of nurturing attention in *Gulliver's Travels*, but usually on the part of creatures so extremely different from him that their surrogacy as mothers has an inevitable element of the bizarre.[39] In two cases these surrogates are of a different species, as well as the wrong sex: the sorrel nag in Houyhnhnmland and the monkey in Brobdingnag who seems to mistake Gulliver for an infant of its own kind, first holding him "as a Nurse doth a Child she is going to suckle" and then, in a grotesque parody of maternal solicitude, cramming food into his mouth and patting him when he refuses to eat (*PW* 11:122). The monkey's misguided maternal impulse almost costs Gulliver his life when he is dropped from the roof. Further, he nearly chokes on the "filthy stuff" the monkey tried to force down his throat (*PW* 11:123). Although Gulliver is rescued by his "dear little nurse" Glumdalclitch, there are a number of other times in the second voyage when she inadvertently exposes him to danger. That Gulliver never blames her for these lapses may reflect Swift's affectionate memory of his own nurse, whose abduction of the infant Jonathan is also singularly unreproached. Nurses as a category fare less well in Swift's writings.[40]

Closely related to the maternal function of suckling a child is the breast itself, an organ that receives a certain amount of unpleasant attention in *Gulliver's Travels*. Throughout his diverse experiences Gulliver will never express attraction to or appreciation of a woman's breast. On the contrary: in Houyhnhnmland he invokes a stereotypical negative image of savage women to describe the Yahoos: "Their dugs hung between their fore Feet, and often reached almost to the Ground as they walked" (*PW* 11:223).[41] In Brobdingnag a number of observed breasts fill him with disgust.

Paul-Gabriel Boucé observes that the maids of honor in Brobdingnag are "archetypal maternal surrogates, endowed with enormous breasts, like huge goddesses of fertility."[42] Yet this is exactly what they are not: whatever sexually-tinged games take place when Gulliver is placed astride their nipples, the result is not procreation, and Gulliver insists that the maids' nakedness was "very far from being a tempting Sight, or from giving me any other Motions than those of Horror and Disgust" (*PW* 11: 119). Just as proximity to these giants is not sexually stimulating to Gulliver, his minuscule size renders him merely an oddity and a toy to the maids, "a creature who had no sort of consequence." The very point of this nude jokery is to demonstrate the impossibility of anything resembling ordinary sex between bodies of such disparate sizes.[43]

Rawson suggests that Swift's satire has an "almost automatic habit of balancing female instances with an exact male counterpart,"[44] as when Gulliver first describes the horrific breast cancer in the Brobdingnagian woman and then the huge wen on the neck of a Brobdingnagian male: "There was a Woman with a Cancer in her Breast, swelled to a monstrous Size, full of Holes, in two or three of which I could have easily crept, and covered my whole Body. There was a Fellow with a Wen in his Neck, larger than five Woolpacks" (*PW* 11:112–13). Swift generally provides such examples in pairs, and he may believe that they are approximately equal. In my reading, the female illustration is invariably more negative.[45] In this instance, the two examples share size, but little else: the cancer is life-threatening as well as disfiguring, and the idea of Gulliver creeping into a cancerous hole, immersing himself in female disease, is peculiarly repulsive. Surrounding Gulliver's flesh with diseased female flesh is suggestive of intercourse with a prostitute who has a venereal disease. More generally, the image communicates male dread of being engulfed and annihilated by the female body.

The breast is "swelled to a monstrous size"; the wen is compared in size to connotatively neutral woolpacks. Moreover, the neck is a part of the body that has much less sexual valence than the breast. Nor is it involved in the inherently maternal role of feeding infants. Because breasts are a significant female site, both natural and cultural, the two examples are only approximate rather than exact counterparts. Keith Crook believes that "compassion for the human condition is behind the disgust at the inflictions of disease on the body" that the cancerous breast provokes in Gulliver.[46] Yet Gulliver's description is clinical—strangely so, given its subject. What governs Gulliver's reaction here, as throughout the Second Voyage, is the transfiguration of things made by size: the ordinary becomes monstrous and any defect or deformity horrific.

A healthy rather than a diseased breast is the object that Gulliver uses to make the point that magnification brings out unexpected flaws. It is worth quoting this passage in full because, unlike the cancerous breast, this breast is engaged in the maternal activity of breastfeeding an infant:

> I must confess no Object ever disgusted me so much as the Sight of her monstrous Breast, which I cannot tell what to compare with, so as to give the curious Reader an Idea of its Bulk, Shape and Colour. . . . The Nipple was about half the Bigness of my Head, and the Hue both of that and the Dug so varified with Spots, Pimples and Freckles, that nothing could appear more nauseous. (*PW* 11:91)

This detailed description is followed by a discourse on perspective, as if to suggest that any object might have served to make the point that great size always alters appearance for the worse. The presumably healthy breast that Gulliver observes here becomes equated with the diseased breast by the use of the same term, *mon-*

strous, to describe it. It seems curious that the healthy albeit spotted breast appears more disgusting to Gulliver than the diseased and truly disfigured breast, especially when the healthy breast is performing its nurturing function.[47] A breast displaying itself sexually might be a more obvious target of criticism.

Gulliver may share some of the ambivalence of his society toward breastfeeding.[48] Writers on the behavior of women were always urging mothers to nurse their own infants as part of maternal duty, yet wet-nursing was rampant.[49] Sir Richard Steele makes a typical plea when he writes that "there is one Duty too much neglected by *Mothers*, and that is the *Nursing* of their Children themselves. . . . No *Quality* can be pleaded in Bar of this Duty, which Nature obliges every Mother to discharge."[50] Valerie Fildes observes that "philosophers, physicians, and some theologians repeatedly condemned mothers who did not breastfeed their own children, but this had little discernible effect on the behaviour of the wealthy."[51] Those who could afford to have others breastfeed their babies generally felt superior to a practice natural to all mammals.[52] It may be this sense of the connection between his own species and the animal kingdom that fuels Gulliver's horror, or it could be the eighteenth-century belief that children could acquire disease and even "lowness of character" from breast milk.[53] A negative reaction to breastfeeding could also be part of the period's construction of women as having "leaky bodies" which bespoke, as Laura Gowing writes of female urinary incontinence, "a thorough inability to keep boundaries."[54]

Simply to illustrate perspective, Swift might have made Gulliver expatiate on any number of other anatomical features, and not necessarily a particularly female part, but he chooses instead to have the most disgusting object Gulliver sees be a breast in the act of feeding an infant, an action with traditional religious meaning: "In both Jewish and Christian traditions, breasts were honored as milk-producing vessels necessary for the survival of the Hebrew people and, later, the followers of Jesus. The example of the baby Jesus suckling at his mother's breast becomes a metaphor for the spiritual nurturance of all Christian souls."[55] The idea of the breast as an agent of nurturance, whether physical or metaphorical, or in any way a positive organ, is absent from this treatment of it and from almost all references elsewhere in Swift's writing. Aside from other reasons for this attitude, Swift may have been repelled by the only breastfeeding he is likely to have seen, that of homeless beggar-women on the streets of Dublin.

Directions to Servants is especially sinister in positing both childbearing and wet-nursing as purely commercial activities in which the well-being of the infant is a matter of indifference. Thus, the direction to the wet nurse is to commodify maternity by contriving "to be with Child, as soon as you can, while you are giving Suck, that you may be ready for another Service, when the Child dies, or is weaned" (*PW* 13:64). No mention is made of the nurse's own child after its conception; that child has served its purpose by facilitating the money-making activity of wet-nursing. The client child must be replaced because it will either die or be weaned: whichever fate is immaterial to the woman who must put aside her own maternity to nurture another woman's child. Positioning death and weaning as equal outcomes is thus another perversion of maternity, one that intrudes a cynical lack of feeling in an area where the scenario of survival would be assumed to be preferable.

The advice to wet nurses is different in kind from the satire aimed at other servants, which targets uncleanliness, laziness, venality, and petty crime. It posits women—themselves mothers—who are indifferent to the deaths of children out of, Swift implies, the same kind of predisposition to evil that elsewhere in his writing makes women worse than men.[56]

In his will, Swift does refer to breastfeeding in the conventional positive way as part of his panegyric description of Queen Anne:

> *Item*: I leave to *Edward* now Earl of *Oxford*, my seal of *Julius Caesar*, as also another Seal, supposed to be a young *Hercules*, both very choice Antiques, and set in Gold: Both which I chuse to bestow to the said Earl, because they belonged to her late Most Excellent Majesty Queen *Anne*, of ever Glorious, Immortal, and truely Pious Memory, the real Nursing Mother of all her Kingdoms. (*PW* 13:154)

The thrust of the entire item description is to magnify the gift of the two seals to a valued friend, and their royal provenance would certainly contribute to this purpose. Still, the final phrase seems an odd choice for Swift, a nostalgic recuperation of the archbishop of York's coronation sermon, which used the image to emphasize Anne's spiritual nurturance of her people.[57] No doubt by 1740, when Swift wrote these words, this positive image overshadowed the late Queen's unhappy personal history of dysfunctional maternity, which had the unfortunate result, from Swift's point of view, of bringing the Hanoverian dynasty to the English throne and thus ushering in the long reign of the detested Whigs. For Swift, Anne is preeminently the last good ruler of England, whose failure at childbearing is forgotten.

The separation between personal and metaphoric levels of maternity in the will's reference to Queen Anne takes a more commonplace form in Swift's life, where he seeks and enjoys maternal function divorced from actual maternity. Just as Gulliver appreciated the maternal attentions of a little girl, Glumdalclitch, Swift was pleased with the maternal ministrations of a number of women, mothers and non-mothers alike. The elderly Lady Orkney, for example, he described as "perfectly kind, like a mother" (*JS* 570). In keeping with her maternal role toward Swift, she provided him with various practical items, including medicine for his numerous ailments. Other women, like Mrs. Vanhomrigh and Stella, nurtured Swift without being thought of as maternal figures, although Mrs. Vanhomrigh had four children of her own. Swift could be like a needy child, once arriving at the Vanhomrigh house long after the dinner hour and demanding that the kitchen find him some food (*JS* 395).

For actual maternity, however, Swift often revealed an antipathy or at best a lack of sympathy. In a memorable passage in the *Journal to Stella*, he tells Stella about a visit paid to an unidentified Lady (Harold Williams thinks this might be Lady Pembroke, age forty-three at the time): "I was to see Lady ——, who is just up after lying-in; and the ugliest sight I have seen, pale, dead, old, and yellow, for want of her paint. She has turned my stomach" (*JS* 443 & n). Swift evidently hated an appearance without cosmetic artifice when the woman needed some agent of improvement, although he also hated the false appearance makeup created. *A Beautiful Young Nymph Going to Bed* ends climactically with the reassembled prostitute a sight to induce a strong reaction:

> Corinna in the morning dizened,
> Who sees, will spew; who smells, be poisoned. (*CP* 455)

Corinna is cosmetically enhanced, yet repulsive in her deception: that, and her life of vice, deserve condemnation. Lady Pembroke seems equally repulsive in Swift's description although she has transgressed only by giving birth.

Granted that eighteenth-century parents might well be overburdened with too many offspring, and a high rate of infant mortality made the loss of children common, Swift's insensitivity about the death of a child is striking: "The evidence of memoirs and autobiographies, of letters and memorabilia like child portraits, suggests that children were wanted, valued and cherished according to the standards of the day and the possibilities open to individual families."[58] Of a woman who had just experienced the loss of a child, Swift remarks, "I pity poor Mrs. Manley; but I think the child is happy to die, considering how little provision it would have had" (*JS* 425). The remark is similar in substance to his feeling about his own existence as a child, how cramped and marred it had been because of reduced circumstances. It also resonates with his many harsh observations about people who produce children they cannot support.[59]

Swift was particularly exasperated with his good friend Abigail Masham because of her great concern over her two-year-old son's illness. In his *Enquiry into the Behavior of the Queen's Last Ministry*, Swift described Mrs. Masham as "a Person of a plain sound Understanding, of great Truth and Sincerity, without the least Mixture of Falsehood or Disguise; of an honest Boldness and Courage superior to her Sex; firm and disinterested in her Friendship" (*PW* 8:153). She was a woman Swift liked and admired, but he could not understand or approve of her allowing her concern for her sick child to take precedence over her court duties: "She is full of grief," he wrote, "and I pity and am angry with her" (*JS* 645). Two weeks later, the boy was still gravely ill and Swift assumed he would die. Having made this judgment, he expected Mrs. Masham also to see the situation in this light, to remember her important responsibilities to the ministry at this time and abandon the care of her son in order to return to the Queen. He commented again, "She is so excessively fond, it makes me mad; she should never leave the Qu, but leave everything to stick to what is so much the Interest of the Publick as well as her own. This I tell her, but talk to the Winds" (*JS* 658). In his edition of the *Journal to Stella*, Sir Walter Scott cannot forebear a note here, saying that "in this advice the Doctor's political zeal seems to have borne down his natural feelings."[60]

But Swift, as his comment to Pope proclaimed, did not have "natural feelings" in this area. Once a child seemed unlikely to survive, he felt that the mother should surmount her anguish, particularly a mother like Mrs. Masham with a significant public role. Thackeray sees the episode as attributable to a Swiftian dislike of children, but Scott was probably closer to the truth: Swift was deeply invested in the success of the Harley ministry and saw Masham as a crucial intermediary between Harley and the Queen.[61]

Swift did seem to feel that a mother's attachment should be, Houyhnhnm-like, confined to rational bounds, an attitude he himself had no difficulty maintaining or attributing to others. He inquired of Stella, "Is my Aunt alive yet; and do you ever see her. I suppose she has forgot the Loss of her son" (*JS* 558). The son had been killed five years before in the battle of Almanza.

In a similar vein Swift wrote a letter of condolence to Mrs. Moore, applying his idea of the reasonable approach by encouraging her to "reflect rather upon what is left, than what is lost." Because she continued to have children of both sexes, "one of them of an Age to be Useful to his Family, and the two others as promising as can be expected from their Age," he told her that "according to the general Dispensations of God Almighty, you have small Reason to repine upon that Article of Life" (W 3:145). This statement recalls the regulation of progeny in Houyhnhnmland, where an annual assembly presides over a swapping procedure that gives every family one male and one female offspring. Should one of these be lost, and the mother past the age of reproduction, another family is appointed to produce a replacement.

Mrs. Moore, having been able to afford the loss of a child according to Swift's calculus, must now avoid caring too much for her remaining children: "which is a Weakness God seldom leaves long unpunished: Common Observation shewing us, that such favourite Children are either spoiled by their Parents Indulgence, or soon taken out of the World; which last is, generally speaking, the lighter Punishment of the two" (W 3:145). This is a conventional religious view, echoing both Biblical passages and writers on maternal duty. Richard Allestree, for example, cautions mothers in a similar fashion:

> The doting affection of the Mother, is frequently punish'd with the untimely death of her Children; or if not with that, 'tis many times with a severer scourge. They live ... *to grieve her eies, and to consume her heart*, [1 Sam. 2:33] to be ruinous to themselves, and afflictions to their friends, and to force their unhappy mothers to that sad exclamation, Luke 23:29. *Blessed are the wombs which bare not.*[62]

In comparing the two passages, identical in content, the difference in occasion seems crucial. Alstree's admonitions are part of an advice manual written to describe theoretical situations for an audience of unknown readers rather than part of a condolence letter directed by a friend to a particular bereaved mother.

The danger of excessive leniency toward children was a recurrent Swiftian theme, an almost automatic reaction to thoughts about his friends' children. In a letter to Mrs. Greenfield, a conventional utterance wishing the family well is followed by an ambiguous subjunctive: "I hope Mr Greenvil [*sic*] and you are in health, as well as your Girl, if you have not spoyled her with Fondness" (W 3:58). Does this final clause mean that Swift would wish the daughter well only if she was being brought up without overindulgence, or is this an allusion to that religious view that such children were better off dead? In context, rather than carrying such negative weight, it seems like a light reminder of proper childrearing.

Given his view of parental fondness, the description of bringing up Lilliputian children probably represents Swift's view of what would be desirable—if impossible—in his own society. In Lilliput, children are raised in nurseries: "Their Parents are suffered to see them only twice a Year. . . but a Professor, who always standeth by on those Occasions, will not suffer them to whisper, or use any fondling Expressions, or bring any Presents of Toys, Sweet-meats, and the like" (*PW* 11:61). A more direct danger brought on by parental doting threatens Gulliver when a Brobdingnagian mother, "out of pure Indulgence," dangles him in front of her infant. The child predictably seizes the offered toy and puts Gulliver's head in its mouth.

In the fourth voyage, Gulliver commends the Houyhnhnms for having "no Fondness for their Colts or Foles" and for showing "the same Affection" to a neighbor's issue as to their own (*PW* 11:268). But Swift must have realized at least in part how inadequate the rational tenor of his letter to Mrs. Moore was to the purpose of consoling a creature who was only *rationis capax* rather than, like a Houyhnhnm, ideally rational. And so his condolence letter concludes with an apology: "I fear my present ill Disposition both of Health and Mind has made me but a sorry Comforter" (W 3:146). Yet, while Swift realizes in a general way that his effort has fallen short, he fails to see that suggesting a child would be better off dead than overindulged is shockingly inappropriate to the occasion and an extreme view under any circumstances. What he finds so attractive, the order represented by the orthodox religious view—indeed, its rationality and justice—simply overcomes his understanding that this is not the way to console a parent for the loss of a child.

Swift's idea of parental consolation is apt to seem inappropriate, since it proposes rationality in the teeth of strong emotion, an effect that verges on the repugnant when his preoccupation with his own condition preempts the effort to assuage a bereaved parent. When Mrs. Whiteway's eldest son, Theophilus Harrison, was dying, Swift wrote to his mother about the young man he had known and valued. His letter begins conventionally, "I pity you and your family, and I heartily pray for both," but it immediately continues, "I pity myself, and my prayers are not wanting: but I pity not him. I count already that you and I and the world must lose him" (*C* 4:460). That settled, in Swift's characteristically forthright and economical way, he proceeds to appropriate Theophilus's approaching death as one of many "disappointments" in his own life: "I was born to a million of disappointments: I had set my heart very much upon that young man" (*C* 4:460). Some conventional sentiments follow: he was too good for this corrupt world; his mother should "take courage from Christianity." Then Swift makes an infelicitous comparison: "I shall also lose a sort of a son as well as you: only our cases are different; for you have more" (*C* 4:461). This suggests that Swift is actually more bereaved than the dying young man's mother, but once again he concludes an excursus into his own condition with a standard injunction: "It is your duty to preserve yourself for them" (*C* 4:461).

A condolence letter may join the writer's own sense of grief and loss to that of the addressee, but this is not precisely the effect of what Swift writes to Mrs. Whiteway. Rather, his loss seems to eclipse hers and unintentionally to become more important. He claims Theophilus as "a sort of son," but whereas Mrs. Whiteway has two more sons (and a daughter), Swift is more bereft in having lost his only progeny. Ironically, what is touching in his before-the-fact condolence letter is a violation of the genre: because Swift was so close to Mrs. Whiteway, he could count on her concern for his own health—even as her eldest son lay on his deathbed. And so he tells her that he is getting over a recent illness, adding, because he is in his late sixties, and the subject of the letter is only twenty-three, "to my shame be it spoken" (*C* 4:461). When Theophilus died a few days later, Swift wrote to his cousin to once again join his grief to hers, and to offer one of his austere consolations: "Some degree of wisdom is required in the greatest calamity, because God requires it; because he knows what is best for us; because he never intended any thing like perfect happiness in the present life; and, because it is our duty, as well as interest, to submit" (*C* 4:463). This is followed by a proposal whose rejection Swift says he will take "very unkindly": Mrs. Whiteway should exchange her house with its sad associations for the deanery, where "all care shall be taken of you . . . and I will be your companion" (*C* 4:464). Having offered himself as a substitute for the dead son, Swift acknowledges that such a move would deprive her of more constant association with the living daughter, who can "sometimes step to see you" (*C* 4:464). No doubt Swift's offer expressed genuine concern for the well-being of his favorite cousin, but it was also an attempt to get her attentions more exclusively for himself. He would remedy his own loss of Theophilus Harrison by corraling Mrs. Whiteway, albeit at the expense of her maternal relationship with her daughter.

Stella evidently shared Swift's insensitivity on the subject of parental bereavement, or perhaps simply reflected it. Swift wrote to her about his cousin "Billy" Swift that he "is dead of his mother's former folly & fondness, and yet now I believe as you say, that her grief will soon wear off" (*JS* 367). Stella had apparently met Billy's mother in Ireland and reported her assessment of the mother's grief to Swift. She was probably already familiar with Swift's attitude that any public display of mourning was hypocritical (*JS* 602).

In writing to Lord Oxford on the death of Oxford's favorite daughter, Elizabeth, who had died in childbirth at the age of twenty-seven, Swift produced the same argument that he proffered to Mrs. Moore; namely, that it is necessary to be comforted by what remains. He did not presume to instruct Oxford on not spoiling his surviving children—Oxford's other offspring were adults, and Oxford was his social superior—but he did conclude the letter with an apology for its inadequacy: "I know not, my Lord, why I write this to you. . . . I am sure, it is not from any compliance with form; it is not from thinking that I can give your Lordship any ease. I think it was an impulse upon me that I should say something" (W 1:550). This declaration reveals yet again Swift's awareness that his approach to condolence is ineffective. He is candid in confessing that he needed to "say something": a loss of such magnitude in someone he knew so well could not go unacknowledged, but Swift realized that he was ill equipped to say something suitable to the occasion. Protestations of inadequacy are conventional in the genre of condolence, but Swift's remarks seem heartfelt.

Comparing John Arbuthnot's comments on Oxford's loss to those of Swift throws into greater relief Swift's inclination to turn to rationality where another person would have an emotional response.[63] Arbuthnot writes to Swift: "I pity his case with all my heart . . . I have a true sense of his present condition for which I know philosophy, and religion are both too weak. . . . I have lost six children. If I am not deceivd I beleive I could have been content to have ransomd the lives of every one of them, ev'n at the hard terms of begging their bread" (W 1:554). Arbuthnot's statement serves as eloquent rebuttal to those present day critics who imagine that the high rate of infant mortality precluded deep parental affection.

Swift, however, would never agree that religion was too weak to address grief. On the contrary, his condolence letter to Oxford labors to produce a religious explanation, complimenting him on a string of achievements and then adducing the conclusion that "God Almighty, who would not disappoint your endeavours for the publick, thought fit to punish you with a domestic loss, where he knew your heart was most exposed." Oxford's daughter, a young mother whom Swift had known and liked, becomes a conventional abstraction, "that excellent creature he has taken from you" (W 1:550). Arbuthnot, as both physician and father, seems more understanding of human sorrow when he advises Swift that he can help his friend more "by turning his thoughts to other objects than by the most rational refflections" (W 1:554). Further, Arbuthnot counsels, Oxford should resume the reins of business as soon as possible, "for I know by Experience, that the best cure is by diverting the thoughts" (W 1:555). Although he did not write to Oxford directly, Arbuthnot's letter to Swift seems superior as a response to Oxford's loss: it genuinely commiserates and then provides a practical remedy.

Swift must have had little fondness for children, which made it possible for him to extol an entirely rational approach to them, as he saw it, one that could regard their deaths with equanimity and even, at times, with a certain satisfaction. His inability to comprehend parental feelings is further exhibited in a tasteless joke about Mrs. Walls's confinement that he returns to a number of times in the *Journal to Stella* as if it is too good to drop. As a prelude, before the child's birth, he expresses exasperation: "I hope she'll have no more. There will be no quiet nor cards for this child. I hope it will die the day after the christening" (*JS* 129). It may be difficult to recover the tone of this remark, made in the privacy of a letter to his closest friend, but at the least it suggests that Swift's response to the expected birth is irritation at the pleasures of his friends inevitably curtailed by the child's arrival.[64] Clearly, he would have preferred for the Wallses not to disrupt the social activities that Stella and Dingley enjoyed (Swift himself was in London, hence unaffected by the baby's arrival). If the baby died, in a world where babies and adults in their prime so often died, Swift would not have been sorry.

Once Stella wrote that Mrs. Walls had given birth to a boy, Swift began to pretend that the child was a girl who had died. He responded to Stella's news, "And so Mrs. Walls is brought to-bed of a girl, who died two days after it was christened;

and betwixt you and me, she is not very sorry: she loves her ease and diversions too well to be troubled with children" (*JS* 156). A month later he exclaims, "What, is not Mrs. Walls's business over yet? I had hopes she was up and well, and the child dead before this time" (*JS* 186). Two weeks later, he remarks that Mrs. Walls is now "pretty well again; I am sorry it is a girl," adding that the father is also sorry: "See how simply he lookt when they told him" (*JS* 196–97). A few days after this comment he pretends to write *as* Stella, making an excuse for not writing to him because of being busy with Mrs. Walls: "We were afraid the poor woman would have died. . . . The child died the next day after it was born, and I believe, between friends, she is not very sorry for it" (*JS* 202–3)—thus putting his own sentiments in Stella's mouth. This is followed by a correction, as if by the real Stella saying, "Indeed, Pdfr, you are plaguy silly tonight, and han't guest one word right; for she and the child are both well, and it is a fine girl, likely to live" (*JS* 203).

There is a further joke in Swift-as-Stella making fun of Swift's inaccuracies: the "correction" contains the major mistake of the child's sex. Would Swift have made such a joke in reverse, that is, if a girl had been born, would she then be described as a boy who died? I think not: that would have been seen as too unhappy an event to joke about, whereas the loss of a girl is not as deeply felt, is even—according to Swift—not minded much by the mother.

Swift makes a similar joking aspersion when Laetitia Pilkington asks him to be the godfather of her expected child: "So! said he, more Demands upon me! Well, if it be a Boy, I don't much care if I do; but if it be a little Bitch I'll never answer for her" (P 310). As Pilkington goes on to recount, "The Hour now came, when the Dean's Promise was to be claim'd; as I brought forth a Son, I wrote to him, but he was in the Country, and in five Days the Boy died: The Dean did not return till I was a Fortnight brought to Bed." When he arrived at Pilkington's bedside, he inquired of his godson and was told that the child was in heaven: "The Lord be praised, said he, I thought there was some good News in the way, your Husband look'd so brisk: Pox take me, but I was in Hopes you were dead yourself; but 'tis pretty well as it is, I have sav'd by it, and I should have got nothing by you" (P 315).

That Swift could greet a parent's announcement of a child's recent death with a joke must separate him from most people of his time—from most people of any time, one might say. Yet this kind of jesting was a mark of his favor, and was so taken by Pilkington, although it would seem to violate his own principle that "some Things are too serious, solemn, or sacred to be turned into Ridicule" (*PW* 12:33). About an hour after Swift's departure, Pilkington received from him a piece of "Plumb-cake, which I did intend should be spent at your Christening" (P 315). Actually, she discovers, the cake is gingerbread, and four guineas wrapped in white paper are labeled "plumbs"—an extension of his joking comment on the situation as well as an example of his complex attitude toward money. Having said that he had saved by the child's death, Swift was determined *not* to have saved by it, in keeping with his practice of donating to charity money allocated for ordinary expenses that he had not had to spend.[65] Pilkington readily entered into the Dean's spirit and sent him back a piece of real plum cake with a witty note.

Evidently, Mrs. Walls continued to produce children steadily, for Swift remarks of the couple little more than a year after his drawn-out joke that "the Cares of the Husband encrease with the fruitfullness of the Wife" (*JS* 541). About another addition to the Wallses' household Swift wrote a congratulatory message to Archdeacon Walls himself: "I received your Notification relating to one Dorothy [Mrs. Walls] and her new Productions, which like other second Parts are seldom so good as the first.[66] I shall be in Town I hope by the time appointed, and contribute as far towards making your new Inhabitant a Christian as one of that Sex can be" (W 1:526). Even to a social superior, Edward Harley, Swift cannot refrain from a light allusion to the preference for sons:

> I was told . . . that the best Lady in the World had lately brought one of her own Sex into it, for which I do most heartily congratulate with Your Lordship and her. And I hope to live long enough to send you half a dozen Letters of Congratulation upon the same Account; onely My Lady must take care now and then to vary the Sex. (W 2:113)

This is typical of the teasing style of compliment Swift used with good friends, and the jocular allusion to female inferiority is no more than a statement of the prevalent opinion of his time. As he wrote in a letter to the Reverend William Tisdall, "Women's prayers are things perfectly by rote, as they put on one stocking after another, and no more" (W 1:150). Such an attitude might not be helpful in making the new inhabitant of the Wallses' household a good Christian, however. A later reference Swift makes to his goddaughter expresses a similar view and ties in with his fear of spoiling children: "I hope to breed her up to be good for Something, if her Mother will let me" (W 1:530). Conventionally, the mother is a model for the daughter, but Swift always chooses men as models for the women he seeks to instruct.

Before the birth, Swift had written to Stella that he had no desire to be a godfather; yet in his subsequent letters to Walls he rarely fails to add some phrase referring to the child: "God bless my godchild" or "I hope my godchild is well." Swift was also fond of Mrs. Walls, often remembering her in his letters to her husband under the familiar name of "Gossip Doll," and on one occasion he commissioned Charles Jervas to paint a portrait of the Wallses' son as a surprise gift for Mrs. Walls (W 2:195n).

Because Swift liked Walls, he expressed himself moderately when he remarked to Stella on his burden of offspring. He also referred to Robert Cope's brood of ten without disparagement, since Cope was another close friend and favorite. But in the case of a man he regarded as "a pest," the Reverend Anthony Raymond, prolific reproduction receives a more severe judgment: "Will Mrs Raymd never have done lying in. He intends to leave Beggars enough" (*JS* 564). Swift finds another instance of ill-considered reproduction in the behavior of the regicide Sir Henry Vane, noting in the margins of Burnet's *History of His Own Times* that Vane's wife "*conceived* of him the night before his execution" (*PW* 5:270). Swift disliked both Burnet and Vane, but he was probably provoked by Burnet's portrait of Vane as a dignified man accepting his fate with composure: such a man would have spent his last night praying.

To avoid such egregious reproduction, Swift makes his rational species, the Houyhnhnms, limit their families to two foals: "This Caution is necessary to prevent the Country from being overburthened with Numbers" (*PW* 11:268). Swift's concern about his own country being "overburthened with Numbers" can be amply documented.[67]

The rational position of the Houyhnhnms seems to overlay an emotional response in Swift himself. When he advises his second cousin, Honoria Swanton, about her wayward daughter, he envisions increasingly bleak scenarios for the young woman. In the first, children are only theoretical: Mrs. Swanton is counseled not to give the daughter "or her children (if she shall have any) a morsel of bread" (W 3:670). In the next, "she must not expect to move your compassion some years hence with the cryes of half a dozen children at your door for want of bread" (W 3:670). Climactically, "her children will have no more title to your charity, than the bratts and bastards of a common beggar" (W 3:670). For Swift, this particular case involves a conjunction of circumstances that he felt strongly about: a woman connecting with a social inferior, which would inevitably lead to the production of beggarly children.

Given his stern attitude toward the children of friends, it is hardly surprising that the children of poverty, who have no chance to be useful to their families, and who are produced in an abundance that strains the resources of the polity, would seem to Swift to be an unnecessary burden on everyone. The most prominent exemplars of the theme of unwelcome reproduction are the wretchedly poor mothers of Ireland in *A Modest Proposal*, whose children, as the subtitle informs us, are "a Burden to their Parents or Country" (*PW* 12:109).[68] The *Proposal's* opening paragraph immediately conflates "*Beggars* of the Female Sex" with mothers and defines their children as constituting in adulthood a negative social group: thieves, traitors, or—at best—emigrants. Swift's hatred of the disorder that this surplus population engenders in the body politic left him open to what Flynn calls "fantasies of annihilation" which "occur with bleak regularity in his work."[69]

A Modest Proposal is Swift's most grandiose fantasy for converting the societal debit of unabsorbable population increase into an asset. These children, "instead of being a Charge upon their *Parents*, or the *Parish*, or *wanting Food and Raiment* for the rest of their Lives . . . shall, on the contrary, contribute to the Feeding, and partly to the Cloathing, of many Thousands" (*PW* 12:110). Motherhood could hardly be treated more reductively than in Swift's conversion of mothers into "Breeders," capable of annually supplying 120,000 infants for consumption through a promiscuous coupling modeled on the breeding of domestic animals. As Marilyn Francus observes, "Women become mothers biologically, but they cannot be maternal, for the material conditions that make nurturance possible are largely beyond their control."[70] Swift's treatment of the unthinkable and unspeakable in relentless detail, as if working out every aspect of the procedure is all that is needed to ensure its acceptability, makes the *Proposal* a tour de force.[71]

In *Directions to Servants*, when Swift casually treats wet-nursing as a commercial enterprise in which the infant's weaning or death is all one, simply the occasion for finding a new client, there is no explicit mention of economic necessity as the driving force behind this industry. In *A Modest Proposal*, grim economic conditions are the rationale embraced by the Proposer, who in his penultimate paragraph challenges those in authority to offer a better solution to the problem: "I am not so violently bent upon my own Opinion, as to reject any Offer proposed by wise Men, which shall be found equally innocent, cheap, easy, and effectual" (*PW* 12:117). All of these seemingly harmless adjectives have a double valence, reverberating against the barbarity of the proposal as well as against the lack of any corresponding plan that could remedy the problem.

Swift often commented with repugnance on untrammeled reproduction, especially among the poor. In Ireland, he wrote in his *Proposal for Giving Badges to the Beggars*, "the Blessing of Increase and Multiply is . . . converted into a Curse" (*PW* 13:135). Not only was fruitfulness a religious injunction, the idea that people were the riches of a nation was a basic tenet of political economy at the time.[72] As John Locke wrote, "Numbers of men are to be preferred to largeness of dominions."[73] Swift intends to demonstrate that Ireland is the unfortunate exception to this rule: his Proposer explicitly confronts the idea that his proposal will lessen the population and asserts that his remedy is tailored to "*this one individual Kingdom of* IRELAND, *and for no other that ever was, is, or I think ever can be upon Earth*" (*PW* 13:116). A similar extreme statement occurs in Swift's late *Proposal for Giving Badges to the Beggars*, where he asserts that Ireland "is the only Christian Country where People contrary to the old Maxim, are the Poverty and not the Riches of the Nation; so, the Blessing of Increase and Multiply is by us converted into a Curse" (*PW* 13:135).[74]

Marriage should be discouraged, his Proposer continues, because it leads to the birth of children whose parents cannot provide for them and consequently force the problem upon the community. The author of *A Letter to a Member of Parliament* (1723) similarly argues that the beggar "eats your Meal, and drinks your Milk, and pays you nothing for it. Instead he fills you with more children."[75] In his own household, as Swift wrote to Lord Bathurst, his elderly housekeeper upheld a policy based on the same premise: "She will not suffer a femal in the house who is younger than her self, under pretence that if it were otherwise, my men and the maids together would multiply my family too much" (W 3:405).

Swift's view of irresponsible reproduction was shared by the Lilliputians, who "think nothing can be more unjust, than that People, in Subservience to their own Appetites, should bring Children into the World, and leave the Burthen of supporting them on the Publick" (*PW* 11:62–63).[76] Writing to Pope about the death of the young Lord Oxford's newborn son, Swift commented that it was "Hard that Parsons and Beggars should be overrun with Bratts while so great and good a Family wants an Heir to continue it" (W 2:622). At this other end of the social scale, the tragedy of unsuccessful maternity in the person of Queen Anne, whose seventeen pregnancies produced no child to survive her, was the most prominent example of a widespread phenomenon in Swift's time; by the age of thirty-five Anne had lost all of her children.[77] The death in childbirth of one of Swift's favorites, Lady Ashburnham, provoked a bitter outburst to Stella: "I hate Life, when I think it exposed to such Accidents and to see so many thousand wretches burthening the Earth while such as her dye" (*JS* 595). When Swift thought of reproduction in all of its phases, the associations were overwhelmingly negative.

If Swift paid little direct attention to human maternity, his description of maternity among the Houyhnhnms may be taken as a model for what he would have liked to see in his own species. To avoid the degeneracy of the race that he lamented in his own family and among both the Irish poor and the English aristocracy, Swift has the Houyhnhnms marry to achieve a perfect combination of strength and beauty in their progeny, in contrast to Gulliver's description of aristocratic offspring in his own society as diseased.

In Houyhnhnmland, as in Lilliput, the young of both sexes are educated equally. The English practice, Gulliver's Houyhnhnm master observes, means that "one half of our natives were good for nothing but bringing children into the world: and to trust the care of their children to such useless animals, he said, was yet a greater instance of brutality" (*PW* 11:269). Just as a lack of education in women poisoned marriage in Swift's opinion, depriving husbands of companions with whom they might enjoy rational discourse, so this same lack poisons maternity. Swift offers an example of the resulting educational practice in one of his *Intelligencer* essays, when he faults an heir's mother for her policy of overprotection: "*Master* must not walk till he is hot, nor be suffered to play with other Boys, nor be wet in his Feet, nor daub his Cloaths. . . . She further insists, that the Child be not kept too long poring on his Book, because he is subject to sore Eyes, and of a weakly Constitution" (*PW* 12:50). The uneducated woman, whether poor or rich, cannot be a good mother. She is merely a breeder of children that she is unfit to educate.

What is most arresting in Swift's attitude toward maternity is the radical rejection of his own birth implied by his practice of reading from chapter 3 of the book of Job on his birthday: "Let the day perish wherein I was born, and the night *in which* it was said, There is a man child conceived" (3.3 *King James Bible*). Such a ritual utterance might be taken in a clergyman as a worthy example of Christian humility, but the despair and negation of the passage chosen seem to go well beyond a religious perspective.

While rationality led Swift to unsympathetic positions in many areas of human weakness, vice, or folly, his criticism of maternity transcends negative manifestations to embrace the condition in its entirety. This can be distinguished from his attitude toward marriage, which recognized the possibility—if not the probability—of acceptable union, although the ideal of marriage Swift shapes is without sex or issue. The paring down of life to a rational kernel, marriage without the complications of passion and offspring, is part of Swift's project to steel himself against loss and grief, although he realized that he could not completely shield himself from these emotions. By the same token, Swift creates a society of rational horses to illustrate what perfect rationality would be and then returns Gulliver to England to demonstrate the impossibility of such a society among human beings.

His only recourse is a God who "did never intend Life for a Blessing" (*JS* 595) and who "hath taken care . . . to prevent any progress towards real happyness here, which would make life more desirable & death too dreadfull" (W 3:335).

This self-protective impulse caused Swift to retreat from love to friendship and to regard propagation with a sweeping displeasure that embraced both sexuality and maternity, beginning with the inauspicious union of his own parents and continuing with his humiliating experience of sexual desire for Jane Waring. In Swift's view, these prime sites of irrationality were impediments to the rational life that seemed to him both so desirable and so unattainable.

6

*T*he Question of Misogyny

The first instance of misogyny given in the *OED* is from a dictionary called *Glossographia*, published in 1656. Here it is defined as "the hatred or contempt of women," a succinct and reasonable definition, only we need to ask what constitutes hatred or contempt of women. The issue of misogyny can be more fruitfully framed in terms of Swift's cultural and personal heritage to determine where, in a writer whose dates are 1667–1745, we can legitimately draw the line between the principle of female inferiority that virtually everyone of his era accepted and the hatred of women that merits the label of misogyny.

If we were to impose our own standards retroactively, everything believed about women in Swift's time was misogynistic, beginning with what John Essex describes as "a Fundamental Law between Man and Wife, that is very near as ancient as the World it self."[1] He was referring to the duty of a wife to obey her husband, based on Paul's plain speaking in Ephesians: "For the husband is the head of the wife" (5:23, *King James Bible*). The system in effect was patriarchal, based on an authoritarian male rule that permeated all gender relations: "a wife had to obey her husband, a daughter her father, a maidservant her master."[2] All women were allotted a narrowly circumscribed role under the dominion of males, who enjoyed great latitude, social and legal, over the persons and property of their subordinate women.[3] Patriarchy as formulated in the seventeenth century by Sir Robert Filmer or John Locke might change in form; nevertheless, as Michael McKeon observes, "male domination and the female subordination of women are constants."[4]

When Milton asks, in the *Doctrine and Discipline of Divorce*, "Who can be ignorant that woman was created for man, and not man for woman?" (2.15), his rhetorical question reminds us that no one at the time would have argued otherwise. The model for behavior in the tradition of Western culture that Swift inherited, compounded of classical antiquity and Christianity, was male. Women are linked with nature and the body, while men monopolize the higher realm of mind and spirit.[5] Sir Thomas Overbury's definition of the perfect wife excludes "much learning and pregnant wit," for "Books are a part of man's prerogative."[6]

However, like all abstract principles, the inferiority of women could be translated into policy with a variety of attitudes and differing degrees of severity. A man might value women and rule benevolently in accord with a marriage sermon preached by the popular cleric Thomas Gataker that advises that "a worthy Woman ... is well worth the seeking. She is a greater blessing than either House or Inheritance."[7] Alexander Niccholes, a clergyman whose treatise concerns choosing the right wife, embroiders the literal words of Eve's creation in a strongly positive manner: "*Adam* lost a *Rib*; but, now being awake ... he hath his Rib again, with Interest and Increase, branched into many *Veins*, and *Ribs*, and *Bones*, and Arteries of wonderful Use, and admirable." Niccholes goes on to say that while Adam was "made of the Slime of the Earth, she was of that better Substance."[8] Practicality might also enter in, as another minister, William Whately, counsels his readers in *Bride-Bush*: "More obedience, and better shall any husband procure to himselfe by this pleasingnes of behaviour, than by all the rigor in the world."[9]

This is the opposite construction from that of early church fathers like Tertullian, who see all women as negative replications of Eve. Addressing women, he writes, "*You* are the Devil's gateway. *You* are the unsealer of that forbidden tree. *You* are the first deserter of the divine Law. *You* are she who persuaded him whom the Devil was not valiant enough to attack."[10] This view continued to be common in the seventeenth century. In the words of John Brinsley, a minister in the Church of England, "As the first Woman was deceived at the first, so are many of that Sex deceived at this very day."[11]

Other indictments are based on the mundanity of relations between the sexes. When the self-proclaimed misogynist Diogenes was asked how to select a wife, he replied with a definition well known in Swift's time: that you should choose one without a head, without a body, and without limbs, "so her Hands shall not offend in Striking, nor her Tongue in Railing, nor her Body in Lusting."[12] Simonides, asked a similar question, defined a wife as "the Shipwreck of Man, the Tempest of a House, the Disturber of Rest, the Prison of Life, a daily Punishment, a sumptuous Conflict, a Beast in Company, a necessary Evil."[13] This sounds more like popular satire, the exaggerations of folk humor that in another time produced such verbal tags as "ball and chain" and "battle axe."

Unlike many of his contemporaries writing about women, Thomas Heywoode unites positive and negative polarities in his nine-volume work *Gynaikeion*, which uses examples from myth and history to illuminate the character of women:

> As there is nothing more divelish and deadly than a malitious and ill disposed woman,
> so there is on the contrarie, nothing more wholesome and comfortable to man than

one provident, gentle, and well addicted; for as she that is good and honest, will upon just necessitie lay downe her life for her husbands health and safetie, so the other will as willingly prostitute hers for his distruction and ruin.

He sums up by pronouncing womankind to be either a "perpetuall refuge" or a "continuall torment."[14] The self-sacrifice of a wife for her husband is extreme, but typical of the patriarchal attitude that Milton's question expressed. Taking for granted that women are intended to be a refuge for men rather than a torment, the question the tracts on women attempt to answer is how to choose the right kind.

Placing Swift in the spectrum of attitudes toward women has never been simple, because his writings are filtered through various speakers and so often employ irony. It can be difficult to formulate what is troubling about a particular representation of a woman—for example, the figure of Betty in a slight poem titled *To Betty, the Grisette*, where a woman's freckled skin is the object of the poet's minute and unfavorable scrutiny:

> Queen of wit and beauty, Betty,
> Never may the muse forget ye;
> How thy face charms every shepherd,
> Spotted over like a leopard!
> And, thy freckled neck displayed,
> Envy breeds in every maid.
> Like a fly blown Cake of Tallow,
> Or, on Parchment, Ink turn'd yellow:
> Or, a tawny speckled Pippin,
> Shrivel'd with a Winter's keeping. (*CP* 447)[15]

The gratuitous quality of attention to Betty's skin is comic, but it is also uncomfortable: it calls to mind the similarly gratuitous character of Gulliver's experience with the "monstrous" Brobdingnagian breast. When Gulliver is nauseated by the sight of the "spots, pimples and freckles" on this breast, he reflects upon the fair skins of "our English ladies, who appear so beautiful to us, only because they are of our own size, and their defects not to be seen but through a magnifying glass" (*PW* 11:75–76). In other words, any skin subjected to the microscope would reveal imperfections; women make more dramatic illustrations of this idea because they are culturally invested with beauty. The question to ponder is whether the magnifying glass of Swift's satiric disapproval of women is properly directed at such natural, innocuous, morally neutral, and non-sex-specific phenomena as freckles, or whether this close examination evinces a revulsion at the female body that has nothing to do with the conventional uses of satire. By directing this kind of pointed attention to Betty's skin, Swift may intend to protest the excesses of a romantic treatment of women, but he actually creates an obverse image that supports the convention from the opposite angle. Had he valorized a freckled complexion, that might have been a thrust akin to that of the Stella poems in hailing mental over physical qualities. Instead, he makes Betty's skin so repugnant that it affirms the romantic standard of beauty.

The poem *To Betty* is puzzling in its entirety. A *grisette*, or *grizette*, is a "French girl or young woman of the working class, especially one employed as a shop assistant or seamstress."[16] The poem fails to clarify why such a person should be the object of so much venom, or even so much poetic attention. Swift at times purposefully observes ordinary people at their quotidian tasks—his descriptions of the morning and of a sudden city shower come to mind—but in those cases the brief portrait is part of a larger context. An urban working-class girl in isolation is an unusual target for Swift's satire. Nothing in the poem suggests that Betty has set up for a beauty, unless the ironic apostrophe, "Queen of wit and beauty," is taken to mean that this is how she sees herself. The poem critiques nothing about her appearance except her freckles.

In contrast, the portion of the poem devoted to Betty's wit gives ample illustration of what the poet dislikes, that is, trite verbal behavior that completely lacks the creative power of genuine wit. However, the idea that a woman in Betty's lowly position, uneducated and poor, would be hailed as a wit strains credulity. The poem's concluding lines satirize those taken in by an imitation of wit that, among other defects, substitutes railing for raillery:

> This, among Hibernian asses,
> For sheer wit, and humour passes!
> Thus, indulgent Chloe bit,
> Swears you have a world of wit. (*CP* 448)

The poem moves, then, from mockery of Betty's physical appearance, which she cannot help, to ridicule of her pretensions as a wit, and beyond that, to what may be the greatest irritant to the poet, Betty's reputation as a wit: it galls him that others, even "Hibernian asses," are taken in and admire Betty's wit. The mixing of legitimate and illegitimate targets of satire is peculiarly Swiftian: must we condemn Betty's skin along with her spurious wit? In doing both, Swift projects a surplus of hostility that we might identify as misogynistic.

We can best examine Swift's ideas on women, and their relation to traditional ideas about women, as they are seriously and forthrightly proffered to Deborah Staunton Rochefort in Swift's *Letter to a Young Lady, on Her Marriage* (1723). Swift is writing to a new bride whom he probably did not know well as an individual but whose parents, the lawyer Thomas Staunton and his wife Bridget, he counted among his longtime friends. However, he had far closer friendships with members of the Rochefort family and regarded the husband, John Rochefort, as his "particular Favourite," as he says in the letter.[17] To his good friend Thomas Sheridan, Swift described John Rochefort as a very agreeable man "except that damn vice of avarice." Such a vice might be expected to loom larger for a wife than for a friend.

Although it was written to an actual person, the *Letter to a Young Lady* belongs to the popular genre of advice treatises directed either to women readers or to men about women.[18] What is most notable about Swift's letter, which contains many striking images of women, is a loss of emotional, as opposed to rhetorical, control that can hardly be intentional. When Swift thinks about a certain kind of woman, the very kind that modern feminists are likely to admire—the kind they are likely to *be*—he appears to forget the governing occasion and turns on the bride with inappropriate anger. Yet the seeds of this anger are present from the beginning, when he cautions her "strictly against the least Degree of Fondness to her Husband before any Witnesses whatsoever" because "this Proceeding is so extremely odious and disgustful to all who have either good Breeding or good Sense" (*PW* 9:86). This inflexible extremism, bristling with absolute injunctions and coupled with threats of severe consequences if it is deviated from by a jot, will characterize Swift's instructions throughout, creating a model that seems well beyond the attainment of an ordinary mortal. Everything in what follows will be exaggerated, as if Swift's real purpose is to write a satire on women rather than lay down some precepts for marital happiness. His advice to a woman whose only fault is to be a woman takes the form of a multitude of prescriptions mixed with general representations of women that reflect both fear and anger.

After the general warning not to despise or neglect his advice, since such disregard will entail the most catastrophic results, Swift elucidates one of the principal tenets of his counsel to those women he undertook to instruct, namely, to avoid the values and behavior of other women. That contemporary male advice books to women reek of condescension is only to be expected, but other than this, their tone varies in keeping with the polarities already mentioned. The books of advice written by the seventeenth-century clergymen Gataker and Niccholes reflect admiration of women. Swift's text, on the other hand, is full of contempt for them, at least for the sort who compose his and the new bride's social sphere. And these references show no sensitivity to the fact that the person addressed belongs to this gender.

Among his negative remarks is a comment worthy of Diogenes that Swift quotes approvingly, something "a pleasant Gentleman said concerning a silly Woman of Quality; that nothing could make her supportable but cutting off her Head; for his Ears were offended by her Tongue, and his Nose by her Hair and Teeth" (*PW* 11:87). *Pleasant* and *silly* characterize their respective gender examples, but there is a more sinister irony at work, the casual association of a bland positive, *pleasant*, with an image of extreme physical violence against a woman, not merely this one woman of quality, we should realize, but any woman whose speech or appearance offends a man. Apparently, one doesn't forfeit pleasantness or social status by advocating violence against women.

Six years after writing the *Letter to a Young Lady*, Swift repulsed Knightley Chetwode's appeal for advice on choosing a wife with uncharacteristic humility, saying that "those who have been married may form juster ideas of that estate than I can pretend to do" (W 3:281). This might simply have been an excuse to get shut of a tedious correspondent, for the *Letter to a Young Lady* exhibits no such restraint, although it does reveal ample evidence of Swift's lack of experience with the marital condition. That a wife might be uneasy at her husband's prolonged and unexplained absence, for example, is something he dismisses as affectation.

Should she greet her spouse's tardy arrival with any question, Swift writes that "a Shrew from *Billingsgate* would be a more easy and eligible Companion" (*PW* 11:87). The sincerity of those wives who demand frequent letters and a fixed date of return from an absent husband is also suspect. This cynicism, jarring in a letter addressed to a new bride, reveals how readily Swift transforms—or deforms—the occasion of advice-giving to a specific person into a satiric indictment of women in general.

Before long, given the nature of the pronoun *you* in English, the woman addressed will be included in this pejorative discourse. At first, it is simply "your Sex" that employs "more Thought, Memory, and Application to be Fools, than would serve to make them wise and useful." But by the next sentence it would be difficult for the bride not to feel implicated, as Swift goes on to say, "When I reflect on this, I cannot conceive you to be human Creatures" (*PW* 11:91). The copy of the *Letter* in the Huntington Library reveals that Swift's earlier version was "I can hardly conceive you to be human Creatures."[19] At some later point he crossed out "hardly" and substituted the absolute "not." Women undergo a satiric metamorphosis here, becoming "a Sort of Species hardly a Degree above a Monkey," but to whom a monkey—in Swift's description—is clearly superior (*PW* 11:91).[20] This is a metaphoric violence often found in Swift's satire, the stripping of human identity. Disengaged readers might take this comparison more lightly as Swift's indulgence in verbal cleverness, an elaborate comparison that values monkeys over women in such a witty and magisterial fashion. But the genre of advice and the surrounding context of the letter would surely have prevented the bride from reading it as a harmless jeu d'esprit.

Swift next turns to his pet project for women, improvement of the mind, a laudable, but also limited, ambition. In reminding the bride in so many words that the term "learned Women" is an oxymoron, Swift makes a comment that is unfortunately repeated as a serious observation in later advice books on women; namely, that however much a woman may study, she "never can arrive in Point of Learning to the Perfection of a School-Boy" (*PW* 11:92).[21] Arresting as this statement is (it may be the only time that anyone has associated the idea of perfection with schoolboys), it is no more than an allusion to the given inferiority of women, a status agreed upon by science and religion.[22]

In spite of having more knowledge of the human body, seventeenth-century science perpetuated the long-enshrined doctrines of Galen and Aristotle whose bedrock premise was that biologically and sexually women were simply inferior men. As Thomas Laqueur writes in his landmark book *Making Sex: Body and Gender from the Greeks to Freud*, Galen "demonstrated at length that women were essentially men in whom a lack of vital heat—of perfection—had resulted in the retention, inside, of structures that in the male are visible without."[23] Renaissance anatomists, in spite of dissecting the human body, did not overturn the one-sex model that denied women their own "ontologically distinct category."[24] If the female body is merely an inferior version of the male, as the seventeenth century continued to believe, then it is understandable that Swift would focus his animus against the body of the sex on which defect was most flagrantly inscribed—the sex which also was not his own.

The belief that women are inferior men can account for Swift's limited vision of their potential. In this reading, when Swift advises the newly married young lady that, whatever her pains, she "never can arrive, in Point of Learning, to the Perfection of a School-Boy," he is merely cautioning her to be realistic. As Bridget Hill observes of this period, "Marriage was regarded as difficult if not impossible to combine with women's education or serious intellectual interests."[25] With their inferior capabilities and domestic responsibilities women could not expect to do more, to achieve intellectually as men did. For Swift, the education of women only leads to better powers of keeping one's spouse's interest, a matter of concern because a woman has "but a very few Years to be young and handsome in the Eyes of the World; and as few Months to be so in the Eyes of a Husband, who is not a Fool" (*PW* 9:89).[26]

Defoe and Swift both want women educated, not to assume the prerogatives of men but to fill their designated roles more capably.[27] But whereas Swift warns women that they can never achieve a great deal, Defoe is full of the rhetoric of encouragement, saying that if women show an aptitude for any branch of learning, they should be allowed to pursue it to its furthest reach.[28] As Paula R. Backscheider writes, a suitor's description of one of Defoe's daughters as having "extensive Knowledge by her Reading gained" indicates that "Defoe practiced what he asserted about women's education."[29]

How uncommon either writer's interest in the academic education of women is may be gauged by a mid-century comment of Lady Mary Wortley Montagu. Writing to Lady Bute, Lady Mary remarked that "Lord Bute will be extremely shock'd at the proposal of a learned Education for Daughters, which the generality of Men beleive as great a prophanation as the Clergy would do if the Laity should presume to exercise the functions of the priesthood."[30] One popular writer, the French nobleman François de Salignac Fénelon, argued that the education of daughters was important because the "Employments of Women . . . are hardly less important to the Publick than those of Men," but he referred only to their traditional domestic duties. He observed that opponents of educating girls offered as a justification the "many Women whom Learning has made ridiculous," a point he agreed with.[31]

Coming from the class of small tradesmen, Defoe also had a view of practical education that increases the possibilities for women. In particular, he was concerned about the widows of tradesmen who find themselves helpless because they have no knowledge of the business: "Women, when once they give themselves leave to stoop to their own circumstances, and think fit to rouze up themselves to their own relief, are not so helpless and shiftless creatures as some would make them appear in the world; and we see whole families in trade frequently recover'd by their industry."[32] Defoe's description of women is not far removed from Swift's representations of modern ladies or those in conduct literature, but rather than simply counseling less vanity and more Bible study, Defoe grasps that women can move from a role of economic uselessness or dependence to one of productivity. But they must be acculturated to see this as a possibility and then given the requisite knowledge to make such a change. Defoe envisions this not in the modern terms of a career choice but rather as an enlightened response to necessity.

For Swift, the great harm of "those who are commonly called learned Women" comes from their rejection of gender boundaries. His extreme statement about the superiority of schoolboys, then, in spite of its discouraging absolute nature, reflects a cultural attitude of limitation rather than misogyny. Virtues and vices have no gender, Swift goes on to say, which has sometimes been taken for a radical piece of enlightened gender thinking. Yet the same overall rule governs here: Swift takes for granted that the scale will be different in men and women because one sex is superior in endowment and suited to the larger arena of the public world. That is, while it may be affectation for women to "fall into fits" at the sight of a mouse or a spider, Swift would not have expected them to confront more formidable animals with equanimity any more than he would have expected Stella's courage in shooting a would-be intruder to be transferable to the battlefield. A woman's practice of such virtues would always be confined to the domestic sphere and therefore small-scale. In Swift's view, the power to perform virtue publicly and thus attain the magnitude of significant action was reserved for men.

Swift was a moralizing satirist rather than a systematic thinker: that women have such petty concerns as lace and brocade because they are denied access to domains of greater societal validation did not occur to him—or, for that matter, to the great number of his contemporaries who wrote on the subject of women. There is no evidence that Swift held men responsible for the defects he found in women, other than his lamentation that women were forced to withdraw after dinner, "as if it were an established Maxim, that Women are incapable of all Conversation" (*PW* 9:90). Swift is suspect here because women constituted such an enthusiastic audience for his own conversation, the "constant seraglio" that Orrery refers to with unbecoming envy. Swift's interest is always male-centered, focused on what improves women for the benefit of men, which he assumes to be a disinterested assessment of the role of women. Since the complacent Stella was his closest woman companion, and his model for female behavior, he may have imagined that participating in a better quality of conversation would also content other women. More likely, he simply felt that it *should* content them because it satisfied his own idea of their role.

Swift was an early advocate of what Lawrence Stone has called "companionate marriage,"[33] a concept that some contemporary historians of gender have regarded with suspicion. In Ruth Perry's words, "companionate marriage is also interpretable as a more thoroughgoing psychological appropriation of women to serve the emotional needs of men than ever was imagined in earlier divisions of labor by gender." She concludes that "educating women to be more interesting companions for men rather than as individuals with their own economic or intellectual purposes is an ambiguous advance."[34]

Not surprisingly, those women who challenge the boundaries of their world on Swift's own ground, that of wit and conversation, receive his most blistering invective. The chief fault of what he characterizes as "a Tribe of bold, swaggering, rattling Ladies" is their use of "rude shocking Expressions, and what they call *running a Man down*" (*PW* 9:93).[35] That is, they appropriate exclusively male speech and male verbal aggression, exactly Swift's own forte, and then turn it against men. It would be better, Swift instructs the bride, for her to associate with "a common

Prostitute, rather than . . . such Termagants as these" (*PW* 9:93). Swift liked to classify and contain a destructive potential, hence his advocacy of the scheme to make beggars wear identifying badges and thus purge Dublin of "foreign beggars," that is, those from some other part of the kingdom of Ireland.[36]

Women, he thought, similarly needed to be confined within boundaries that were clearly delineated and enforced. In seventeenth-century texts on women, their "gadding about" or circulating freely was seen as ominous, the inevitable forerunner of a challenge to patriarchal authority. As Matthew Griffith wrote portentously in 1633, "Many evils come from women's gadding."[37] What some of these evils are is specified by another seventeenth-century writer, Joseph Swetnam, whose popular work *The Araignment of Lewd, Idle, Froward and Unconstant Women*, first published in 1616, went through at least ten editions in eighteen years. For Swetnam, "Twenty to one that if a woman love gadding, but that shee will pawne her honesty, to please her fantasie."[38] Physical and sexual liberation might also be accompanied by the liberation of mind that resists patriarchal control.

The common prostitute, who goes about in her true colors, already denied social status, if not humanity, is thus a less dangerous acquaintance to the young lady. The structure of the sentence—I would recommend this rather than that— does not mandate one or the other alternative. It is a lesser of two evils, or the labeled immorality, less dangerous because it is circumscribed and therefore not to be feared as much as the unnatural and highly contagious immorality of adopting certain male prerogatives. Prostitutes were effectively placed and contained, confined by their occupation to certain bad streets and alleyways and off the map of society. The swaggering, rattling ladies, on the other hand, may be encountered in polite company, unrecognized as a dangerous aberration and thus posing a more active threat to an unformed young woman.

Swift's ploy, designed to emphasize the danger of such ladies, is rhetorical: a clergyman and family friend would not seriously advise a young bride to associate with a prostitute. Nevertheless, it is a measure of Swift's anxiety, anxiety that his culture shared, about women circulating freely in society.[39] The conclusion of this passage reflects the full measure of his feeling: "I have often thought that no Man is obliged to suppose such Creatures to be Women; but to treat them like insolent Rascals, disguised in Female Habits, who ought to be stripped, and kicked down Stairs" (*PW* 9:93). In all women, it seems, lurks the potential for suddenly throwing off their "female habits" and revealing the beast within.[40] Assume the prerogatives of men, Swift warns, and rather than the gentlemen these women pretend to be, they will be treated like what they are in actuality: rascals in drag who should be exposed and physically punished. The stripping and kicking must be literal rather than metaphorical, for only nakedness would truly reveal the body's sex.

Swift does not deny that these creatures are women: his point is that if they violate the conventions of female behavior men need no longer treat them with the respect due to women. He thus acknowledges that gender is a social construction without precisely saying so. We cannot know if Swift actually wanted to see those learned ladies who freely criticized men treated violently—passages in his work that offer violence are often ambiguous in this respect—but the eighteenth-

century version of Joe Sixpack could adduce Swift's *Letter* to justify physical measures against an assertive woman, or merely one he didn't like.[41]

As if this outburst has abated his rage, Swift closes the *Letter* with a gentler
recapitulation of his main ideas and the reiterated injunction to pay attention:
"I desire you will keep this Letter in your Cabinet, and often examine impartially
your whole Conduct by it" (*PW* 9:94). "Your whole Conduct" reemphasizes at the
very end of the letter the absolute and rigorous nature of Swift's counsel when he
is addressing a woman seriously at an important juncture of her life.

If we are to believe Pilkington, Mrs. Rochefort did not appreciate Swift's
advice. Pilkington remarks that "the Lady did not take it as a Compliment, either
to her or the Sex" (P 30). Another negative view was offered in Samuel Richardson's *Pamela*, where the protagonist proclaims her resentment of Swift's contempt
for women, which she found in most of his works, "particularly in his *Letter of
Advice to a new-marry'd Lady*: A letter writ in such a manner as must disgust,
instead of instructing; and looks more like the Advice of an Enemy to the *sex*,
and a bitter one too, than a friend to the *particular lady*."[42] This is a more accurate
description than that found in Louis Landa's introduction to the letter in volume
9 of the standard edition of Swift's prose works, where he refers to it as "a very
charming letter" (*PW* 9:xxvii).

There is a striking parallel between the *Letter to a Young Lady* and one of the
letters of the early church father, Saint Jerome. A young man asked Jerome to
write to his mother and "virgin sister" to advise them about proper Christian com-
portment. Dismissing the mother at the beginning of his letter to address himself solely to the daughter, Jerome undertook to demonstrate to her that almost
anything she might do would be sexually provocative. His vivid description of the
allurements of female dress, even when the apparel in question is a "coarse and
sombre" robe, rises to a crescendo, much as Swift's indictment does: "Your shawl
sometimes drops, so as to leave your white shoulders bare, and then, as though
unwilling to be seen, it hastily hides what it unintentionally revealed. And when in
public it hides the face in a pretence of modesty, with a harlot's skill it shows only
those features which give men when shown more pleasure."[43] I am not suggesting
that Swift was specifically influenced by this or similar letters, but rather that for
both Swift and Jerome, the gulf between an innocent young woman and a harlot
can be readily bridged. Referring to both Jerome and Tertullian, Karen Armstrong
remarks that "Christian love for women easily modulates into sexual hatred."[44]
The same pattern can be found in Swift's letter to the bride, which moves from
gravely offered advice to intemperate railing against women.

Both Jerome and Swift exemplify the major concern of the vast literature
of instruction written about women by men: its prescriptive intention to control their behavior. Where Jerome sternly commends the young woman to her
brother's authority, Swift constantly reminds the young lady he addresses that
"the grand Affair of your Life will be to gain and preserve the Friendship and
Esteem of your Husband" (*PW* 9:89). The bride's husband should choose her
male acquaintances and "interpose his Authority to limit you in the Trade of
Visiting" (*PW* 9:88). Both men fear that left to their own discretion, women will

circulate from their assigned places into those dubious precincts of the harlot, metaphorically if not literally.

Additionally, Swift fears that women will encroach upon his own sphere and present themselves as "learned ladies." As Anne Finch wrote in 1713,

> Alas! a woman that attempts the pen
> Such an intruder on the rights of men,
> Such a presumptuous Creature is esteem'd,
> The fault, can by no vertue be redeem'd.
> They tell us, we mistake our sex and way;
> Good breeding, fasshion, dancing, dressing, play
> Are the accomplishments we shou'd desire.[45]

Women who spoke in public particularly encroached upon the domain of men; hence, Swift satirizes not only "learned ladies" in general, but women preachers and, in the person of the *Examiner*'s Miss Faction, women who speak about politics (*PW* 3:103–4). Yet, Swift did not want to restrict women to their usual ornamental pursuits or to forbid them "to write, or read, or think, or to enquire" as Finch asserts most men do; rather, he wanted them to keep their intellectual attainments within the traditional compass of subordination.

Swift as a conservative churchman would naturally condemn sex before marriage, but a quatrain he is said to have composed extemporaneously reveals how deep his distaste was. In a rainstorm, so the story goes, Swift found himself sheltering under a tree with a couple going to Chester to be married, although she was already noticeably pregnant. He helpfully proposed to save the couple the trip by marrying them, but when the woman requested a certificate of marriage, he produced this verse:

> Under an oak, in stormy weather
> I join'd this rogue and whore together;
> And none but he who rules the thunder
> Can put this whore and rogue asunder.[46]

The lines communicate Swift's displeasure, not only by labeling the couple disparagingly as *whore* and *rogue*, but by the chiasmus of the repetition which replicates their violation of the prescribed sequence of events. By producing a mock certificate, Swift satirizes what he perceives as the couple's mockery of the sacrament of marriage. From another perspective, the couple's marriage restores the social fabric. But, for Swift, it would seem, it merely legitimizes hypocrisy.

In two of Swift's "progress" poems, narratives are constructed around other versions of the wayward bride: Phyllis, the protagonist of Swift's poem *Phyllis or, The Progress of Love* (1719); and the lady in *The Progress of Marriage* (1722) meant to represent Lady Philippa Hamilton. *Phyllis* is not one of Swift's most celebrated texts, perhaps because its subject is the un-Swiftian one of love based on sexual attraction followed by marriage. We might reduce the narrative structure of *Phyllis* to this banal trajectory: on her wedding day, the bride spurns the suitor agreed upon by her parents in order to elope with the man she loves, John the butler. This socially ill-assorted couple suffers the usual waning of sexual desire and disillusionment of such unions and then achieves an accommodation that might approximate that of many marriages. If they do not live happily ever after according to the romantic vision with which Phyllis began matrimony, they do remain together in a kind of bottom-feeding equilibrium, low-life counterparts of Swift's other romantic couple, Strephon and Chloe, who "find great Society in Stinking." The poem concludes with the pair operating an inn:

> They keep at Staines the Old Blue Boar,
> Are cat and dog, and rogue and whore. (*CP* 192)

Or, as Thomas Gataker wrote in one of his early-seventeenth-century marriage sermons, which also characterizes a married couple as cat and dog, "they live together . . . not as *Man* and *Wife*, but as bruit *beasts*."[47] As the Yahoos of *Gulliver's Travels* illustrate, finding beastliness rather than humanness is one of Swift's most devastating metaphorical reductions of human behavior.

Phyllis expresses certain attitudes toward women more clearly than other Swiftian texts. Like the other progress poems Swift wrote, the title is ironic: the life journeys that the characters in the progress of love, beauty, or marriage undertake follow a declining curve. In addition to satirizing the idea of a progress as progress of any sort, each poem subverts the positive valence of its subject, those abstractions that lend themselves to idealizing formulations. The narrative of *Phyllis* does not simply deviate from an expected or sanctioned course of love: it presents the very idea of love as contaminated.

Swift described his feeling for Stella with the peculiar term "violent friendship," a condition to which he accorded the same status as what he called "violent love," except, he said, that violent friendship was more enduring. *Violent* in Swift's comparison has the eighteenth-century function of an intensifier: "great friendship," "great love." But the more common meaning of *violent* also bleeds into its use as an epithet for love, since the idea that deep attraction to another person must be violent, and therefore destructive, is the classical sense of passion. For Swift, this kind of love invariably reduces to sexual attraction alone, which, even if other circumstances are favorable, will fade and need to be replaced with some nonphysical mutuality. As he writes about another poorly matched couple, the old divine and the young girl in *The Progress of Marriage*:

> No common ligament that binds
> The various textures of their minds,
> Their thoughts, and actions, hopes, and fears,
> Less corresponding than their years. (*CP* 243)

Phyllis and John have no bond beyond the sexual, nor do they have the material prosperity that cushions the incompatibility of the divine and his wife. Unlike that wealthy couple, Phyllis and John must limit their aspirations by necessity to the realm of economic survival. The narrative moves the couple inexorably from low to lower, so that the parody of marital harmony achieved at the poem's conclusion, which the narrator calls "exact Poetick Justice," is the worst punishment. Instead of recoiling in horror at her debasement, Phyllis has accepted her lot, that of a whore married to a rogue. Begging from door to door with an honest man, as Phyllis extravagantly told her father she was willing to do, would have been morally preferable although—considering Swift's feelings about beggars—not by much.

Swift had at hand other possible outcomes within the paradigm of marrying down: had Phyllis and John been truly committed to each other, the conclusion might have been honorable poverty. The couple might have ended up running a tavern without being reduced to the level of beasts committing immoral and illegal acts. But Swift wants to punish Phyllis for her disobedience and puncture her romantic illusions, so she is brought to the lowest possible ebb, prostitution and venereal disease. Pairing *Phyllis* with the mock marriage certificate, which also labels the couple as rogue and whore, suggests that for Swift sexual desire automatically reduces human beings to the lowest category, although, in the case of the pregnant bride, "an unchaste or lewd woman" is the most likely meaning of whore.[48] Phyllis must become an actual prostitute to exemplify Swift's belief in conservative social arrangements for marriage; the couple who met under the oak are equally labeled as if their prenuptial sex had tarred them irrevocably and completely.

Phyllis's protestations of enduring love for John are followed by the travails of the wedding journey, which immediately destroy their feeling for each other: hence the ephemeral nature of an attraction that has no basis other than sexual. Instead of having a fixed position in the social scheme, the two have become a "wandring Pair," "well bemir'd" literally to correspond to their tarnished moral condition. This kind of circulation, leaving one's proper place in any sense of the word, is repeatedly represented by Swift as a violation of order: psychic, social, and moral. "But what adventures more befell 'em / The muse hath now no time to tell 'em" (*CP* 191): Swift dismisses the couple in a peremptory fashion as no longer of interest except for a few broad strokes of degradation and the cynically harmonious conclusion.

If the *Letter to a Young Lady* alludes to presumptuous and disobedient women as a group, and poses theoretically the dangers of associating with them or modeling oneself on them, *Phyllis* presents the case of one such woman. The deception that Swift condemns elsewhere in physical terms—the gaudy tulips concealing their origin in dung as an image of the fashionable lady, for example—is in this text a sham of behavior.[49] As a maiden, Phyllis counterfeits modesty and piety successfully for other characters in the poem, although the narrator's language conveys that her demeanor in church is actually coquettish. The omniscient narrator aside, such behavior foregrounds one of the key issues that preoccupied men about women: their ability to simulate virtue successfully. As Laura Gowing writes in *Common Bodies*, "The distinction between 'virgin' and 'whore,' central to prescriptions for virtuous feminine behaviour, was at best unstable, and at root unsustainable."[50] And yet, it was essential for a society based on the subjection of women to make a range of such distinctions about them. The consequences of misreading Phyllis's behavior before her sudden elopement is a rent in the social and moral fabric.[51]

When Phyllis is missing on the day of her wedding, parents and groom at first imagine that the cause is bashfulness over the coming transition from maiden to wife. They have been completely deceived. Whatever prompted her flight, the instruction to bring Phyllis back "alive or dead" inscribes the overriding importance of filial obedience, a value mocked not only by her behavior but by her language. Just as Phyllis's showy modesty had concealed a coquette, so the letter she leaves behind employs insincerely the rhetoric of paternal respect. It begins with the salutation, "much honoured father," an empty form, echoed in the closing, in which she styles herself "his most obedient daughter." Both expressions are false. Phyllis has flouted her father's authority as completely as possible, and her assessment of this transgression is as wrongheaded as her behavior: rather than repent her mistake, she asserts that "She'd do't if 'twere to do again" (CP 191). Although her utterances are swallowed up and discredited by the authoritative speaker of the poem, that Phyllis's words appear in the text gives her a novel voice in the group of Swift's poems often accused of misogyny. These poems are overwhelmingly creations of the male gaze observing a silent and objectified woman.

Phyllis's attitude that distinctions of wealth and class can be overcome by love and by ignoring parental wishes could hardly be further from Swift's thinking on the subject. His was the orthodox religious view of the time, as *Matrimoniall Honour*, a popular seventeenth-century treatise on marriage, attests. Here the Reverend Daniel Rogers discourses on the consequences of failing to obtain parental consent:

> As for the beggery you bring upon your selves, who should pitty them, who wrong themselves willingly, and chuse themselves such a portion? Oh! but (say some of these) we did it in a suddaine passion of love, and is not that to be pitied? I answer, considering what constant misery your short passion hath procured you, your selves are likely to have the worst of it: it were well, if others would learne to be wiser by pittying your folly.[52]

The disobedient couple should not expect aid or forgiveness from the parents. In conclusion, Rogers decrees that even a bad parent does not forfeit authority over his child: "He must have the honour of thy consent, though thou canst not enjoy the good of it."[53] Prescriptions similar to those of Rogers can be found throughout the literature of seventeenth- and early-eighteenth-century tracts devoted to the proper place and behavior of daughters.

And such a prescription can also be found in Swift's real-life advice to his second cousin, Honoria Swanton, who had evidently consulted Swift about her wayward daughter. The young woman had left her mother's house, taking her possessions with her. Swift wrote to the mother that he had made inquiries and "been assured that there is a man in the case . . . some beggarly rascal, who would pass for a Gentleman of fortune" (W 3:669). Swift advises Mrs. Swanton to send for the daughter three times: "If she still refuseth; Let her know, in plain terms, that you will never have the least correspondence with her, and when she is ruined, as will certainly be the case, that you will never see her, nor give or leave her or her children (if she have any) a morsel of bread" (W 3:669–70). Swift concludes his instructions on "so disagreeable a Subject" with a stern directive that his cousin renounce her child and any possible progeny completely and permanently. An orthodox response, yet it seems excessive. For one thing, Swift's advice is not aimed at reconciliation but rather at a legal protection of Mrs. Swanton from any later assault on her property by her daughter. The mother is to deliver the ultimatum in the presence of witnesses and keep a copy of it. The three appeals to the daughter are not designed as genuine overtures but as "fair warning" of consequences. Swift obviously believes that the daughter is already beyond saving: "If she will run into destruction with her eyes open, against common sense, and the opinion of all rational people, she hath none to blame but her self" (W 3:670). The future of ruin that he imagines suggests his satisfaction in this outcome—and a disregard for the advice he gave himself in 1699 under the heading "When I come to be old." At that time he resolved "not to be over severe with young People, but give Allowances for their youthfull follyes, and weaknesses" (*PW* 1:xxxvii).

Like Phyllis, Mrs. Swanton's daughter touches a nerve in Swift: his strong negative reaction to matches involving social disparity, especially where the woman is of gentle birth and the man beneath her. The daughter has been "enticed by some Servant," itself a violation of decorum, "to run into the arms" of a man pretending to a higher social status than he has, a deceptive self-presentation that Swift was bound to hate.

The fiction of Phyllis and the incident of Mrs. Swanton's daughter can be meaningfully compared with an anecdote related by Sir Walter Scott in his life of Swift:

> A young clergyman, the son of a bishop in Ireland, having married without the knowledge of his friends, it gave umbrage to his family, and his father refused to see him. The Dean being in company with him some time after, said he would tell him a story: "When I was a schoolboy at Kilkenny, and in the lower form, I longed very much to have a horse of my own to ride on. One day I saw a poor man leading a very mangy lame horse out of the town to kill him for the skin. I asked the man if he would sell him, which he readily consented to, upon my offering him somewhat more than the price of the hide, which was all the money I had in the world. I immediately got on him, to the great envy of some of my schoolfellows, and to the ridicule of others, and rode him about the town. The horse soon tired and laid down. As I had no stable to put him into, nor any money to pay for his sustenance, I began to find out what a foolish bargain I had made, and cried heartily for the loss of my cash; but the horse dying soon after upon the spot, gave me some relief." To this, the young clergyman answered, "Sir, your story is very good, and applicable to my case; I own I deserve such a rebuke"; and then burst into a flood of tears. The Dean made no reply, but went the next day to the lord-lieutenant, and prevailed on him to give the young gentleman a small living, then vacant, for his immediate support; and not long after brought about a reconciliation between his father and him.[54]

Two particulars seem significant in the supposedly true story: Swift's instruction of an individual person, and the young man's proper response to this instruction;

that is, a genuine remorse, expressed in both words and tears. That the man is a clergyman and the son of a bishop with whom Swift was on friendly terms might have made Swift *less* likely to intervene if the culprit had not been repentant.

Finally, the factor of gender is all-important. The narrative does not include any particulars about the woman whom the young man married: his fault was marrying without asking advice, and we can assume that he did not ask because his parents would not have approved of the match. Had he married beneath him, however, the results would not have been as extreme as the cases of Honoria Swanton's daughter and Phyllis, since women, unless they had great status in their own right, took their social position from their husbands.[55] Like Phyllis, and like the schoolboy Swift, the young man gave no thought to the morrow. Swift's intervention repaired the breach and drew the errant son back into the world of respectable society, reconciled with his family and able to support his wife.

That Swift envisions no such outcome for Phyllis or his cousin's daughter is completely consonant with the religious and social thinking of his time, the interests that culminated in the prohibition against the clandestine marriage of minors enacted in the 1753 Marriage Act.[56] The act of the all-male parliament to regulate elopements was not gender-blind: it was worse for women to make these errors, since they were supposed to be obedient, and there was no recovery from significant lapses such as loss of chastity. Randolph Trumbach observes that "stealing a son . . . was not the great crime. It was, rather, the theft of a daughter that was the real nightmare. For a woman's property became her husband's, and she took his social standing."[57]

Swift's distaste for women attracted to inferior men recurs elsewhere in his writings, both fictional and historical.[58] As he wrote to Stella, one alliance particularly upset him because of disparities of status and fortune in the couple: "Deuce take lady S——; & if I know D——y, he is a rawboned-faced fellow, not handsome, nor visibly so young as you say: she sacrifices two thousand pounds a year, and keeps only six hundred" (*JS* 28). This couple is mentioned again a few months later: "I know all that business of lady S——. Will nobody cut that D——y's throat? Five hundred pounds do you call poor pay for living three months the life of a king? They say she died with grief" (*JS* 148).

Directions to Servants describes the romance of a footman and a court lady who "had an honourable Employment, was Sister to an Earl, and the Widow of a Man of Quality" (*PW* 13: 42) The lady married her footman in a chapel one day, and he "came home in the Chariot by his Lady's Side," a sudden elevation in status that Swift condemns as a violation of social caste. The husband "unfortunately taught his wife to drink Brandy, of which she died, after having pawned all her Plate to purchase it, and *Tom* is now a Journeyman Malster" (*PW* 13:42).[59]

The women of Laputa, as Gulliver recounts, are similarly extreme instances of capricious sexuality:

> I was told that a great Court Lady, who had several Children, is married to the prime Minister, the richest Subject in the Kingdom, a very graceful Person, extremely fond of her, and lives in the finest Palace of the Island, went down to *Lagado*, on the Pretence of Health, there hid her self for several Months, till the King sent a Warrant to search

for her, and she was found in an obscure Eating-House all in Rags, having pawned her Cloths to maintain an old deformed Footman, who beat her every Day, and in whose Company she was taken much against her Will. And although her Husband received her with all possible Kindness, and without the least Reproach; she soon after contrived to steal down again with all her Jewels, to the same Gallant, and hath not been heard of since. (*PW* 11:150)

This is a typical Swiftian narrative of female desire outside its proper sphere skewed so far as to be an exemplary tale of the patriarchal tradition. The errant wife of an ideal husband is not given the choice of a handsome but lowborn or penniless lover: that would be blameworthy enough but understandable. Her swain must be anomalous in every respect so that her conduct can only be regarded as completely perverse, inexplicable to any reasonable person by any standard of love or policy. Frank Boyle writes of this narrative that "a superficial feminist reading will project Gulliver's misogyny onto Swift and dismiss the episode as typical of male views of women at the time."[60] There is much to consider in Boyle's projection of a straw feminist reading, but I would note in passing that he is rather too fond of setting up such figures as extreme alternatives to his own reading. The same page of his text also refers to the "misogynist reader," "the conventional male reader," and the "angry female reader"—with the assumption that these terms are self-explanatory. Boyle finds fault with all of these genderized perspectives, not surprisingly since, by representing one narrowly biased approach, each has been set up to fall short of his own comprehensive reading.

It will be useful to begin with the person who tells this prejudicial story. Boyle objects to reading misogyny back to Swift, but it should not be read back to Gulliver either: he merely recounts a tale told to him. In keeping with the naïf side of his character, Gulliver repeats the anecdote of the "great Court Lady" without the kind of indignation that informs the treatment of Phyllis. The prime minister's wife chooses the same situation twice, so we may presume that she is happy living in poverty with her lover. Gulliver, unlike the speakers in *Phyllis* and *The Progress of Marriage*, mildly observes of the Laputan story that "the Caprices of Womankind" transcend national boundaries, although there are undertones of the cynical speaker of *The Lady's Dressing Room*, who embraces the ooze along with Aphrodite. The specific anecdote is recounted after some general observations about the women of the island, whose interests Gulliver denominates matter-of-factly as strangers, then gallants, and finally lovers. Gulliver introduces the narrative with another low-keyed remark, one that does not seem a matter of condemnation so much as a difference of opinion: Gulliver thinks Laputa "the most delicious Spot of Ground in the World" while the ladies of the land "long to see the World, and take the Diversions of the Metropolis" (*PW* 11:149). All of this occurs within the context of the foolish men of Laputa who neglect every important aspect of life, including their wives, in order to pursue crackpot schemes. In Gulliver's nonjudgmental telling, blame seems to be apportioned to both parties, or barely apportioned at all.

Boyle is undoubtedly right that both the conventional male reader and the misogynist will interpret the anecdote as evidence of female irrationality and perfidy, but he fails to note that a narrative that elicits the same response from a conventional male reader and a misogynist, that is, which requires a non-misogynist to produce a misogynistic response, is suspect. Gulliver can be acquitted of inventing a story that unfairly discredits women, but the story he tells has all the earmarks of the Swift who takes the idle social conversation of ladies as evidence that women are "a Sort of Species hardly a Degree above a Monkey."

For Swift, these women deserve punishment because they have committed multiple violations, but we sense that a personal dislike clothes itself in orthodoxy rather than orthodoxy shaping an individual judgment. The irrational choice of a social inferior illustrates the dangerous unpredictability of women, their tendency to transgress the boundaries of their prescribed existence in ways that cannot be accounted for or anticipated, ways that mock rationality and wreak social havoc in the process of eluding legitimate male authority. Just as the fictive *Phyllis* can be paired with Swift's advice to Mrs. Swanton, the telescoped anecdote about Lady S—— and D——y in the *Journal to Stella* is a real-life counterpart of the fictions Swift creates in *Directions to Servants* and *Gulliver's Travels*. In all cases the presentation of the data, whether fictive or real, evokes a conventional response of condemnation, coupled with the heightened exasperation of a satirist who finds these violations of natural and social order particularly offensive.[61] Instead of rational choice based upon compatibility of temperament and equality of social rank and fortune, the women who flout these criteria exemplify for Swift a dangerous sexual desire embedded in an anarchic self-assertion.

The narrative of *The Progress of Marriage* was inspired by another kind of matrimonial imbalance, the marriage of Swift's longtime acquaintance and coeval Benjamin Pratt, dean of Down and former provost of Trinity College, to a young girl, Lady Philippa Hamilton.[62] Less than a year later Pratt was dead at the age of fifty-two. Swift had always supported Pratt, writing to Archbishop King in 1716 that the then provost was "a very honest Gentleman, perfectly good-natured, and the least inclined to speak ill of others, of almost any Person I have known." If Pratt had a fault, it was that "he hardly ever makes Use of any other Counsellor than him self" (W 2:188). Swift also wrote to the duke of Ormonde on his friend's behalf, saying that Pratt and Dr. Elwood "have more merit and candour than a hundred of their detractors" (W 2:13). Swift had recommended to Archbishop King that Pratt be given a "rich deanery" to remove him from some difficulties at Trinity College, and King had concurred entirely with Swift's assessment. The provost became dean of Down in 1717, four years before his death.

Swift was moved by the unexpected passing of "one of the oldest Acquaintances I had," but Pratt's sudden demise also provided food for reflection: "He has left a young Widow, in very good Circumstances. He had Scheems of long life, hiring a Town-house, and buiding a Countrey, preparing great Equipages and Furniture. What a ridiculous thing is Man" (W 2:404).[63]

The poem based on Pratt's marriage develops a satiric narrative in which the disparity in age is only a vehicle for a common Swiftian example of matrimonial folly, the bringing together of two people who have no basis for intellectual compatibility. As a result, differences between male and female cultures are exacerbated by differences in predilection and habit: the divine, although rich, is cheap and dresses poorly; the wife, predictably, is preoccupied with matters of dress. He rises early while she sleeps until noon; he prefers dining at one, but finds his wife having dinner at four. The real Dean Pratt "was fond of society, something of a *bon vivant*, and incurred criticism for spending too much of his time in London" (*PS* 2:289),[64] but in *The Progress of Marriage* the fictional dean is devoted to his religious duties while his wife is a gadabout:

> And drops him at the church, to pray
> While she drives on to see the play. (*CP* 244)

The satire against the young wife becomes more pointed when the subject becomes the clergyman's efforts to get an heir. Swift first wrote that in less than a twelve-month "poor Lady Jane has thrice miscarried"—something within the realm of possibility—then changed it to an impossibility, "his lady has twelve times miscarried" (*CP* 720n, 245). Against his inclination, the dean takes his wife to Bath, where, Swift hints, her desire is amusement more than reproduction. In attempting to perform beyond his age-diminished capacity, the husband catches a fever and dies. His wealthy young widow will now be surrounded by lovers. The poem concludes with the poet's venomous wish:

> Oh, may I see her soon dispensing
> Her favours to some broken ensign!
> Him let her marry for his face,
> And only coat of tarnished lace;
> To turn her naked out of doors,
> And spend her jointure on his whores:
> But for a parting present leave her
> A rooted pox to last forever. (*CP* 246–47)

The germ of this opprobrium, the fact that Pratt has left "a young Widow, in very good Circumstances," develops into full-blown resentment, yet, since marriages were arranged by men, with women having at best the power of refusal, it would seem that Dean Pratt was more culpable in proposing marriage to a young woman than she was in accepting him. The poem never loses sight of the defects of age, treated so much more harshly here than they were in Swift's self-representation in *Cadenus and Vanessa*, but the final lines, rather than focusing on the foolishness of human schemes as Swift's letter did, fantasize a severe punishment for the young widow. Why? If the dean died, "a victim to the last essays / of vigour in declining days" (*CP* 246), the narrative suggests that his eagerness to get an heir is to blame.[65] Swift can lay no heinous crimes at the door of Lady Jane, yet he nevertheless wishes her a terrible fate, as if to survive an elderly spouse is in itself a crime, and to be left with a fortune, doubly so.

Writing so soon after Pratt's death, Swift could not know how his widow would comport herself, but his poem prefers to imagine the worst, not as a lamentable outcome but as a source of malicious pleasure for the poet.[66] In this coda, Swift replicates the conclusion of *Phyllis*, degradation and venereal disease, but with less apparent reason. Phyllis and other women who choose sexual partners beneath them violate social order and thus incur a condemnation that the moral culture of Swift's time would support. Lady Jane married an older man, a situation Swift's society approved, which would seem to make it a different case entirely. Nevertheless, Swift wants to visit upon her the same extreme punishment. This cannot be otherwise explained than by the hypothesis of a subterranean emotion that Swift could not have understood or easily justified—an irrational motive in this man who valued rationality above all.

Swift may have been unusually sensitive to this societal commonplace because of his own susceptibility to younger women, a tendency he foresaw at the age of thirty-two and made two resolutions against: "Not to marry a young Woman" and "Not to hearken to Flatteryes, nor conceive I can be beloved by a young woman" (PW 1:xxxviii). The second resolution continues in Latin, "to hate and avoid those who seek to get themselves written into wills." In other words, as a young man Swift already feared being victimized by someone who would flatter him into marriage in order to become his heir. Viewed cynically, Lady Philippa fit Swift's paradigm as too much younger to genuinely care for her husband and therefore an unworthy beneficiary of his wealth. What Swift regarded as his own vulnerability he projected onto his old friend.

This censure spills over into misogyny when Swift suggests that all women are prone to such follies, a totalizing rubric that he extends to the innocent Lady Jane. For her to fulfill Swift's hope would illustrate the danger that widowhood represented in the popular imagination, that of a woman's sexuality unchecked by some societal restraint. A popular late-seventeenth-century text on women asserted that two of the three possible states for women—virginity, marriage, and widowhood—are states of subjection. Being a widow is "the most desolate and deplorable" because God "reckons them most miserable, when they are most at liberty."[67] Women existed in the law and in ideology as always under the protection of a father, a husband, or some other male relative.[68]

There may also be a motive of resentment that the subordinate partner, the wife, should ever outlive the man to whom she owes obedience. Such a fear is articulated in one of the satiric "parliament of women" pamphlets, which portrays women assembling as a parliament to wrest power from men. One such woman remarks, "I know no reason why a Woman that kicks off three or four Husbands, or forty or fifty, one after another into the other World, ought not to be rewarded."[69] Protecting a man's estate from his widow, particularly from her using it to enrich some other man, has been the thrust of a branch of English law since medieval times.[70] For Swift, who was indignant that the inferior D——y had received "five hundred pounds . . . for living three months the life of a king" (JS 148) in his marriage to Lady S——, Lady Philippa presented another case of unmerited reward, having inherited a fortune after less than a year of marriage. His poem, which places the worst construction upon her, is Swift's idea of poetic justice. In the case of D——y he thought of someone cutting the man's throat, but for the dean's young widow in The Progress of Marriage the punishment was more elaborate and indirect: thralldom to an abusive husband and venereal disease.

A contribution Swift made to Harrison's *Tatler* also illustrates the interface between conventional thought and misogyny. Through the persona of Isaac Bickerstaff, Swift presents the material of the essay in the form of a dream inspired by some bedtime reading that a lion would never hurt a true virgin:[71]

> I dreamed that by a Law of immemorial Time, a He-Lion was kept in every Parish at the common Charge, and in a Place provided, adjoyning to the Church-yard: That, before any one of the Fair Sex was married, if she affirmed her self to be a Virgin, she must on her Wedding-Day, and in her Wedding-clothes, perform the Ceremony of going alone into the Den, and stay an Hour with the Lion let loose, and kept fasting four and twenty Hours on purpose. (*PW* 2:179)

Women only pretending to be virgins were condemned and horribly slaughtered by the lion in the presence of spectators. Although no one was forced to have her virginity tested in this barbaric manner, if a woman refused, no one would marry her and everyone had the right to call her a whore.

Michel DePorte remarks of this fantasy "the relish with which the cruel logic of its premise is worked out."[72] In one parish no women have presented themselves and therefore no one will marry them. They have all taken vows of virginity and entered a nunnery: "This Manner of Ladies entering into a Vow of *Virginity* because they were not *Virgins*, I easily conceived; and my Dream told me, that the whole Kingdom was full of Nunneries, plentifully stocked from the same Reason" (*PW* 2:180). In another parish the speaker and an accompanying friend see a lady approach the lion:

> We observed the Beast smell her with great Diligence; he scratched both her Hands with lifting them to his Nose, and laying one of his Claws on her Bosom, drew Blood: However he let her go, and at the same time turned from her with a Sort of Contempt, at which she was not a little mortified. . . . Methought the whole Company immediately understood the Meaning of this; that the Easiness of the Lady had suffered her to admit certain imprudent and dangerous Familiarities, bordering too much upon what is criminal. (*PW* 2:181)

The final case is a "famous Prude," who has been held up as an example to neighborhood daughters: "The Sight of a Man at twenty Yards Distance made her draw back her Head. . . . Her Father had much ado to make her dine without her Gloves, when there was a Man at Table" (*PW* 2:183). She appeared to be extremely fearful, but this was attributed to the presence of so many male spectators. The lion immediately "gave the deadly Sign; at which the poor Creature . . . miscarried in a Fright before us all."[73] She confessed that "*this was her third big Belly* and when her Friends asked, why she would venture the Trial? She said, *her Nurse assured her, that a Lion would never hurt a Woman with Child*" (*PW* 2:183). The lion dispatches her, and with this climactic example Bickerstaff awoke.

This extraordinary text seems to have been neglected by Swiftian critics of all stripes. It is, first of all, an example of Swift's abiding hatred of hypocrisy, the claiming of virtue by vice, and his equally abiding conviction that all virtue that calls attention to itself is in fact hypocrisy. Yet the fantasy of Harrison's *Tatler* is so extreme in its punitive cruelty that it is reasonable to ask why this particular example of transgressive and deceptive behavior, loss of virginity before marriage, merits such a horrific fate.

Julia O'Faolain and Lauro Martines observe that a woman who was not a virgin on her wedding day "could scarcely, it was thought, remain chaste thereafter; and this sort of thing made paternity uncertain, mongrelized the family, and endowed the unworthy with property."[74] This rigid view, with its sweeping, even catastrophic consequences, would have been congenial to Swift's temperament. According to Bridget Hill, however, in the course of the eighteenth century prenuptial pregnancy was to become the condition of forty percent of all brides. She writes that "getting pregnant was a way to get married since there was communal pressure to support one's children and keep them off the poor rolls."[75] If Swift's fantasy does not mean that he literally wanted to see nonvirginal brides devoured by lions, we are entitled to ask what it does mean: within the paradigm of response to transgressive women, the solution he offers is extreme, even if it is presented as Bickerstaff's dream and not reality. Once again, there is an excess of hostility that intensifies the orthodox condemnation of loss of virginity before marriage.

In Swift's poetry, three texts involving the male discovery of female excretion have sometimes been labeled misogynistic: earlier times found them shocking and obscene. The most problematic of this group, *The Lady's Dressing Room*, continues to baffle by its withholding of essential information. We do not know exactly what the relationship among the three principals is, nor do we know enough about the mysterious speaker. Strephon, for all his silliness, exposes the truth when he sneaks into the empty dressing room, or *a* truth—although he does not contextualize it well. And, predictably in Swift's treatment of women's bodies in poetry, something disgusting is out of place, the excremental taint on Celia's petticoats escaping the chest to circulate through society. Celia recedes, overwhelmed by the particulars of a disorder that was inert and matter-of-fact in her life but enormous and dreadful in Strephon's experience.

As readers we can easily see that Strephon's behavior is foolish and extreme. For his pains, Strephon ends in obsessive-compulsive behavior or even paranoia, but the poem has described his journey through the lady's dressing room in such compelling language that against our better judgment we, too, may be tempted to link each dame we see with all her stinks. We, too, would not want to use towels "Begummed, bemattered, and beslimed / With dirt, and sweat, and ear-wax grimed" (*CP* 449). The power of the image trumps logic: is it likely that Celia's towels are *that* dirty, or that she needs to extract worms from her nose? Betty the maid is technically responsible for cleaning up, but the poem focuses on the condemnation of Celia as if dandruff and other products of the body were culpable by their very existence, much like the freckles of Betty the Grisette.

The speaker accepts the blanket condemnation of women, but with equanimity, asking rhetorically, "Should I the queen of love refuse, / Because she rose from stinking ooze?" (*CP* 452). The pungently negative reframing of Aphrodite's birth resonates against the standard idealized image of this mythic event. The epithet "queen of love" should not obscure that the speaker does not reject Strephon's experience; he merely envalues it differently. In the speaker's view, Strephon ought to exchange one kind of blindness for another.

Just as the speaker affirms the connection between women and filth, he also generalizes as Strephon does—and as the reader must if he or she is to remain within the parameters of the text. The link between women and filth is inextricable and serious: more than a state of mess, it is presented as a moral indictment. Strephon, possessed of the romantic vision of women that exists in both poetry and painting, cannot bear it. The speaker doesn't care: he believes it should be overlooked in the interest of sexual pleasure.

What makes the poem so puzzling is the unsatisfactory nature of its conclusion. Throughout the narrative the speaker has seemed to be a voice of reason, superior to Strephon, whom he regards patronizingly—referring to him playfully as "the rogue" in line 13, as "poor Strephon" in line 43, "frighted Strephon" in line 61, and finally "wretched Strephon" in line 129. The only words spoken by Strephon in the poem is the memorable exclamation, "Oh! Celia, Celia, Celia shits!" (*CP* 451)—as if Strephon can neither think nor say anything else. *Shits* is climactic, but *Celia* is uttered three times: the trauma is not in the excrement familiar to Strephon from his own bodily functions but in its association with a vision of Celia so misleading that he had to handle the contents of the chest to verify the unwelcome knowledge.

The speaker is not presented as the recipient of Strephon's story: rather, he functions as a secondary voyeur who observes Strephon throughout and knows his every thought, translating it into the comic diction that is a hallmark of Swift's satire. This narrative omniscience invites the reader to endow the speaker with authorial certitude as he tells Strephon's story. Having become accustomed to the distance between Strephon and the narrative voice, we find our own reaction comfortably confirmed by it; namely, that Strephon is a fool. But the speaker affirms an equally misguided stance that is itself a form of romantic distortion. His "ravished" vision ignores all but outward appearance, and this means ignoring a great deal: the last word of the poem, after all, is *dung*.

Commenting on Bahktin's interpretation of Rabelais in terms of an opposition between the grotesque body and the classical body, Peter Stallybrass observes that "if it [the grotesque body] privileges an area, it is the anus and it celebrates dung as the fertilizer of material life, whereas the classical emphasizes the head as the seat of reason."[76] Such an opposition seems useful in reading Swift as well as Rabelais, with the caveat that Swift's adherence to reason as an (unattainable) ideal is straightforward and unchanging, while his texts both complicate and ambiguate the idea of the grotesque body. *The Lady's Dressing Room* hides Celia's grotesquely oozing and dirty body in layers of finery, but the speaker coyly reminds us that this unseen body is a source of sexual pleasure as well. When Swift's texts describe the monstrous Brobdingnagian breasts or the decaying parts of his diseased streetwalker protagonists, the language is at its most comically pungent, "the language of festive obscenity and abuse."[77] The grotesque female body as it exists in Swift's poetry is both horrific and funny, its horrors treated wittily and thus distanced.

This interpenetration of horror and comedy has created difficulties of interpretation in all of the poems of this sort. Some modern commentators have read
the unblinking scrutiny of *A Beautiful Young Nymph Going to Bed* as an expression of sympathy for its struggling subject, a prostitute removing various artificial parts of herself as she gets ready for bed.[78] Such readings must overlook
the decisive final assertion—"Corinna in the morning dizened, / Who sees, will
spew; who smells, be poisoned" (*CP* 455)—or add an unspoken corollary like the
conclusion of Baudelaire's *Au Lecteur*: "Hypocrite lecteur, —mon semblable, —
mon frère."[79] But Swift's poem has no such corollary: the subtitle, "Written for
the Honour of the Fair Sex," signals comic irony, and the narrative that follows,
although it is third-person observation, presents Corinna's unironic perspective on
her life enclosed within the ironic frame of the speaker. This same dual perspective informs *The Progress of Beauty*, with its drawn-out metaphysical comparison
of "rotting Celia" to the moon. Like the litany of Corinna's woes, the particulars
of decay are so vividly incised that a temptation exists to view them unironically,
liberated from the framing context of the waning moon and Celia's unsanctioned
profession.

Are these unsympathetic representations of rotting streetwalkers misogynistic? John Middleton Murry was one of Swift's severest critics in finding the horror
of these poems "not confined to the nausea evoked by the hideous detail; it proceeds equally from the writer's total lack of charity, his cold brutality, towards the
wretched woman who is anatomized. It is utterly inhuman."[80] Like many readers, Murry experienced "hideous detail" and "lack of charity" as an uncomfortable
mixture: the very particulars exposed would seem, in our time, to require the sympathetic response of a common humanity. Moreover, the ridiculing of any sort of
misfortune does not sit easily with moral sanctity, and the one-dimensionality of
the satiric portrait is unforgiving.

Nevertheless, as an orthodox churchman of his time, Swift might reasonably
make poetry condemning women mired in a life of vice without incurring the
charge that he was expressing hatred of women as a sex. To Swift, Corinna's trade
was not a human misfortune but the choice of a life of sin, properly punished by
venereal disease and social ostracism.[81] He was far from embracing any mitigating
sociological explanation of prostitution. In Swift's traditional religious conception
of human life, individuals, regardless of circumstance, had the power to make moral
decisions and should be held accountable for those they made. But Swift also knew
the world, where the rich and powerful often escaped the consequences of their
behavior. This injustice did not excuse others from obeying moral precepts.

The issues of uncleanliness and excretion, which exist outside the province
of morality, are more problematic than prostitution. In *Strephon and Chloe*, Chloe,
like Celia in *The Lady's Dressing Room*, appears to be flawless:

> You'd swear, that so divine a creature
> Felt no necessities of nature.
>
> .   .   .   .
>
> Her milk-white hands, both palms and backs,
> Like ivory dry, and soft as wax. (*CP* 455)

She is in fact assimilated to Venus in the poem's second stanza. But unlike Celia, whose fair appearance is constructed on a foundation of mess and dirt, Chloe is only guilty of "the necessities of nature" that the poem finds incongruent with her appearance of bodily perfection. This alone is sufficient to dethrone her in her bridegroom's estimation. The comic clash of ideal and real on the couple's wedding night is predictable: when Chloe uses the chamber pot, Strephon is first incredulous, then disillusioned. Like other wrong-headed males in Swift's poetry, he has literalized a metaphoric comparison and in doing so ignored both biology and religion: no human being can transcend the body or be "faultless."

Strephon and Chloe addresses a topic that was central to Swift's thinking on marriage: how to keep its natural intimacy from degenerating into a wallowing in the physical. Early in life he had hinted at this concern when he told Varina that cleanliness of person was more valuable in his eyes than beauty. He articulated his fear more directly in *Hints towards an Essay on Conversation*, where he wrote that "a little Grain of the Romance is no ill Ingredient to preserve and exalt the Dignity of human Nature, without which it is apt to degenerate into every Thing that is sordid, vicious and low" (*PW* 4:95).[82] That was Swift's view in 1710. By the time *Strephon and Chloe* was written, in 1731, any grain of romance seemed suspect, but the importance of preserving dignity within intimacy remained paramount—without, one might add, Swift having any reasonable idea of how to achieve it. In Felicity Rosslyn's words, "Swift has no advice to give Chloe except, lamely, that she hide her needs—though if she did, he would doubtless round on her for hypocrisy."[83]

The conclusion of *Strephon and Chloe* recalls Swift's *Letter to a Young Lady on Her Marriage*, that nonfictional document written to a real bride to whom Swift intended to give good marital advice. Somehow he ended up writing an attack on women, comparing them (unfavorably) to monkeys and saying that those who failed to observe proper boundaries should be stripped of their clothes and kicked downstairs. The same kind of shift happens here, although less dramatically. After treating Chloe's excretion in an entirely unrealistic way, a way that recommends a prurient voyeurism to men, the speaker moves on to the marital relation in a more general sense.[84] Then he abruptly states:

> What various ways our females take,
> To pass for wits before a rake! (*CP* 462)

Chloe has shown no propensity for such behavior, or for any deception for that matter, but just as Swift in his own person was particularly sensitive to and censorious of women who go about "running a man down," the speaker of *Strephon and Chloe* rails against this same target:

> Some call it witty to reflect
> On every natural defect. (*CP* 462)

By the poem's conclusion the speaker is no longer preoccupied with women excreting: now he is concerned with various abstract qualities that might be seen

as the equally unrealistic counterpart of the romantic feminine ideal that was originally satirized. This is Swift's most explicit delineation of the "body of reason" as
opposed to the leaking and offensive "grotesque body."

Cassinus and Peter, subtitled "a tragical elegy," is a less ambitious, purely comic
version of the same primary issue of *Strephon and Chloe* and *The Lady's Dressing
Room*, the disturbing revelation that women have the same need of chamber pots
that men do.[85] Unlike the two Strephons, Cassinus, discovered by his friend Peter
moping in his room, is unclean and untidy. The poem's structure is a series of questions and answers designed to build toward a dramatic revelation: attempting to
pin down what transgression of Celia's accounts for Cassinus's extravagant condemnation, Peter runs through the conventional causes of lovers' quarrels, only to
be told that such calamities as Celia's death or her "playing the whore" would be
trivial compared to her real offense. Peter cannot imagine, nor can the reader, that
the "crime to all her sex unknown . . . the blackest of all female deeds" (*CP* 466),
the discovery of which has claimed Cassinus's sanity and plunged him into despair
is—defecation. Cassinus claims to have seen Celia with his own eyes, but doing
what isn't revealed until he pronounces the poem's final line: "Oh! Celia, Celia,
Celia shits" (*CP* 466).

It is tempting to think that this simple poem antedates *The Lady's Dressing
Room*, which contains a lengthy response to that identical line. *Cassinus and Peter*
may not go further than the revelatory utterance because both speakers are "college sophs," similarly unsophisticated and given to a romantic vocabulary, whereas
the speaker of *The Lady's Dressing Room* offers both a contrasting perspective and a
superior sophistication to the primary voyeur figure. *Cassinus and Peter* ends with
"Celia shits," the unvarnished act to which, it would seem, there can be no mitigating reply on Peter's part. *The Lady's Dressing Room* reaches that climactic percep-
tion in line 118 but does not conclude until twenty-six lines later, lines devoted
to the speaker's presentation of an opposing view. Its closing image, "such gaudy
tulips raised from dung," substitutes an aesthetic process for the action of Celia
shitting. The speaker does not suggest any direct aesthetic byproduct of human
defecation on the order of dung enriching the soil that produces tulips, and in the
process becoming part of them: strictly speaking, Celia's shit is a waste product
that does not contribute to the beauty of her public self in the way that dung plays
a role in producing the beautiful tulip. Nevertheless, the analogy between Celia
and a showy tulip shifts the subject from the image of Celia shitting to the final
product of her toilet.

In poems such as *Cassinus and Peter*, *Strephon and Chloe*, and *The Lady's
Dressing Room*, we should not accept the argument that Swift's satire is pointed
exclusively at the foolish men who idealize women, for women are the principal
victims of this idealization, expected to conform to an exaggerated role and then
condemned when they fail to do so. A woman like Celia, resplendent in tis-
sues and brocades, has fashioned an unreal and perfect figure that she presents
as a total and unchanging self: the rotting Diana, the dismembered Corinna,
the bodily functions, all mock the woman who has created herself as an artifact.
Klaus Theweleit observes that in European painting of this era "a pictorial convention placed women in constant opposition to an ideal image, as well as to their

own bodies and those of other women." He concludes that "the road to 'beauty' thus did *not* pass through woman's experience of her own body: it was simply one more road to her constitution as object and representation."[86] Women undertake self-creation as the ideal beautiful object because this is a standard valorized by male attention, with its financial and psychic rewards. By the twentieth century, Simone de Beauvoir could describe this process as calculated in a way that Swift does not articulate and would hardly approve: a woman's appearance, she writes, is "a rich possession, capital goods, an investment ... for not only does the woman of fashion project herself into things, she has chosen to make herself a thing." Beauvoir concludes that women embrace this artificiality: "It is this identification with something unreal, fixed, perfect as the hero of a novel, as a portrait or a bust, that gratifies her [the woman dressed]; she strives to identify herself with this figure and thus to seem to herself to be stabilized, justified in her splendor."[87] This deception provokes a Swiftian antipathy directed toward the substitution of a misleading facade of artistic perfection for what in actuality is human and imperfect. Swift regards men who are taken in by this feminine self-creation as individual naïfs: he chooses not to acknowledge the male desire that has invented, imposed, and rewarded that artifice.

This attitude typifies the overall paradigm of patriarchal domination in which women are kept in subjection yet accused of running rampant. In one form or another Celia will feed the outrage of a Strephon or a Cassinus. And she will feel the consequences of this outrage as well. Men were not required to be of irreproachable character in order to claim their superior gender status in Swift's time. As Rachel Weil sums up Mary Astell's view, "The duty to obey does not arise from the fact that men deserve their power but from the fact that they have it."[88]

In another arena, Swift waged a long and unprofitable battle against Ireland's importation of foreign goods, an economically ruinous policy that he blamed primarily on women. Here, too, he focuses on the phenomenon in isolation, rejecting the possibility of a rational cause by constantly attributing the pattern of female consumption to a failure of character. This hatred of Irish women's preference for imported goods does not drive his negative representations of women: many other habits and characteristics equally inspire his condemnation. Love of imported luxuries is simply one example of female weakness, albeit one that inspires a particular ferocity in Swift.[89] His animus toward women who use imported goods is apt to find expression in a jeremiad indicative of his desperation over the always worsening condition of the kingdom.

In the Irish tracts, characterized by frustration and despair, Swift saw women as the prime agents of economic ruin, just as he saw their bodies as repulsive and their pastimes as frivolous. To Swift, their refusal to obey his instruction and curb their consumption of imported products demonstrated their incorrigibility, and it produced some of his fiercest accusations.[90]

The *Proposal that All the Ladies Should Appear Constantly in Irish Manufactures* shows Swift making his familiar case for the wearing of Irish textiles in the restrained terms of a rational argument. In this essay, he makes his argument by means of numbers in the manner of *A Modest Proposal*: so many pounds of imported articles at such-and-such a cost. There is a moment of choler when Swift wishes that those ladies who resist wearing native manufactures "may go in rags" (*PW* 12:127), but this brief intemperance is immediately followed by a politic compliment: "Let them vie with each other in the fineness of their native linen: Their beauty and gentleness will as well appear, as if they were covered over with diamonds and brocade" (*PW* 12:127). Swift may imagine this to be a strong argument, although "diamonds and brocade" could only be read as more powerful examples of finery than ordinary "linen." The tract concludes with an appeal to the men who govern Ireland to pledge themselves, their families, and their circles of influence to use only Irish products. Quixotic as such an idea may be, it is based on the hierarchy of gender and class Swift's society subscribed to, in which men have power over their families and other dependents like tenants; yet, as Swift must have realized, most men would be unlikely to challenge the women of their households on a question of fabric, let alone coffee and tea. Nor, since their wives and daughters reflected their own status, would they be willing to see them clothed simply in a society where finery commanded respect.

Swift's *Letter to the Archbishop of Dublin, Concerning the Weavers* pursues the question of male authority over women in indicting the "cowardly slavish indulgence of the men to the intolerable pride, arrogance, vanity and Luxury of the Women" (*PW* 12:67). This indictment faults both men and women, although for different behaviors. Men are culpable for sins of omission in not controlling women, women for the zealous commission of sins. While both may be regarded as blameworthy, a larger share of blame belongs to women as the evil in need of checking.

The tone and language of *An Answer to Several Letters from Unknown Persons*[91] most tellingly illuminate the difference between Swift the rational critic of mercantile policy and Swift the misogynist. The essay introduces its topic of profligate consumption by comparing the importation of nonessential products to "the beggar who could not eat his Veal without Oranges" (*PW* 12:80), a telling linkage. Swift abhorred beggars, a class that drew from rather than contributed to society, and he would accordingly regard a beggar's expecting a fancy dish rather than simple sustenance as a violation of social and moral principle. This is followed by an assertion that begins as a rhetorical question but then becomes a periodic sentence, gathering force as it sweeps majestically through a number of damning clauses to conclude where Swift's deepest fears and quarrels with women are always situated, the female body:

> Is it not the highest Indignity to human nature, that men should be such poltrons as to suffer the Kingdom and themselves to be undone, by the Vanity, the Folly, the Pride, and Wantonness of their Wives, who under their present Corruptions seem to be a kind of animal suffered for our sins to be sent into the world for the Destruction of Familyes, Societyes, and Kingdoms; and whose whole study seems directed to be as expensive as they possibly can in every useless article of living, who by long practice can reconcile the most pernicious forein Drugs to their health and pleasure, provided they are but expensive; as Starlings grow fat with henbane: who contract a Robustness by meer practice of Sloth and Luxury: who can play deep severall hours after midnight, sleep beyond noon, revel upon Indian poisons, and spend the revenue of a moderate family to adorn a nauseous unwholesom living Carcase. (*PW* 12:80)

This full bill of particulars is a relentless catalogue of female sins. Swift's style is direct and energetic, but the passage is more of a pulpit remonstrance than a literary tour de force. It concludes with the speaker invoking a merciful God to "look down upon a nation so shamefully besotted" (*PW* 12:80). The very nature of manliness is at stake in this issue, for part of what establishes a man as a man is his authority over women. For this to be in question is, Swift asseverates, "the highest Indignity to human nature."[92]

Rather than the *Proposal*'s abstract characterization of "this insupportable grievance of bringing in the instruments of our ruin," the *Answer* vividly evokes apocalypse: the "Destruction of Familyes, Societyes, and Kingdoms." In the *Proposal* tea is merely "the common luxury of every chambermaid, sempstress, and tradesman's wife" (*PW* 12:126),[93] a mild reflection of the beggar demanding oranges with his veal.

The global indictment of women for expense and luxury has a long history: like a beggar, a woman signifies the absence of productivity, but she goes beyond this lack to represent "a prodigal consumption of resources."[94] Readers should keep in mind that "pernicious forein Drugs" and "Indian poisons" are not heroin and hashish but coffee, chocolate, and tea—which were enjoyed by many men, including Swift. Men at this time also wore lace and other embellishments of costume, yet Swift never indicts *them* for adorning a "nauseous unwholesom living Carcase." He is prompted to criticize women for their preference for foreign textiles, a practice that increases the misery of the Kingdom of Ireland, yet the body he represents as repulsive would be equally nauseous and unwholesome if it were concealed by Irish cloth, and Swift would be equally repulsed by it—if more approving of the covering. The implication of the climactic example here is that the female body is always nauseous and unwholesome, in keeping with Swift's description of women in a letter to Vanessa as "beasts in skirts." This characterization of the female body is the most predictable form of Swiftian misogyny.

7

$\mathcal{J}$wift and Women Critics

Anecdotal evidence establishes that women read Swift and commented on his writings from the time his texts first appeared, but the systematic attention that results in a book-length critical study would not be undertaken until the twentieth century. Some nineteenth-century essayists, such as Anna Jameson, Margaret Wood, Margaret Oliphant, and Lady Wilde, were drawn, like their male counterparts, to speculate on the by-then notorious triangle of Swift, Stella, and Vanessa without being similarly drawn to any analysis of Swift's writings. In the latter part of the eighteenth century, however, the popular writer of conduct literature, Mrs. Hester Chapone, engaged one of Swift's texts, the *Letter to a Young Lady, on Her Marriage*, in her own letter of advice addressed to a newly married niece—and did so in a way that seems to reflect differences of gender experience.

In her earlier *A Matrimonial Creed*, Chapone had stated her belief in a husband's divine right to "the absolute obedience of his wife . . . as her appointed ruler and head, he is undoubtedly her superior."[1] Such a position can readily be inferred from Swift's *Letter* but is not stated outright. Swift assumed that everyone acknowledged male superiority: it informs his pronouncements rather than being baldly stated. Chapone intends to be disarming in her assertion, for she continues by affirming her equally strong belief in exceptions to this rule.

Chapone's *Letter to a New-Married Lady* reiterates the commitment to female subjection and obedience in marriage, but throughout her letter she exhibits qualities of flexibility and common sense that cannot be found in Swift's letter to Deborah Rochefort. Chapone makes no such extreme pronouncements as Swift does when he advises the bride not to join that company of ladies who "affect abundance of uneasiness while their Husbands are abroad" and make such a fuss when he comes in late that "a Shrew from *Billingsgate* would be a more easy and eligible Companion" (*PW* 9:87). Part of this difference is probably due to Chapone's experience, albeit brief, of the married state, and part is due to her more intimate knowledge of the young woman she is writing to, whom she regards as a person of good sense. On the topic of displaying affection in public, Chapone agrees that "Dean Swift, in his coarse way, says very sensible things on the subject." But she goes on to add that the subject of affection in public "may safely be left to your own natural delicacy."[2]

A profound part of the difference between the two advice-givers is a matter of approach to their subject and audience. Swift, for example, distrusts the behavior of those wives who exaggerate their pain at a separation from their husbands by demanding frequent letters and a fixed date of return. "I can only say," he proceeds to say with relish, "that in my Observation, those Ladies who are apt to make the greatest Clutter upon such occasions, would liberally have paid a Messenger for bringing them News that their Husbands had broken their Necks on the Road" (*PW* 9:87). Such comments addressed to a young woman who is a new bride are insensitive. Chapone, whose frequent allusions to Swift's *Letter* reflect careful reading of it, draws a distinction between women who deserve censure and those who do not. "Your husband," she writes, "is untainted with that base opinion of women, which a commerce with the worse of the sex always inspires" (110). In view of her references to Swift, this could well be a pointed observation.

In writing to a bride, Swift not only takes the opportunity to critique women as a gender, he constructs—as he does in the poem *Strephon and Chloe*—an ideal of marriage that would be impossible to adhere to, even if it were desirable. Chapone is far more practical, describing Swift's advice that the bride have no friends among her own sex as "preposterous." She immediately notes the danger such behavior would bring to a woman's reputation and even her morals. But aside from this, she writes, "surely a woman who despised her own sex, and would converse with none but men, would be not less ridiculous than a man who should pass his whole time among women" (125). Yet, as she knows and accepts, this simple reversal leaves out the issue of male superiority. Swift's injunction is designed to improve the bride's mind by exposing her to intellectual superiors; unlike a woman who conversed only with men, a man who conversed only with women would be subjecting himself to a constant diet of the intellectually inferior.

Chapone's solution, like the idea of male superiority itself, would hardly satisfy women of our time. She begins promisingly, "I cannot but flatter myself that the ladies are mightily improved since the time when Dean Swift . . . exhorts his fair pupil to make no friendships with any of her own sex" (124). She continues, "You may find advantages in the conversation of many ladies, if not equal to those which men are qualified to *give*, yet equal at least to what *you, as a female*, are capable of *receiving*" (126). Thus Chapone and Swift do not disagree on the basic premise of superior/inferior, just on the feasibility of exposure to the superior sex alone. Chapone suggests, as Swift does not, that women cannot converse on the same level as men. Once again, this is more of a difference of style than substance: Chapone, as a woman, wants to establish that she is no radical intent upon claiming male prerogatives for women. Swift would have felt no need to argue that women were less able conversationalists than men.

Swift's most cherished principle about marriage is that it should be founded upon an enduring friendship rather than a fleeting romantic attraction. He tells the new Mrs. Rochefort that "the grand Affair" of her life will be "to gain and preserve the Friendship and Esteem" of her husband (*PW* 9:89). If she fails in this, the prognostication for the marriage will be grim: "You will, in Time, grow a Thing indifferent, and perhaps contemptible, unless you can supply the Loss of Youth and Beauty with more durable Qualities. You have but a very few Years to be young and handsome in the Eyes of the World; and as few Months to be so in the Eyes of a Husband." (*PW* 9:89) Accordingly, Swift advises the bride to cultivate her husband's interests and to improve her mind. The happy result will be to "produce in your Husband a true rational Love and Esteem for you, which old Age will not diminish" (*PW* 9:90).

In respect to the ideal of friendship in marriage, Mrs. Chapone once again provides a more nuanced view, although she begins with the same premise, invoking Swift's pronouncement "that the passion of love in men is infallibly destroyed by possession, and can subsist but a short time after marriage" (110). She agrees both with the idea that violent passion does not last and with Swift's recommendation that during the brief time of romantic attraction, the bride must "build the solid foundation of a durable friendship" (111). The bride should cultivate "a hearty desire of conforming to [her husband's] inclinations and sharing in his pleasures" (115). Yet elsewhere she pragmatically advances a view subversive to Swift's: "Many an honest woman, who would make a faithful and obedient wife, is utterly unqualified to be a friend in the highest sense of the word: and many marriages are tolerable easy, if not happy, where friendship was never once thought of, either in the making, or in the course of the union."[3] Swift, no doubt, had observed marriages of the sort that Chapone describes, but he had an investment in the idea of a marriage in which all other qualities were subordinated to his concept of friendship. Ruth Perry's criticism, that this is merely another requirement imposed on women, would not have been entertained by either Swift or Chapone since both believed that this is what a wife's role *should* be.

In keeping with her more pragmatic approach to marriage, Chapone has some advice on getting along with people who make no appearance in Swift's letter: the bride's mother-in-law and her husband's relations in general. She sensibly counsels her niece to avoid quarrels with them. More tellingly, Chapone does refer to one matter that is completely and startlingly absent from Swift's advice, namely, children. Although women in the early part of the century were not defined as exclusively by the maternal role as they would come to be by the end of the century, it was still assumed that having children was a primary conjugal activity, indeed, in religious doctrine, a duty. Swift, if the *Letter* is any evidence, thought of a wife's role exclusively in terms of her husband.

James Boswell describes how a Scottish lady once asked Dr. Johnson if he believed that no man was naturally good. Johnson replied, "No, madam, no more than a wolf." Boswell then asked, "Nor no woman, sir?" and received the predictable response, "No, sir." At this, Boswell recounts, "Lady MacLeod started, saying low, 'This is worse than Swift.'"[4] Her comment, made in 1773, reflects a woman's view of Swift that might serve as a rejoinder to Margaret Doody's assertion that "in every century exclamations over Swift's foul-mindedness have been much more common" among men.[5] Whether she means that we should disregard or merely remark this gender difference, the observation fails to consider the informal criticism of women like Lady McLeod voicing their objections in conversation or Lady Mary Wortley Montagu writing to her daughter. Nor does it take into account how few women critics there were in comparison with men in earlier periods. "Throughout the eighteenth century," Terry Castle writes, "it was commonly held that literary judgment was—or should be—reserved for men. A woman who set forth literary opinions in public exposed either her folly or her presumption."[6] Before the modern period, conventions of decency would have prevented a gentlewoman from alluding to such forbidden topics as Swift treats in his most notorious poems on women. For these reasons, the gender difference that Doody has noticed may not be attributable to the cause she suggests, namely, that women are not bothered by Swift's negative portraits of them.

Swift's representations of women became a subject of debate, often vitriolic, beginning in his own lifetime. He had no sooner published *The Lady's Dressing Room* than Lady Mary penned a response attributing the negative portrait of Celia in the poem to Swift's impotence.[7] An anonymous author, identified only as Miss W——, produced *The Gentleman's Study, In Answer to [Swift's] The Lady's Dressing Room*.[8] Laetitia Pilkington's mother made her own negative comment by promptly vomiting after reading the poem (P 314). And in one of the anecdotes collected in *Swiftiana*, Swift received a rebuke from "a widow lady of a very respectable family, Mrs. Seneca, at Drogheda," where he spent a night: "In the morning he made a violent complaint of the *sheets* being *dirty*. 'Dirty, indeed,' exclaimed Mrs. Seneca. '*You are the last man, Doctor, that should complain of dirty* SHEETS.' He had just then published the '*Lady's Dressing Room*,' a poem which wants nothing but *delicacy*."[9] Whether Swift was upbraided by an indignant landlady in actuality, the circulation of such an anecdote makes a commonsensical point: women might well be offended by his satiric characterization of their sex. Until our own unshockable times, unfavorable pronouncements on the scatological poems, as they were then referred to, and on Swift's relations with particular women, appeared with regularity: a persistent tide of moral condemnation reached its apogee in the nineteenth century. As Donald Berwick writes in his study of Swift's reputation, "More and more . . . hatred of the Dean was to center on his treatment of women."[10] This approach receded before the aesthetically-based critiques of post–World War II criticism that separated Swift from the speaker of the offensive passages or pursued other interpretive strategies that eliminated the possibility of misogyny attributable to Swift the man.[11] The rise of feminist scholarship has produced new appraisals of Swift on the subject of women, and we are now in a second phase of this period, one that has moved away from the most notorious textual examples to undertake a broader inquiry. This welcome effort to consider Swift and women has expanded to include his relations with women who were professional writers and his influence on women poets of the later eighteenth century.[12]

Nora Crow, in her essay "Swift and the Woman Scholar," has documented a number of reversals of opinion as feminist criticism moved from assessment to reassessment.[13] The earlier stage seems predictable: Swift was a great literary figure who had been celebrated in twentieth-century criticism for his art, while his negative representations of women were ignored. In their influential *The Madwoman in the Attic: The Woman Writer and the Nineteenth-Century Imagination*, Sandra Gilbert and Susan Gubar condemn Swift for creating "monstrous females," a term they use interchangeably with "female monsters."[14] They adopt, in other words, a straightforward reading of Swiftian texts in which negative images are what they seem to be, representations of women as disgusting, unclean, deceptive, foolish, and frivolous. According to Gilbert and Gubar, such representations should be read as Swift's revulsion against women, a revulsion which—they quote Simone de Beauvoir—projects man's "horror of his own carnal contingence."[15]

This forthright interpretation also informs Katharine M. Rogers's *The Troublesome Helpmate*, a book that appeared well before feminist criticism of Swift could be identified as a theoretical approach or a body of work. Rogers asserted that Swift's satire often "moves from woman's corrigible follies and vices to her very nature. From his works, in fact, it is possible to collect a comprehensive indictment of the physical aspects of woman."[16]

Second-wave feminist critics have instead returned to the earlier twentieth-century male critiques that contextualize negative representations of women within the perspective of a satirically rendered speaker. The poem *Cassinus and Peter*, according to this argument, does not blame Celia for the natural function of excretion: it ridicules Cassinus for his investment in an unrealistic version of Celia. And so on down the line: wherever we might criticize Swift for pejorative versions of women, a created character is the responsible party. Swift, the inventor of many personae and many indirections, should therefore be exculpated from misogynistic intentions.

Deborah Baker Wyrick exemplifies this approach in her discussion of the frequently disputed conclusion of *The Lady's Dressing Room*: "Swift de-authorizes his figural reinterpretation, emphasizing the excremental part of the image, through the order/ordure pun, assonance, and terminal placement of the word *Dung*. The tell-tale clothes, shed like serpent's skin, have exposed woman's body, man's metaphorical imagination, and Swift's radical ambivalence toward both."[17] Each insight taken alone is persuasive, and their polished conjunction is powerful enough to momentarily obscure its evasion of the conclusion's meaning. The emphasis on excrement is buttressed on all sides, but what does it mean? Does the poem valorize the exposure of the female body and the male imagination to the same degree? Are men and women equally at fault? The "radical ambivalence" ascribed to Swift might cover a multitude of interpretations. It is finally noncommittal.

In *The Brink of All We Hate*, Felicity Nussbaum similarly de-emphasizes misogyny by inserting Swift in an ancient literary tradition of attacking women: his "antifeminist posture and his obscene language are not at all original."[18] This has a mitigating effect, but the existence of a literary genre does not necessarily illuminate or explain away any individual author's choice. The justification that "everybody does it" will not exonerate you if you are caught breaking the law; moreover, everybody *doesn't* do it: the selection of a subject and an attitude toward it necessarily reveals something about the writer. Swift might have chosen another of many established literary traditions to write in or confined himself to other subjects within the tradition he chose. Simply positioning him within a long line of writers swallows up his individuality and reduces it to blandness. If he "hates all of womankind," according to Nussbaum, "it seems to be in the same way he detests the whole of mankind."[19] How to interpret that statement is not immediately clear, for if Swift did hate all women *as women*, this would surely meet some definition of misogyny. Further, Swift's satiric treatment of women—*pace* Juvenal and Ovid—is far different from his treatment of men. Men are satirized as corrupt politicians, vain beaus, ignorant scholars, clods, and fools, but they are not satirized simply as men.[20] Nor are they indicted, historically and globally, as Swift indicts women in a letter to Jane Waring, as "those who have been these 5000 years using us ill" (W 1:124). Cassinus and Peter, for example, are "college sophs," rendered as immature and therefore foolish individuals. Their object of discussion, the unseen Celia, may be more readily generalized as all women.

In a later book, *Feminism in Eighteenth-Century England*, Rogers joined the second-wave feminists who see Swift's critique of women as proof that he valued them. Misogyny is now brought up to be explained away. Swift's contempt for women, Rogers wants us to believe, actually springs from an egalitarian impulse: "He found their empty-headedness disgusting because he saw no more excuse for failings in women than in men."[21] One can agree that insofar as failings could be categorized as moral, Swift accepted no excuses. But "empty-headedness" suggests a cultural component, and if Swift had held such a view of women's intellectual failings, he would have been far less discerning about his society than we usually imagine. This is possible, of course, but Rogers wants to construct an insightful rather than an unthinking Swift. Substituting different terms in her statement suggests its weakness. Suppose Swift saw no more excuse for failings in the racially or politically oppressed than in their oppressors. One wonders if Rogers would have accepted this idea so readily. She does, after all, admit that Swift "condemned everything that is distinctively female," which might well qualify as misogyny.[22]

Rogers also repeats from her earlier book that Swift "never patronized women," a strange comment following hard upon her quotation from a letter he wrote to Pilkington that seems completely patronizing.[23] Swift admonished the young woman, "You must shake off the leavings of your sex. If you cannot keep a secret and take a chiding, you will quickly be out of my sphere. Corrigible people are to be chid; those who are otherwise may be very safe from any lectures of mine" (P 54). The letter illustrates Swift's strategy in addressing a promising young woman like Pilkington: if she wishes to be a member of Swift's exclusive circle, she must abandon the bad habits of her sex and accept his chiding. Such behavior will demonstrate her superiority to those women who are not worthy of Swift's attention. Swift was always instructing women in this fashion, and one can only conclude that Rogers shares his opinion of women as habitually in need of such instruction.

In Rogers, as in other adherents to this view of Swift, there is a necessary vagueness about the definition of *woman* or *female*, reminiscent of the convertibility of female monsters and monstrous females in Gilbert and Gubar. To gain Swift's approval a woman had to model herself on a man, eschewing "everything that is distinctively female." Even so, a woman's prospects are severely limited, although Rogers does not refer to the often cited passage from *A Letter to a Young Lady, on Her Marriage*, where Swift asserts that women's best efforts to improve their minds will fall short of "the Perfection of a School-Boy" (*PW* 9:92). Far from having no more excuse for failings than men have, women seem, in Swift's opinion, to be genetically determined to at least intellectual inferiority.

Can a belief in the limited educability of women be reconciled with regarding them as equals? Hardly, but I would also observe that the ground of the argument has shifted between Rogers's first and second assessments of Swift on women. Her later text does not revisit the "comprehensive indictment of the physical aspects of women"—and with good reason.[24] Women might gain Swift's approval by adopting male habits of mind and foregoing feminine finery and frivolity, but they could do nothing to change the bedrock of their physical existence as women, and this, Swiftian texts repeatedly affirm, is a source of disgust independent of whoever is speaking or observing.

The relationship of Swift and Delariviere Manley, a woman who worked with him in the male world of the *Examiner*, has received much attention from women critics in recent years. These commentators, who see Manley sympathetically as a female counterpart of Swift, have uncovered some notable differences between the treatment accorded her by male and female critics. Oddly enough Manley has been characterized in terms of her physical existence more by Swift's male biographers than by Swift himself. Melinda Alliker Rabb finds that Ehrenpreis is unable to mention Manley "without a reference to her body or to her sex life,"[25] a habit that Swift himself is free from. Frequently identified as the mistress of the printer John Barber, and physically unpretentious, "poor Mrs. Manley"—as Swift referred to her in the *Journal to Stella*—was a known quantity rather than the kind of woman who incurred Swift's ire by deceptive self-presentation. Rabb finds that Ehrenpreis and Herbert Davis gave little attention to the Swift-Manley relationship, "yet a relationship undoubtedly exists."[26] Whatever the omissions or misrepresentations of scholars such as Ehrenpreis and Davis—here as elsewhere eager to keep Swift at a distance from scandal—the relationship they have ignored is not apt to provide evidence that Swift had a modern appreciation of Manley the writer.[27] While he sympathized with her ill health and precarious finances, and she mentioned him in her will as her "much honored friend,"[28] Swift would have been unlikely to see the similarities between them that both Rabb and Carole Fabricant adduce. Fabricant states that "if Manley was a 'kept' woman, after all, her status was not all that different from Swift's, who was likewise a hireling of 'my lord keeper,' Robert Harley."[29] Both Swift and Manley were Tory propagandists, true, but Swift could appear publicly with government ministers and eat at their tables—where he was made to feel witty and valued. Harley's error of thrusting money into Swift's hand as payment for his work was not repeated; instead, he conveyed to Swift that he was a friend and confidant.

Writing to Addison in 1710, Swift makes a brief comment on Manley's novel *Memoirs of Europe*, in which Addison was a recognizable character: "It seems to me as if she had about two thousand Epithets, and fine words putt up in a bag, and that she puled them out by handfulls, and strowd them on her Paper, where about once in five hundred times they happen to be right" (W 1:287). The best efforts of present-day critics to envision a bond between the two writers is apt to founder on this dismissive appraisal. Swift regarded only other male writers as peers: however much his path as a political writer crossed or paralleled Manley's during this time, however much he appreciated her talents in their mutual endeavor, he would have experienced a gulf between them that encompassed not only gender but social class. Until the disastrous end of Harley's ministry, Swift had high expectations; Manley, plagued by medical and material difficulties, struggled to survive.[30] Most significantly, as Rosalind Ballaster has noted in her appreciative essay on Manley as a satirist, "Manley could not receive remuneration in the form of public office for her activities on behalf of the Tory party."[31] From the vantage point of the early twenty-first century, we may emphasize that both writers were at one time fellow employees of the Tory ministry, but we should keep in mind that the world they lived in would have recognized and acted on the many distinctions between them.

For some time now we have been able to read the misogyny in Swift's writings not as central and all-consuming but as embedded in fictive contexts whose positive values reduce its power. To engage in this critical practice, however, is not to obviate the effect of Swift's negative representations of women, which are essential parts of the texts they inhabit, or to defend them as reasonable critiques of women, but rather to absorb them within a system that intellectualizes them and thus harnesses their disturbing power in the service of a larger design.

My last two examples of this practice on the part of women critics, the first feminist, the second postcolonial, demonstrate how ideological zeal can alter a Swiftian text almost beyond recognition. Or, as Helen Vendler has recently written about lyric poetry, "The poem is too often conscripted into illustrating a social idea not germane to its own inner workings."[32]

Ruth Salvaggio goes further than most critics who explicate a text according to a particular theoretical approach to Swift by maintaining that his negative representations of women should be read as valorizing the feminine. To do this she posits a side of Swift that wants to be "like the women he described, to write the kind of disruption they embodied."[33] From wanting to be like a woman to actually *being* one occurs in the same paragraph: "Recovering the 'woman' in Swift means recovering the positive potential of fluid phenomena that he figured only in disparaging terms" (81). Author and character express the same desire: "Swift, like Gulliver, ultimately finds more of a home in the disordered sea" (90). Although Gulliver at least sets sail often in *Gulliver's Travels*, Salvaggio never presents evidence that either Swift or Gulliver identified the sea as a "home." Swift is also

merged with his subject matter in her reading in order to transform his negative representations of women into positives. One might ask how Swift would
have expressed real disparagement—by creating attractive portraits of women?
Salvaggio's Swift might be compared to the Milton characterized by Blake as
being of the devil's party without knowing it.[34] But there is a crucial difference:
Blake's judgment has credibility to the extent that Satan is an *attractive* figure in
Paradise Lost. Reading as Salvaggio does, a repulsive portrait of Satan would be the
evidence that Milton belonged to the devil's party.

"Perhaps," Salvaggio concludes her discussion of Gulliver, his vulnerability "is
the desire—despite his search for systems—to return again and again to the disorder of the sea" (89). Perhaps, but in the spirit of Dr. Johnson kicking the stone
to refute Bishop Berkeley, one might prosaically point out that once Swift had
decided to write a travel narrative he could hardly move Gulliver from one exotic
place to another without repeatedly taking him to sea. Does Swift's choice of this
popular genre express a desire for disorder? I believe instead that *Gulliver's Travels*
satirizes various systems, not with the idea of embracing disorder as an alternative
but with the traditional satiric purpose of opposing a better system to the multiform follies of human practice. As a native of an island nation in the early eighteenth century, Gulliver could travel nowhere outside his country without taking
to the sea, nor could he conclude one adventure and move on to another without
a sea voyage. How can this necessity be separated from a desire "to return again
and again to the disorder of the sea," and what might differentiate Swift/Gulliver's
desire from that of any seafarer of his time? In my reading, what Gulliver desires
when he returns to the sea (at times without other alternative) is to escape from
adventures turned unpleasant and to find a way back to his real home. What Swift
desires at these junctures is to end a particular episode of his narrative. This will,
perforce, require Gulliver to launch himself upon "the disorder of the sea."

Aside from the reality that requires a sea voyage to get from one island to
another, Gulliver is the protagonist of a recognizable literary genre, one of the
most popular and enduring. In Northrop Frye's words, "Of all fictions, the mar-
velous journey is the one formula that is never exhausted."[35] In such texts, which
include the classical epics of Homer and Virgil, the sea is the path to foreign
adventure as well as an obstacle to it, as it also is to the obverse of adventuring—
returning home.

The problem with the Freudian-cum-deconstructive symbology that Salvaggio wields is how and when to get it to stop operating. Salvaggio declares
her acceptance of both conscious and unconscious motives, as I assume all post-
Freudian critics do: the question is how to distinguish between these two realms
of human intentionality. Vendler suggests that "all poems . . . contain within themselves implicit instructions concerning how they should be read,"[36] but the desire
to impose ideas upon a text may be equally strong, overriding such genre impera-
tives as I have referred to above. "Critics," Vendler observes, "continue to emphasize the imaginative or irrational or psychological or 'expressive' base of poetry;
it is thought to be an art without a science."[37] Although in Salvaggio's reading
the Gulliverian sea sometimes means female disruption and sometimes maternal

security—two rather different phenomena—it *always* symbolizes the female, and Gulliver's return to it is always a return to the feminine.[38]

To coerce Gulliver's preference for female disruption, Salvaggio must set up an either/or situation in Laputa in which "we might regard Swift's satire as having less in common with the systematic scientists who inhabit the island, and more in common with the women—the wives and daughters of the scientists—who flee the island in search of 'Diversions'" (78). Both the preoccupied men and the desperate women can also be seen as part of the satiric treatment of a system that, like so many objects of Swift's sardonic thrusts, privileges fantasy over reality. The escape of their women from constituted male authority extends the satiric portrait of the foolishly absorbed scientists without validating the female desire for "Diversions." For Swift, the problem with the systems of the Laputan projectors is not that they are systems per se but that they are nutty, unworkable systems.

Gulliver does move through masculine social and cultural systems, as Salvaggio asserts—even his far-flung travels discover no other kind—but she is wistfully theoretical in imagining that women are the disruptive forces in these systems, or that women are responsible for Gulliver's departures from the societies he visits on each voyage. In two of the voyages, women are disruptive only to Gulliver and only briefly: the maids of honor play with Gulliver in a way that diminishes his self-esteem but does not threaten his life as the male monkey did, and the female Yahoo expresses aggressive sexual desire toward him, again to his discomfort but not to his safety. Neither case is truly a crisis: Gulliver is not forced to spend further time with the maids, and as a grown man with a Houyhnhnm protector close at hand, he is in no real danger from a female Yahoo of eleven. Yet he reacts more violently in the latter instance because he instinctively knows that he and the girl belong to the same species and realistically could engage in sex. Gulliver's sojourns in the superior societies of Brobdingnag and Houyhnhnmland are not ended by these incidents involving women, and against the saucy maids of honor we might balance the sympathetic queen of Brobdingnag and Gulliver's appealing young nurse, Glumdalclitch. Salvaggio wonders why Swift in the second voyage "chose to deal with women as large and overpowering rather than small and submissive" (85). But surely a land of giants would contain women as well as men: one apparently needs to kick the same stone again and again when progressing through Salvaggio's *Gulliver*.

In Lilliput, although the first article of Gulliver's impeachment is his violation of the statute against making water "within the precincts of the royal palace," a reference to his unorthodox method of extinguishing a fire in the queen's apartment, the queen is not given agency in the article, which refers to her only as "his Majesty's most dear imperial consort." Moreover, the other articles, having to do with military matters concerning the enemies of the kingdom of Lilliput, are obviously of more importance. Skyresh Bolgolam, the Lillliputian High Admiral, hates Gulliver for his success against Blefuscu, and Flimnap, the High Treasurer, has become his enemy because he believes, ludicrously, that Gulliver and his wife may be lovers— an accusation Gulliver forcefully denies just as if it were a reasonable charge.[39] Women function here as they do in the real eighteenth-century world: as objects of male control and justifications for certain masculine behavior. In Lilliput, male enmity causes the man-mountain to fall out of favor.

In three of the four places where Gulliver makes an extended stay there is no evidence that women as a gender are "disruptive." Only in Laputa, the one venue inhabited by humans of ordinary size, does Gulliver remark that the caprices of women transcend climate and nation, but although the Laputan women exhibit more agency than those elsewhere in *Gulliver's Travels*, Swift is at pains to make their behavior appear capricious and foolish rather than liberating. Given Swift's delight, both in reality and fiction, in punishing women who stray from their social position to mésalliances with their inferiors, there is not much evidence to redeem the great court lady who abandons her husband and children for an "old deformed footman" who beats her. What we can read into this exemplum, I believe, is Swift's hostility to what he regarded as the inexplicable desires and behavior of women—his version of Freud's exasperated "what do women want?" and a typical stereotype of female alterity.[40] Such hostility takes a light form in *Daphne*, where the speaker remarks of his subject that "the folly of her sex / Makes her sole delight to vex" (*CP* 433).

Salvaggio's exegesis of Gulliver is only one example of her thesis that men are identified with the solidity of systems and institutions from which women, defined as the fluid other, must be excluded: "They [women] are not the stable and cohesive material of which systems are made" (100). But Salvaggio ignores that women are as much a part of these systems as men, just as slaves are as much a part of the system of slavery as slaveowners: the marginalization in each case is one of power, not presence. Both systems, patriarchy and slavery, require people to be ruled as well as people to rule. Further, the systematizing sins against women that Salvaggio attributes to Swift's time period, the necessity "to isolate and confine this disruptive feminine phenomenon" (16), can be found throughout history. The Enlightenment may have regarded its systems as superior to those of earlier historical periods, but its representation and confinement of women were hardly original, either in theory or practice.[41]

In its most extreme form, Salvaggio's need to distort the text to achieve congruence with a theoretical proposition results in separating Swift schizophrenically into a man responsible for upholding systems and a woman (within) who, by writing "vivaciously and disruptively" (79), undermines such systems. This is a long way from Virginia Woolf's meditation on Coleridgean androgyny:

> I went on amateurishly to sketch a plan of the soul so that in each of us two powers preside, one male, one female; and in the man's brain, the man predominates over the woman, and in the woman's brain, the woman predominates over the man. The normal and comfortable state of being is that when the two live in harmony together, spiritually cooperating. If one is a man, still the woman part of the brain must have effect; and a woman also must have intercourse with the man in her.[42]

Woolf's vision is of a harmonious interaction that creates complementarity, not an evocation of Guy Fawkes in the subterranean passages scheming to blow up the parliament above, an internalized war of the sexes.

With the overt ascription of gender, Salvaggio's dichotomy at first seems much like the topographical metaphor Ann Cline Kelly employs to capture Swift's dual allegiance: "Although the cultivated lawn of traditional discourse represented all that was safe and civilized, Swift had an irresistible urge to explore the jungle beyond."[43] Yet there is a world of difference between a statement that deprives Swift of conscious agency when he is writing "disruptively" and one that contrasts his conscious attraction to both the traditional and the experimental. Swift knew that he wrote disruptively and did so in the service of a conservative ethos. His intention is to disrupt practices that have undermined this ethos, not introduce a radical revision of society that would bring about the liberation of women.

Presumably Salvaggio's first Swift is the Tory political writer and preacher of Anglican doctrine whose satires promulgate a conservative worldview, while the second Swift, his feminine self, is the genius who "writes disruption" with such brilliance.[44] In Salvaggio's assessment, it appears that everything of real value in Swift and his age can be attributed to women: those supposed embodiments of Swiftian rationality, the Houyhnhnms, become through the resemblance of the word *Houyhnhnm* to *homonym*, representatives of the opposite of rationality, that is, women. This argument needs to be given in some detail:

> I suspect that what lurks within the homonym game is that Houyhnhnm is a hom-onym for *homonym*, and that to play the homonym game is to play a game of end-less repetition and referral—endless "diversion." That Houyhnhnm may actually be a homonym for *homonym* makes it possible for us to see these ostensibly rational and controlled creatures as themselves inscribed by a language that—through its endless referrals and deferrals—moves beyond their control. . . .
>
> *Houyhnhnm* as "homonym" may well be what subverts Gulliver's ideal existence among these rational creatures. And if this is so, then *Houyhnhnm* as "woman" may well be the disruptive feminine force within this subversion. (87)

Here, another feminist reading of Swift that draws upon unconscious motiva-tion may be usefully compared to Salvaggio's. Nora Crow Jaffe's analysis of *Death and Daphne* begins with a number of puzzling questions about the poem that can be answered by assuming that the figure of Death is a "stand-in for Swift himself."[45] She connects, in other words, the recognizable figure of Swift with the unconscious motive she attributes to him in *Death and Daphne*. Rather than an arbitrary, hence untestable, linkage between author and character, Jaffe pro-duces an interpretation that offers evidence for equating the poet with the figure of Death: "An old, celibate scholar and clergyman, with a system of pedagogy that covers such matters as eating and walking, binds to himself . . . a young and agreeable woman who might be much better suited to other activities. It is Death courting Life in another sense."[46] By demonstrating congruence between Swift's life and the text, Jaffe provides a coherent interpretation of the poem. Or, by artic-ulating all terms of her comparison, she offers the material necessary to judge its plausibility and justify its existence. The transformation of *Houyhnhnm* into *homonym* into *woman* provides no test of its plausibility and sheds no light on the text of Gulliver's fourth voyage. It implies, rather, that the Guy Fawkes lurking in

Swift's subconscious was insanely powerful, effortlessly turning his most thought-fully contrived rational structure into its opposite. My point is not that such a process is impossible, merely that there is no chain of evidence that the reader can follow to test this supposition.

Language itself draws Salvaggio's Swift into the disorder that he thought himself to be ordering through its instrumentality: "It is possible to view Swift's own immersion in chaotic and fluid matters, especially the world of language, as an immersion into a distinctly feminine domain" (90). In this species of feminist theory, the appropriation of language as "a distinctly feminine domain" substitutes for the lack of a real domain within the space of political power and societal insti-tutions. If language is indeed "a distinctly feminine domain," it is nevertheless one that men have mastered and used to enforce their power over women. Judith But-ler goes further in cautioning that "the category of 'women,' the subject of femi-nism, is produced and restrained by the very structures of power through which emancipation is sought."[47]

What the polarity of conscious male system and unconscious female sea dis-regards in Swift is his conscious complicity in writing "disruption." In *A Beauti-ful Young Nymph Going to Bed*, his obvious enjoyment in disassembling Corinna into all of her unlovely parts does not require an attraction to her or a releasing of "the woman within" but rather an enjoyment of his ability to explore and contain such disorder within a poetic structure. Swift's attention may be prurient, but his voyeuristic exploitation does not express identification. Lecturing readers on the "gross and filthy" can be a pretext for wallowing in it poetically, but Swift invokes the unpleasant in a complicated rather than a reductive way. He is drawn to the exposure of women as gross and filthy not because he is attracted to this state of things but because he wants to find a way to defuse that very anarchic potential that energizes his treatment of them. Swift does not proclaim his hatred of certain phenomena because he actually loves them; it is more that his hatred has dimen-sions that he does not—indeed, cannot—acknowledge: not the woman within seeking egress but the misogynistic male whose fear of women reveals itself at times in an uncomfortable surplusage of hatred.

A slippage between the real and the metaphoric continually threatens the theoretical package that Salvaggio's arguments construct. Swift feared the decay of the female body, she writes, just as he "feared that his own writing would decay into nothingness" (93). He did explore in *Verses on the Death of Dr. Swift* the pos-sibility that his writings would no longer be read after his death, but it seems to me more likely that he saw in the decay of the female body an analogy to the decay of the male body and thus his own body. It is striking that what he critiques in women's bodies is usually not what is peculiar to those bodies but what they share with male bodies.

Elsewhere, Salvaggio finds that those women of Laputa who escape from their indifferent consorts resemble Gulliver, "who cannot seem to stay at home on his own island," and also resemble Swift, "whose own career took him through the tempestuous worlds of political, religious, and literary controversy" (81). Two instances of moving from one geographical location to another on the part of fictive characters are thus conflated with real activity within different sectors of society. This chain of analogies, enforcing a similarity between Swift the author, Gulliver the male protagonist, and some undifferentiated women characters, is part of the overall project of "recovering the 'woman' in Swift" and thereby "recovering the positive potential of fluid phenomena that he figured only in disparaging terms" (81)—fluid phenomena meaning at different times bodily secretions and excretions, the "disordered sea," women, and chaos.

Salvaggio admits that what is found in Swift's writing—she might say in spite of himself or in spite of the woman within—are negative representations of women. She believes that Swift created these unflattering portraits because his conscious adherence to systems overmastered the part of himself that was attracted to disruption, whereas I believe that Swift was drawn to various taboo subjects in the way that people are drawn to highway accidents or news footage of disasters: not because they truly want this experience for themselves but because it is titillating to be in the presence of disruption without having to be a part of it, to experience it at a remove as we do media violence, without having to suffer the consequences in our own lives. Swift arranges a voyeuristic experience for the reader in some of his most notorious texts, but unlike the voyeur lurking outside the uncurtained window, the reader-voyeur participates only at a significant distance.[48] Swift was always fussily arranging his life and withdrawing from the offer of passionate commitment: today we can label this behavior as "repression" and wish that Swift, for his own sake, had engaged in less of it. Returning to the real Swift, I see no evidence that he wanted to abandon himself to disorder, whatever name we give it. The biographical and literary evidence will point the other way: this was a man almost cripplingly committed to order. The energy and brilliance of his representatives of disorder vividly express his terror of it—not his attraction to it.

Ironically, Salvaggio's construct of a divided Swift replicates the actual relation of men and women in Swift's world, where male consciousness confined the feminine and regarded it with suspicion. There is a further irony that might amaze at least the conscious Swift; namely, that the image of woman that Salvaggio releases from Swift's unconscious is in fact a familiar pernicious stereotype of the male consciousness—woman as disorder and chaos.

In the current phase of feminist criticism, readings that explain away the negative representation and substitute something entirely different have been all too frequent. A case in point is the controversy over *A Beautiful Young Nymph Going to Bed*, in which some critics, Felicity Nussbaum and Carol Barash among others, ascribe to Swift sympathy with its prostitute protagonist. In this reading, neither the morally condemned nor the comically rendered streetwalker survives. Corinna is instead an object of compassion.

Twenty-first-century readers may be more comfortable with this enlightened view, but it seems dubious as the intention of an eighteenth-century divine who never represents sexual relations as entirely guiltless or free of disgust and whose comments about moral lapses are more apt to be harshly punitive than charitable.[49] We know from Swift's personal life as well as his nonfictional writings that he was particularly sensitive to uncleanliness and endlessly critical of feminine cosmetic deception. That he might also entertain or express sympathy for a prostitute goes against everything else we know about him as man and author. The reading that finds women such as Corinna "heroic in their dismemberment"[50] mirrors instead the attitude of our own time toward the lives of women like Corinna.

Laura Brown's reading of Swift as a locus of intertwined colonialist and gender motives merits lengthier consideration as a more radical step in displacing Swift from his texts. Brown frankly labels the major poems in question misogynistic, but this is merely a stepping-stone to other matters. Quoting from *The Progress of Beauty*, where venereal disease inexorably strips the prostitute Celia of hair, nose, teeth, eyes, cheeks, and lips, she asks rhetorically, "What is the status of a misogyny that, while claiming to condemn an essential corruption, so quickly substitutes the accoutrements and ornaments of the female body for the woman herself?"[51] Her answer is that Swift's real object of satire is not the diseased whore but the enterprise of mercantilism that provides adornment for the female body and in the process, as Swift so often wrote in prose tracts, despoils Ireland.[52] Once again, the central representation of the poem is displaced to make way for a radically different figure, in this case not a figure at all, but the cosmetic and medicinal paraphernalia that surrounds the wasted body.

My answer to Brown's question equally affirms the hostility that dwells so eagerly and mockingly on the destruction of the female body. Sinful behavior leading to disease has brought Celia down, a perfectly predictable outcome in Swift's orthodox religious view—a view that can be labeled misogynistic only if one is willing to similarly indict the vast majority of Swift's fellow Christians who believed in the reality of human choice and the consequences of sin. Swift does not *substitute* accoutrements (or, in other poems, ornaments) for the woman but relates with mock concern the failure of these inadequate materials to hold her together. It is her misfortune that they cannot substitute for her decaying body, which remains foregrounded while the "poor Supplies" convey only their limitations. In his inventory of the streetwalker's ironically feeble aids, the speaker savors the gulf between their paltry resources and the impossible job they have been called upon to perform:

> Two balls of glass may serve for eyes,
> White lead can plaster up a cleft,
> But these alas, are poor supplies
> If neither cheeks, nor lips be left. (*CP* 195)

"These" are not only "poor supplies," they are ludicrous responses to Celia's cataclysmic physical collapse.

In Brown's reading of Swift, the figure of the woman "appears as the essential incarnation of the evils of luxury and accumulation" (181). I have several difficulties with the series of connections and displacements necessary to arrive at this conclusion. First, the animus of Swift's representations of women overwhelms and at times eclipses the satire on finery and other such luxuries. When Swift compliments Vanessa by asserting that compared to her other women are like "*bestes en juppes*" (W 2:305), animals in skirts, the emphasis clearly falls on the animal, which seeks to clothe or disguise its bestial nature by putting on garments. "Skirts" in this instance bears no suggestion of that excessive costuming that Swift satirizes elsewhere. Without disturbing the thrust of the analogy it could be sackcloth, or the homegrown textiles Swift urged on the women of Ireland. "Skirts" simply functions as a synecdoche for female clothing in this arresting image. Swift's serious *Letter to a Young Lady on Her Marriage* similarly foregrounds the nature of the beast upon which the finery is hung, and the Celia whose dressing room Strephon explores incurs criticism because her skirts, whatever they are made of, are not clean. Swift wanted women to use Irish cloth and other Irish products, but it strains credulity to believe that if they had, and if they had foregone luxurious dress, his antipathy *toward their bodies* would have been pacified.

Brown finds that Gulliver also smacks of mercantilist meaning because he is dressed by Glumdalclitch in Brobdingnag, becoming a "miniaturized, commodified female figure," something like the fashion dolls that were popular at the time (187). She refers to Gulliver's treatment by the maids of honor, who undress him and sit him astride their gigantic nipples, along with other sexualized play that he only alludes to. In the fourth voyage he is also a victim of the female Yahoo's attack. In all these cases Gulliver occupies the passive or female role and then, by virtue of this association, becomes the colonized native, to which Brown's ingenious argument has been pointed all along—although she writes that "neither Swift's contemporaries nor Swift himself would have been able to move ... from the misogynist attack on women to an understanding of its historical basis in commodification and trade" (198). It might be noted here that the long history of misogyny antedates the capitalistic expansion it supposedly exemplifies in Brown's reading of the Swiftian text. Perhaps what is most disturbing in this progression is the intimation that Swift would be of little value if we could not somehow find the colonized subject in his pages.

The misogyny Brown freely ascribes to Swift does not become respectable in her reading, as it does in earlier readings where it has been redefined as an element within a complex artistic design. Instead, it is diminished to irrelevance because it is only seen as a stepping-stone to what Brown calls liberationist politics. "The unpromising materials of misogyny," she writes, "enable us to perceive the critique of racism" (199)—thus making a silk purse out of a sow's ear. In Brown's politicized hierarchy, racism exists as the final step in the equation, the significant discovery.

Brown is aware that this process might require explanation. She writes that "the sacrifice of women might seem a high price to pay for the problematization of racial difference" (199–200). This putative self-criticism could simply be turned into a statement and elaborated: the sacrifice of women *does* seem a high price to pay for the problematization of racial difference, especially in a context where racial difference cannot be plausibly problematized. Furthermore, it seems like a frightening price, a kind of intellectual triage that demands the ranking of forms of oppression in order to privilege the most worthy. But there is no explanation for why racism trumps sexism; it is a given of Brown's argument.

The problem with a forced reading is that, of necessity, it is radically and arbitrarily selective, imposing its vision on the totality of the text. One could counter

Brown's idea of the passive Gulliver in Brobdingnag and Houyhnhnmland with the aggressively masculine Gulliver of Lilliput and the ordinary male of the third voyage. Even in Brobdingnag, the minuscule Gulliver wields his knife and his hanger against threatening insects and takes the initiative whenever the opportunity presents. Just as the requirements of travel literature send Gulliver to sea, those occasions of Gulliver's passivity occur to fulfill narrative purpose: to exploit the anomaly of a human being reduced in size or subjugated to horses. While the elephant in the text goes unnoticed, Brown and Salvaggio pursue a fantasmic mouse.

What has captivated recent feminist critics of Swift is what they regard as his enlightened departure from essentialism. In *A Letter to a Young Lady, on Her Marriage* he stated uncategorically, "I am ignorant of any one Quality that is amiable in a Man, which is not equally so in a Woman . . . nor do I know one Vice or Folly, which is not equally detestable in both" (*PW* 9:92–93).[53] Read critically, this statement does not endorse gender equality: it takes for granted the separate and unequal spheres of men and women while affirming that positive and negative qualities are the same for both. Those who read the statement in feminist terms should keep in mind the prescription that Swift advances in the same text. Those women who do not display the proper deference to males, who wish to pass for "learned Ladies," need not be supposed to be women, he wrote. They should instead be treated like "insolent Rascals disguised in Female Habits, who ought to be stripped, and kicked down Stairs" (*PW* 9:93). This position definitively rejects one of the most cherished principles of feminism: gender equality.

Swift's ideal woman is actually divested of any quality identifiably female except the docility to take instruction. She is then endowed with the desirable qualities of men without any corresponding enlargement of her sphere of activity. Instead of making the argument for equality for women, Swift makes the conservative argument of merit, the merit of male qualities or merit as determined by himself. Stella and Vanessa were assiduously formed by Swift, and he hoped that Deborah Staunton Rochefort, the bride to whom the *Letter* was written, would follow in their footsteps. The reader who applauds Swift's assertion of genderless qualities of character must be equally prepared to recognize his sustained diatribe against women, the generality of whom he pronounces unworthy of respect and of limited educability. Perhaps Swift genuinely believed in one set of qualities for both sexes, but we will look in vain in his writings for the consequences that such a belief might be expected to produce.

I wish to conclude by returning to Vendler's argument that it is a poor use of a poet's "inventive genius" to look to his work for large inferences about the social phenomena of his world. *Gulliver's Travels* is prose fiction and satire, so we can learn a good deal from it about the author's world; nevertheless, to use it merely or solely "as a means of cultural illustration" can only be reductive.[54]

Conclusion

Swift, we can be certain, did not consider himself to be a misogynist: after all, in addition to his long-term special relationships with two women whom he admired extravagantly, he liked many women as friends or protégées, enthusiastically extolling their talents and generously encouraging their intellectual development. He did refer to himself as a misanthrope, but one who made exceptions for individuals. Whether this declaration included women by default, as was the grammatical custom of the day, it defines Swift's attitude to women as well as men. On a personal level he had, at all periods of his adult life, women friends whose company he enjoyed and who returned his friendship. His correspondence attests, through letters written and regards conveyed through others, to the presence in his life and thoughts of women he liked. To the music master of his cathedral, John Worrall, Swift wrote in 1728, "Pray give Mrs Worrall a thousand thanks from me for her kind present and workmanship of her fairest hands in making me two night caps" (W 3:199). The gratitude seems heartfelt, and also typical both of women's interest in him and his reciprocity. To his cousin Martha Whiteway, he wrote on New Year's Eve, 1739, "You are much more friendly to me than a thousand of them [unmentioned others]."[1] With the last young woman in his life, Mary Pendarves, he could invoke negative stereotypes of women with a light tone, responding when she had visited a country house called Paradise, "With great submission I am sorry to find a lady make use of the word paradise, from which *you* turned *us out* as well as *yourselves*; & pray tell me freely how many of your sex bring it along with them to their husband's houses?" (C 4:455). Women he liked, such as Lady Acheson and Stella, are individualized in his poetry: we experience their personalities, their

171

likes and dislikes, some of their habitual behavior. In the spirit of true friendship, Swift did not allow his annoyance with what he regarded as their faults to alter his feeling for them.

Nevertheless, in spite of the women he valued, whenever Swift thought in sweeping terms about humanity, he focused on its terrible defects. Women, as the acknowledged inferior sex, were more culpable and thus more likely to become a general gender stereotype in his texts.[2] Celia, Corinna, Chloe, and similar figures make no claim on us as distinct personalities, but rather illustrate deception in appearance and behavior. Swift's detailed descriptions of them are at bottom superficial—their garments, their repulsive bodies, the messes that they leave behind.

Throughout his writings and with characteristic passion, Swift expresses the desire to contain women in a circumscribed space, both physical and nonphysical. In this respect, he differed little if at all from the majority of both men and women living at the end of the seventeenth and beginning of the eighteenth century. He judged sternly even those women he knew, like Laetitia Pilkington, who strayed beyond the strict confines of acceptable behavior, and in this, too, he did not differ from the quotidian positions of his world. The violation of boundaries considered impermeable explains a great deal of Swift's negativism toward women, but not all. Why, for example, does Gulliver say of the Struldbruggs that the women were more horrible than the men? Possibly because decaying female bodies are the more shocking in contrast to the literary image of woman as goddess, but whereas Swift's poems make this point unambiguously, the message in *Gulliver's Travels* is unclear. Gulliver's comment seems to convey a spontaneous reaction of disgust that the author does not repudiate. In a similar fashion, *The Last Speech and Dying Words* that Swift made up for the criminal Ebenezor Elliston blames his many crimes on "those odious common Whores we frequent" (*PW* 9:39). Instigators of crime to feed their extravagance, they reward their robber-lovers with nothing but treachery and the pox. If this is only the skewed perspective of the criminal Ebenezor Elliston rather than the opinion of Jonathan Swift, it nevertheless stands undisputed in the text except for the obvious thought that a man of this stripe, on his way to the gallows, would naturally blame someone else for his misspent life. The indictment, like so many when Swift considers women in the aggregate, persuasively embodies the satirist's own voice. It is possible to dismiss Elliston as a wretch while retaining the bill of damning particulars assembled against the whores, much as the silly Strephon of *The Lady's Dressing Room* can be disregarded without rejecting the disorder and filth of Celia's dressing room.

Where Swift most openly exhibits misogyny is in his tendency to make Strephon's mistake in *The Lady's Dressing Room* and imagine that *all* women are as dirty as Celia. As readers, we can easily see that Strephon's obsessive-compulsive disorder, a kind of behavior we sometimes find in Swift's own life, is comical. For his violation of Celia's privacy, a violation the poem neither censures nor explains, the foolish Strephon becomes an unhappy extremist, but *The Lady's Dressing Room* does not suggest that his conclusion, that any woman is other than a gaudy tulip raised from dung, is wrong.

In other texts, notably the *Letter to a Young Lady, on Her Marriage*, Swift's condemnation of women is so sweeping that to Penelope Wilson it appears to be almost femicidal. She writes that "in Swift the otherness of women, and of a woman's world, is something to be as far as possible eliminated."[3] A position like Wilson's is untenable because the interface between patriarchy and misogyny is by its nature so ambiguous. The male body, male institutions, male values, were the norms of Swift's culture, buttressed by the authority of Holy Writ. "Remember thy sex is crazy ever since Eve sinned," Daniel Rogers advised women in his marriage manual.[4] While women were assumed to occupy a lesser and subordinate place, part of what made them inferior to men was the frivolity of their social world. To wish to eliminate a behavior centered on dress and amusement, and instill more masculine habits and values in women while retaining their subordinate status, seems unjust today, but not necessarily a product of hatred of women. It is more likely to be the result of a self-serving and self-perpetuating ideology, which uses women as convenient targets for practices common to both sexes. As a satirist, Swift had a desire, often expressed in violent images, to eliminate many human practices and to punish those who engaged in them, but with women he had an equally strong desire to instruct and reform. It would not have occurred to him that stripping away their otherness and remaking them in the image of men would eliminate their identity as "women." Stella and Vanessa were proof to Swift that women could be sensible and serious and still be women.

Swift was hardly unique in praising women for masculine qualities: the accepted superiority of men in his time contextualizes his criticism and advice as a mode of improvement, one that, in fact, women have followed in order to claim equality of opportunity in educational institutions and the workplace. As early as 1581, Queen Elizabeth I proclaimed, "I have the heart of a man, not of a woman and I am not afraid of anything."[5] If the construction of femininity in the early eighteenth century entailed inferiority, then the advancement of women required the renegotiation of its terms in the direction of what was recognizably superior. No people—whether configured as a gender, a race, or a religion—have achieved equality by claiming it on the basis of their inferiority.

To characterize Swift as a "notorious misogynist," as so many have done, requires a disregard of all that is not single-mindedly and sweepingly negative in his treatment of women.[6] Swift may more accurately be described as a writer whose representations of women sometimes cross the line into misogyny by promulgating the idea that women are evil in some natural and inexplicable way as a sex and a gender rather than as individuals. Thus, Isaac Bickerstaff's lion fantasy suggests that there are no virginal brides: that all women are deceitful and therefore deserving of punishment—if not that of being devoured by lions then by being, as the *Letter to a Young Lady* argues, stripped of their clothing and kicked downstairs. In eluding understanding, that is, male understanding, women become susceptible in Swiftian texts to being redefined as other than human, as worse than monkeys or as animals in skirts. Swift could joke about his satires on "the fair sex," but the last century has amply instructed us that dehumanizing the other in words like his is a slippery slope indeed.

When Swift crosses the line, he represents women as vehicles of mental confusion, frightening sexuality, disgusting physicality, and disease. Why he crosses this line between the standard view of women as inferior and the misogynistic view of them as violators of order in every realm can only be a matter of conjecture. As Alexander Welsh has written in another context, "Most things of a mental order—feelings, memories, intentions—cannot be seen at all."[7] Swift at one time had envisioned a conventional personal life married to Jane Waring. After his humiliating experience with her, his diligence in controlling Stella and Vanessa, along with his constant worries about exposure and scandal, suggest that he felt fear and vulnerability in connection with women. By choosing celibacy for himself, Swift may have come to feel that all eroticism was tainted, not merely the sort he castigates in beggars producing brats, women running off with their social inferiors, and couples who are not sufficiently concerned with nonsexual companionship.

Much of Swift's criticism of women is not sex-specific in reality, but it functions as all stereotypes of alterity do, as a way of shifting the feared and the undesirable from self to other. And while Swift's ability to render detail so effectively foregrounds the reality of particulars, the paradigm illustrated by a poem like *The Lady's Dressing Room* need not be restricted to gender but could be adapted to race or other categories of identity. For whatever reason, society defines some groups as other and seeks to keep them within a limited space of existence and opportunity. To do so, it must invent a rationale of difference and predict a consequence of catastrophe if the other attempts to claim a space that has been denied, and it must punish severely any violations. For Swift, otherness centered on the female body, "the unalterability of biological difference."[8]

We should not seek to dilute the impact of Swift's misogynistic representations by explaining them away. Like other prejudices, misogyny has been a long-enduring human phenomenon: by giving it such memorable expression Swift reminds us that we need to comprehend its appeal and challenge its premises, not pretend that it does not exist.

NOTES

INTRODUCTION

1. Warren Montag observes that in *Gulliver's Travels* "there is no hint of sexual intrigue or feeling at all except aversion" (*The Unthinkable Swift*, 155).

2. Commenting on this feminine topos in history, Klaus Theweleit notes parenthetically that "in most men's minds, they continue to exist as blabbermouths and fucking-machines" (*Male Fantasies*, 358).

3. *Anatomy of a Woman's Tongue*, in *Harleian Miscellany*, 2:175. See Swift's *Hints towards an Essay on Conversation* and *Hints on Good Manners* (*PW* 4:85–95, 219–22) for his rules on proper conversation.

4. Anthony Fletcher observes that "the woman who speaks neither in reply to a man nor in submissive request acts as an independent being" (*Gender, Sex and Subordination*, 14). The extreme of this figure is found in the female preachers in *A Tale of a Tub* (*PW* 1:99 and n.).

5. *Anatomy of a Woman's Tongue*, in *Harleian Miscellany*, 2:170.

6. Richard Feingold embraces the same view when he writes, "The style of the Drapier is the style of the Dean, nor was there any desire for that identity to be a subject for playful speculation" (*Moralized Song*, 55).

7. An illuminating comparison of the two writers' knowledge of each other can be found in Novak's "Swift and Defoe." J. A. Downie discusses Swift and Defoe as propagandists who, without knowing each other's efforts, were skillfully coordinated by Harley (*Robert Harley and the Press*, 131–48).

8. Pope's relationship with Martha "Patty" Blount is discussed in Rumbold, *Women's Place in Pope's World*, chapters 5, 9, and passim.

9. Rumbold, *Women's Place in Pope's World*, 103.

10. Ross, *Swift and Defoe*, 33. Richard I. Cook states that "as a Dissenter and a representative of tradesmen, Defoe stood for everything Swift found most threatening to the social order he valued" (*Jonathan Swift as a Tory Pamphleteer*, 96).

11. Defoe, *Meer Nature Delineated*, 45.

12. Katharine M. Rogers, "The Feminism of Daniel Defoe."

13. Defoe, *Conjugal Lewdness*, 47, and *Harrison's Tatler, No. 5 (PW* 2:178–83).

14. See Astell, *Some Reflections upon Marriage*; see also Makin, *An Essay to Revive the Antient Education of Gentlewomen*, and Defoe, *An Essay upon Projects*.

15. The purpose of this identification was to prevent "strolling beggars" from begging outside their own parishes. The poor at that time were considered to be the responsibility of their home parish.

16. Linda Woodbridge remarks that in early-seventeenth-century texts women who in any way challenged their traditional role were regarded as "monsters of unnaturalness" (*Women and the English Renaissance*, 145).

17. The violent images in Swift's writings may not be literally meant, but Swift once wrote to Stella that an Irish politician, Dick Tighe, "used to beat his wife here; and she deserved it" (*JS* 360). Swift doesn't specify what Mrs. Tighe did to "deserve" a beating.

CHAPTER 1

1. My discussion will refer to Esther Johnson and Esther Vanhomrigh by the names invented for them by Swift, not only because of custom but in recognition of the fact that history has been interested in these women only because of their association with Swift.

2. Swift uses monkeys both positively and negatively; on the one hand, they are parodic versions of humanity in the *Letter to a Young Lady, on Her Marriage*, where they are specifically female, and in the poetic apologia *To a Lady*, where the narrator asks (rhetorically): "Should a monkey wear a crown, / Must I tremble at his frown?" (*CP* 518). On the other hand, in the *Journal to Stella* Swift addresses the ladies affectionately as "little monkies mine" (*JS* 79) and "saucy monkies" (*JS* 296).

3. See Swift's letter to the Rev. John Kendall, Feb. 1691/92 (W 1:104).

4. Ehrenpreis, in particular, is associated with this interpretation, but his work is preceded by Evelyn Hardy: "In both cases [Stella and Vanessa] the girl, or woman, was fatherless and Swift, whose protective tender side was drawn to shield and guide her, involved her in a relationship which must be largely sterile" (*The Conjured Spirit*, 137).

5. For further discussion of Swift's mother, see Chapter 5.

6. See Swift's letter to the Rev. John Worrall, Jan. 18, 1728/29, in which he remarks of Betty Jones, "my prudent mother was afraid I should be in love with her; but when I went to London, she married an inn-keeper in Loughborow" (W 3:207).

7. W 1:127n.: "Dr. John Lyon, writing c. 1762–1765 . . . noted three further letters."

8. Thomas Sheridan to J. Oughton, Nov. 3, 1736, cited in James Woolley, "Thomas Sheridan and Swift," 94, 110n.

9. Gregory King, *Natural and Political Observations*, 88. In King's population study there is a surplus of women over men for every age group above sixteen years.

10. Cited in Hill, *Eighteenth-Century Women*, 11–12.

11. W 1:128n: The letters referred to by Dr. Lyon were dated Dec. 20, 1695, June 29, 1696, and Aug. 28, 1697.

12. And later still, about Lady Acheson: "All her spirits in a flame / When she knows she's most to blame" (*Daphne, CP* 433).

13. This explanation was advanced in the eighteenth century by George-Monck Berkeley (*Literary Relics*, xxviiii), and was revived in the twentieth century by John Middleton Murry (*Jonathan Swift*, 60).

14. Mandeville, *Treatise of the Hypochondriack and Hysterick Diseases*, 246.

15. Fraser, *The Weaker Vessel*, 3.

16. Mandeville, *Treatise of the Hypochondriack and Hysterick Diseases*, 244.

17. Le Brocquy, *Cadenus*, 36–37.

18. Jordan, *Charities of London*, 28.

19. Gregory King, *Natural and Political Observations*, 89.

20. Swift's fulminations against Varina's family, on the other hand, are similar to Pope's ongoing distress over Martha "Patty" Blount's subordination to a domineering sister. See Rumbold, *Women's Place in Pope's World*, 254–57 and passim.

21. Berkeley, *Literary Relics*, xix.

22. Ann Cline Kelly provides the most recent review of this material (*Jonathan Swift and Popular Culture*, 105–26).

23. Scott, "Memoirs of Jonathan Swift, D.D.," 2. Venturo, "Concurring Opponents," 196.

24. Orrery, *Remarks*, 84, 159.

25. Beddoes, *Hygeia*, 3:193.

26. A woman critic who also embraces this view is Sophie Shillito Smith. She believes that we cannot "blame Swift for what happened [to Vanessa] nor can he reasonably be made responsible for any part of this unfortunate episode in his life" (*Dean Swift*, 174).

27. Cited in Newman, *Jonathan Swift*, 267.

28. Patrick Delany, *Observations*, 123.

29. Davis, *Stella*, 55. Davis repeats the phrase "she failed him" on 60.

30. Johnston, *In Search of Swift*, 173.

31. Thackeray, *The English Humourists*, 40.

32. Johnston, *In Search of Swift*, 136.

33. Thackeray, *The English Humourists*, 40.

34. Ehrenpreis is the most nuanced critic in this respect; Davis, *Stella*, and Nokes, *Jonathan Swift*, are similar to Victorian admirers of Stella while rejecting the language of the earlier century. Le Brocquy, on the other hand, subjects *On the Death of Mrs. Johnson* to rewarding critical scrutiny, almost sentence by sentence, in *Swift's Most Valuable Friend*.

35. Orrery, *Remarks*, 82.

36. Orrery, *Remarks*, 159.

37. Orrery, *Remarks*, 155. Deane Swift, in *An Essay upon the Life, Writings, and Character of Dr. Jonathan Swift*, undoubtedly intended his own comment as a rejoinder: "Thus died at *Cellbridge*, worthy of a happier fate, the celebrated *Mrs. Esther Vanhomrigh*, a martyr to love and constancy" (264).

38. Crow, "Swift and the Woman Scholar," 233.

39. Swift, *Of the Education of Ladies*: "This question is generally determined in the negative by the women themselves, but almost universally by the men" (*PW* 4:225).

40. Kelly, *Jonathan Swift and Popular Culture*, 124.

41. Hill, *Women Alone*, 3.

42. Davis, *Stella*, 51.

43. Jaffe, *The Poet Swift*, 86. In her illuminating discussion, Jaffe remarks that Swift "transforms all the love motifs he uses" (88).

44. Swift's praise of Henrietta Cavendish Holles, the noblewoman who married Edward Harley, would also seem to challenge Swift's distaste for this kind of hyperbole. He does not call her a goddess in his congratulatory poem on their marriage; he says that she is equal to one goddess and superior to another: "Thus Cavendish, as Aurora bright, / And chaster than the Queen of Night" (*CP* 130).

45. Rogers's note to these lines identifies Jim as probably James Stopford and the "favourite clan" as the Grattan-Jackson cousins, "clergymen who were versifiers and punsters dear to Swift" (*CP* 729n).

46. Cf. "His beauty shall in these black lines be seen, / And they shall live, and he in them still green" (Sonnet 63, *Against my love shall be as I am now*). In reality, in most of the sonnets the poetic artifact eclipses its subject rather than serving it.

47. When Stella was dying, Swift wrote in *Holyhead*: "Absent from whom all climes are cursed, / With whom I'm happy in the worst" (*CP* 330).

48. Joseph Horrell, in Swift, *Collected Poems*, 1:394n.; Davis finds the same motive of avoiding "the possibility of offence" (*Stella*, 67).

49. See Rawson, "Rage and Raillery," for a full discussion of this aspect of the poem.

50. *Codicil to Swift's Will* (*PW* 13:198–99). The will referred to was probably destroyed although the instructions survived. Swift is buried in St. Patrick's Cathedral, Dublin.

51. Satan asserts, "Better to reign in Hell than serve in Heaven" (1:262); Achilles tells Odysseus, "Better, I say, to break sod as a farm hand / for some poor country man, on iron rations, than lord it over all the exhausted dead" (11.489–91; the translation is Robert Fitzgerald's).

52. Craig, "The Buildings," in *The Legacy of Swift*, 40.

53. Cave, "Dramatising the Life of Swift," 25.

54. Le Brocquy, *Cadenus*, 102.

55. Mahony, *Jonathan Swift*, xi, xvi, and passim.

56. Lady Wilde, *Notes on Men, Women, and Books*, 88.

57. Jameson, *Memoirs of the Loves of the Poets* [1829], 439.

CHAPTER 2

1. Real, *Securing Swift*, 109.

2. Patrick Delany, *Observations*, 57, 66, passim.

3. See *PS* 2:736 for a discussion of this attribution, which I find persuasive.

4. Dingley's reason for attaching herself to Stella, her social inferior, may require little explanation beyond her very slender means. Margaret Doody states that Dingley had only £14 a year ("Swift and Women," 96).

5. Le Brocquy, in *Swift's Most Valuable Friend* (12–20), reproduces in its entirety the anonymous letter asserting the relationship that appeared in *The Gentleman's and London Magazine* (November 1757, 487–91). Johnston (*In Search of Swift*, 114) has a lengthy discussion, culminating in the conclusion that Swift could not marry Stella because they were uncle and niece.

6. Nokes remarks that when Stella moved to Ireland she may not have known of Swift's "resolution 'not to marry a young woman'" (N 58). This was one of seventeen resolutions Swift wrote out in 1699 under the title "When I come to be old" (*PW* 1:xxxviii). It would not have applied to his life in the early part of the eighteenth century, when he was not yet old.

7. Hufton, "Women without Men," 355. See also Hill, *Women Alone*. Hill finds that in the two hundred years covered by her study, "the position of spinsters changed relatively little" (11).

8. Gillis, *For Better, For Worse*, 15. These distinctions may be seen as a subset of the increasing polarization of the "hierarchies of class and gender" described by Amussen (*An Ordered Society*, 187).

9. Lady Mary Wortley Montagu to Philippa Munday, 12 Dec. [1711], *Complete Letters* 1:112.

10. Wilkes, *Letter of Genteel and Moral Advice*, 33–34.

11. Hayley, *A Philosophical, Historical, and Moral Essay*, 3:187.

12. Hayley, *A Philosophical, Historical, and Moral Essay*, 1:37.

13. Le Brocquy, *Swift's Most Valuable Friend*, 77.

14. Such was the case with Pope's principal female friend, Martha Blount. See Rumbold, *Women's Place in Pope's World*, 256.

15. Wall, "Women Alone in English Society," 310.

16. Woolf, *Collected Essays*, 3:73.

17. Jameson, *Memoirs of the Loves of the Poets*, 437; Manch, "Jonathan Swift and Women," 205.

18. Lane-Poole in Swift, *Letters and Journals of Jonathan Swift*, 165.

19. Lecky, "Biographical Introduction," lv.

20. Maurice Johnson, *The Sin of Wit*, 49.

21. Longe, *Martha, Lady Giffard*, 226. Longe does not consider the possibility that women did not attend funerals at this time, but in any case her hypothetical is merely a specific instance of a general pattern: Stella lived her life in keeping with Swift's convenience, not vice versa.

22. Taylor, *Mark Twain's Margins*, 45.

23. Oliphant, *Historical Characters*, 99–100.

24. Woods, "Swift, Stella, and Vanessa," 1246.

25. Stella's will contained the following provision: "I desire that a decent monument of plain white marble may be fixed on the wall, over the place of my burial, not exceeding the value of twenty pounds sterling" (cited in William R. Wilde, *The Closing Years*, 97). Apparently the memorial tablet was erected not long before the year 1780 (Ball 4:462n). Wilde observes: "Both her own name and that of Steevens are misspelled in it. The precise date of its erection has not been ascertained; but it does not appear to have been set up during the Dean's lifetime" (121n).

26. Le Brocquy notes that this epitaph "annoyed the King, when it was repeated at the English Court" (*Swift's Most Valuable Friend*, 78).

27. Little more than a year later, Swift was to write of the death of William Harrison, a poet he had befriended: "No loss ever grieved me so much" (*JS* 620).

28. Stephen Karian believes that Swift was mourning Stella's death when he inscribed a verse from the *Aeneid* onto a blank page in a copy of *Verses on the Death of Dr. Swift* ("Swift's Epitaph for Stella"). Were this to be the case, and the argument is tenuous, it would hardly qualify as the public memorial Stella had in mind.

29. Connery, "Self-Representation and Memorials," 157.

30. Maynard Mack comments on Pope's addressing Patty Blount as "friend" that this is "the one word in the language that denotes relationships of equality and permanence" (*Alexander Pope*, 632).

31. Heywood, *Gynaikeion*, 6:282–83.

32. Woolley, "Friends and Enemies," 216.

33. Peake, "Swift's Birthday Verses to Stella," 176. Crow also believes that Swift was "in love with" Stella, "even against his will and his principles" ("Swift in Love," 49).

34. Hardy, *The Conjured Spirit*, 173.

35. R. Wyse Jackson refers to her as "Dear Brainless Dingley! The Fat White Woman whom Nobody Loves," but at the same time records that "any household accounts which survive are in her handwriting" (*Swift and His Circle*, 44, 47).

36. "Of the Report about Dr. Swift's Marriage," cited in Johnston, *In Search of Swift*, 164.

37. Orrery, *Remarks*, 81–84; Patrick Delany, *Observations*, 60–61; Deane Swift, *An Essay*, 92–98; Sheridan, *Life of the Rev. Dr. Jonathan Swift*, 29, 29n, 62.

38. Berkeley, *Inquiry into the Life of Dean Swift*, in *Literary Relics*, 36. William Monck Mason, whose life of Swift is part of his *History of the Collegiate and Cathedral Church of*

St. Patrick near Dublin, says of the Berkeley story that from 1716, when the ceremony was supposed to have taken place, to the time of Bishop Ashe's death the following year, Berkeley was out of Ireland and could never have received the confidence (302).

39. Johnston, *In Search of Swift*, 155.

40. Quintana, *Mind and Art*, 233.

41. Sheridan, *Life of the Rev. Dr. Jonathan Swift*, 322.

42. Sheridan, *Life of the Rev. Dr. Jonathan Swift*, 323; modern commentators have generally accepted Williams's cautious attribution of the poem "On Jealousy" to Stella (*PS* 2:736). Murry discusses Stella's jealousy of Vanessa (*Jonathan Swift*, 279–80), as does Nokes (N 217). Both believe in the secret marriage.

43. Swift to Thomas Sheridan: "I have been long weary of the World, and shall for my small Remainder of Years be weary of Life, having for ever lost that Conversation, which could only make it tolerable" (W 3:1).

44. Lady Mary Wortley Montagu was an early proponent of the impotence theory. See *Complete Letters*, 1:273–76 and 3:56, 56n.; see also Stephen, *Swift*, 140, and Powys, *Cup-Bearers*, 14. The consanguinity hypothesis rests on the idea that both Swift and Stella were natural children of members of the Temple family, and it, too, has had a long history. See note 5 above.

45. Cited in le Brocquy, *Swift's Most Valuable Friend*, 18. Bruce Arnold offers this explanation for the mysterious initials: "In a note to the first edition of his *In Search of Swift*, Johnston writes on page 19: 'Mr. R. G. Leigh, of Shankill, Co. Dublin, at one time a cryptologist in the Foreign Office, write[s] that he is satisfied that this list of consonants represents CUM PAGANUS [sic] SATANAS.'" The meaning, according to Arnold, is "I am speaking the truth while the devils are with the pagans" (Arnold, "Jonathan Swift," 44–45).

46. Krafft-Ebing, *Psychopathia Sexualis*, cited in Gold, *Swift's Marriage to Stella*, 130.

47. Freeman, *Vanessa and Her Correspondence*, 104. David Woolley's note to this letter describes Little Master as "evidently a child, unidentified" (W 2:103n).

48. Stella's will contained the following bequest: "I bequeath to Bryan McLoghlin (A child who now lives with me, and whom I keep on charity), twenty-five pounds to bind him out apprentice as my executors or the survivors of them shall think fit" (cited in William R. Wilde, *The Closing Years*, 100). Wilde is the best source for Stella's will, which is no longer extant.

49. Le Brocquy, *Cadenus*, 52.

50. Glendinning, *Jonathan Swift: A Portrait*, 195.

51. Le Brocquy notes that the twenty-five pounds bequeathed to M'Loghlin was a considerable sum of money at a time when "the fee paid to apprentice a boy was 3 pounds and a suit of clothes" (*Cadenus*, 115).

52. Essex, *The Young Ladies Conduct*, xv.

53. John Gregory, *A Father's Legacy to His Daughters*, 94.

54. Wrigley, "Marriage, Fertility, and Population Growth," 146. These data are not divided by sex.

55. Ehrenpreis, *The Lady of Letters*, 22. He comments that Swift "assembled a little, disappointing collection of her *bons mots*."

56. John Hawkesworth's description of Stella's wit reverberates ironically against this incident: her wit "was under the direction of such sweetness of temper, such general kindness, and reluctance to give pain, that she never indulged it at the expence of another" ("An Account of the Life of the Reverend *Jonathan Swift*, D.D.," in Swift, *The Works of Dr. Jonathan Swift*, ed. Hawkesworth, 1:49).

57. This idea is restated in the definition of good manners as "the Art of making those people easy with whom we converse" (*PW* 4:213).

58. Samuel Johnson, *Lives of the English Poets*, 3:42.

59. Samuel Johnson, *Lives of the English Poets*, 3:42.

60. Meynell, *Essays*, 207–8.

61. Davis, *Stella*, 51. Moreover, these recollections contain most of the surviving examples of Stella's speech.

62. *The Concise Dictionary of European Proverbs collected by Emanuel Strauss* attributes to England "Kings have long armes and rulers large reches" (249, n.1690). Cordry, *The Multicultural Dictionary of Proverbs*, identifies "Kings hae lang hands" as Scottish (147, n.10110). The saying is also found in Swift's *Thoughts on Various Subjects* (*PW* 4:246): "Kings are commonly said to have *long Hands*."

63. Patrick Delany, *Observations*, 58.

64. Patrick Delany, *Observations*, 207; Virgil, *Eclogae* 9:28: "Alas, Mantua, too too close to wretched Cremona."

65. Patrick Delany, *Observations*, 71n.

66. Patrick Delany, *Observations*, 207.

67. Sociolinguistic studies indicate that male speakers conversing with women take longer speech turns, interrupt more frequently, and are generally more assertive speakers. See Zimmerman and West, "Sex Roles, Interruptions and Silences," 105–25; Gumperz, *Discourse Strategies*, 154–55; and Graddol and Swann, *Gender Voices*, 170–72.

68. Swift, *The Correspondence of Jonathan Swift, D.D.*, ed. Ball, 4: 436n.

69. *The Anatomy of a Woman's Tongue*, 5th ed., in *The Harleian Miscellany*, 2:168–76.

70. Du Boscq, *The Compleat Woman*, 22.

71. *Miss More's Essays*, in *The Ladies Pocket Library*, 19–20; see also John Gregory, *A Father's Legacy to His Daughters* in the same volume. He advises his daughters to be "rather silent in company. . . . People of sense and discernment will never mistake such silence for dullness. One may take a share in conversation without uttering a syllable" (93).

72. See *Polite Conversation, On Good Manners and Good Breeding, Hints on Good Manners*, and *Hints towards an Essay on Conversation*, all in *PW* 4.

73. Patrick Delany, *Observations*, 75.

74. As Richard Allestree writes in the section on virgins of *The Ladies Calling*, "She that listens to any wanton Discourse has violated her ears; she that speaks any, her tongue" (161). According to Patricia Meyer Spacks, *The Ladies Calling* was widely read in the late seventeenth and early eighteenth centuries (*Gossip*, 39).

75. "The greatest number of her acquaintance was among the clergy" (*On the Death of Mrs. Johnson, PW* 5:233). That Stella's social life was focused on the church reflects not only her relationship with Swift but her status as a spinster. See Hufton, "Women Without Men," 368.

76. Gowing, *Common Bodies*, 11. Many seventeenth- and eighteenth-century texts on women express the same view. William Kenrick, in *The Whole Duty of Woman* (1753), cautions women against seeking after male knowledge. The modest woman "inquireth not after the knowledge improper for her condition" (38); James Fordyce, in *Sermons to Young Women* (1787) states, "I had rather a thousand times for a young lady carry her bashfulness too far, than pique herself on the freedom of her manners" (65).

77. Scott, "Memoirs of Jonathan Swift," 50n.

78. A comic negative view of Dingley also appears in Sheridan's poem *To the Dean of St. Patricks* (1724), where she is described as "grumbling poor complaining Dingly" (*PS* 3:1041).

79. He similarly erupts inappropriately in the *Letter to a Young Lady, on Her Marriage*. See my discussion of this text in chapter 6.

80. Swift to Miss Jane Waring, May 4, 1700: "These are the questions I have always resolved to propose to her with whom I meant to pass my life; and whenever you can heartily answer them in the affirmative, I shall be bless'd to have you in my arms, without regarding whether your person be beautiful, or your fortune large. Cleanliness in the first, and competency in the other, is all I look for" (W 1:143).

81. In this instance Swift might have been unreasonable: Lewis Mumford documents a scarcity of water among the poor in large urban centers at the beginning of the Industrial Revolution (*The City in History*, 463 and passim).

82. John Nichols first called the letters *Journal to Stella* in 1779 (*JS* ln).

83. I have followed the recent practice of restoring Swift's own name for himself, *Pdfr*, where Deane Swift had substituted *Presto*, the Duchess of Shrewsbury's nickname for Swift.

84. To a less intimate friend, the Rev. John Worrall, he wrote more circumspectly: "Upon my Advice they both came to Irel^d and have been ever since my constant Companions" (W 2:655).

85. Woolf, *Collected Essays*, 3:73.

86. DePorte, "Night Thoughts in Swift," 650.

87. Williams (*JS* 794) lists fifty-five occasions in the *Journal* when Swift dined at Mrs. Vanhomrigh's.

88. See Frederik N. Smith, "Dramatic Elements," for a discussion of Swift's ways of dramatizing the material of his letters.

89. I disagree with Downie that Swift did "his utmost to restrict references to the Vanhomrighs in general, and to Esther in particular in the *Journal to Stella*" ("'The Coffee Hessy spilt,'" 67). In the early part of the *Journal* he refers to Mrs. Vanhomrigh and her house frequently. Only later, probably when he becomes interested in Vanessa, does he cease to reveal how often he is at the Vanhomrigh house. However, any mention of Vanessa might be considered gratuitous and could have easily been avoided.

90. Cited in Downie, *Robert Harley and the Press*, 132.

91. There are many references to the ladies playing cards throughout the *Journal to Stella*. Swift himself played cards and always mentioned the amounts he won or lost.

92. Downie draws a picture of a self-deceived Swift manipulated by Harley and Bolingbroke while believing himself to be influential and independent (*Robert Harley and the Press*, 131–32 and passim).

93. With the exception of Alice Meynell, who believes that Swift loved Dingley as well as Stella. She writes, "No one else in literary history has been so defrauded of her honours. . . . Dingley's half of the tender things said to MD is equal to any whole, and takes nothing from the whole of Stella's half" (*Essays*, 201). The proof of this particular pudding is Swift's failure to maintain a close relationship with Dingley after Stella's death and his deprecation of her in letters to friends.

CHAPTER 3

1. Sybil le Brocquy attributes the failure to publish the correspondence soon after Vanessa's death to the influence of the Irish clergy, particularly Archbishop King, whose motive would have been to avoid scandal to the church (*Cadenus*, 107–8).

2. Freeman, *Vanessa and Her Correspondence*, 39. Many of the letters first appeared in Sir Walter Scott's edition of Swift's complete works (1814).

3. Freeman, *Vanessa and Her Correspondence*, 48.

4. Freeman, *Vanessa and Her Correspondence*, 43.

5. Le Brocquy, *Cadenus*, 89. She refers to *Swift to Miss Esther Vanhomrigh*, Aug. 7, 1722 (W 2:430). See also *Swift to Miss Esther Vanhomrigh*, Jun. 1, 1722 (W 2:421), telling Vanessa that his travels so far had been miserable: "It would have been infinitely better once a week to have met Kendall, and so forth, where one might pass 3 or 4 hours in drinking Coffee in the morning, or dining tête à tête, and drinking Coffee again till 7."

6. Patrick Delany, *Observations*, 123.

7. Acworth, *Swift*, 92.

8. Masson, *The Three Devils*, 267.

9. Howard Williams, *English Letters and Letter-Writers*, 170n.

10. Woods, "Swift, Stella, and Vanessa," 1239–40.

11. Alyse Gregory, "Stella, Vanessa, and Swift," 759.

12. This was not an unreasonable fear. An anonymous pamphlet, published under the title *Dr. S——'s Real Diary* and other titles (London and Dublin: 1715) could only have been written by someone who had seen at least one of the letters now collected as the *Journal to Stella*.

13. This would be even more the case if *Cadenus* is not an anagram for *Decanus* but, as le Brocquy has ingeniously argued, an anagram for "*Cad Es Vn*," meaning "*the familiar spirit of Esther Van (Homrigh)*" (*Cadenus*, 156). Swift wrote in a 1726 letter to Thomas Tickell that the poem had been written fourteen years before, that is, in 1712, before he had been appointed dean (W 2:649). Swift is not totally reliable on dates, however.

14. The original reads: "soyez assurè que jamais personne du monde a etè [plus] aimee honoreè estimeè adoreè par votre amie que vous" (W 2:386).

15. I agree with Nokes that the coffee references "do not refer to intercourse, but rather to a special sexually-charged sense of intimacy" (N 258); however, I do not agree that this "originated at their first meeting at Dunstable when Vanessa spilt some coffee." The sense of intimacy develops later.

16. Margaret Doody reaches a different conclusion. She believes that letters between Swift and Vanessa "are undeniably the letters between lovers who have consummated their relationship" ("Swift and Women," 104).

17. P. V. and D. J. Thompson in Swift, *The Account Books of Jonathan Swift*, xli.

18. Doody, "Swift Among the Women," 22.

19. Or so many biographers have believed on the evidence of Vanessa's will, which makes no mention of him, and her instructions to her executors to publish both the poem and her correspondence with Swift, actions she knew would embarrass him severely. See Swift, *The Correspondence of Jonathan Swift, D. D.*, ed. F. Elrington Ball, 3:462, and Nokes (N 263–64). Ehrenpreis disagrees (E 3:388–89).

20. In neither of the letters that mention *Cadenus and Vanessa* does Swift use its title.

21. Scott, "Memoirs of Jonathan Swift, D.D.," 231.

22. The next-to-last letter, dated July 13, 1722, also mentions the questions: "I can sincerely answer all your Questions, as I used to do" (W 2:425).

23. Deane Swift, *An Essay*, 263–64.

24. Mitford in Swift, *The Poetical Works of Jonathan Swift with a Memoir by the Rev. John Mitford*, lxxi. Stella, too, rejected her clergyman suitor. The higher ranks of Vanessa's suitors correspond to her higher social class. She had a fortune of £5,000, as Swift remarks in *Cadenus and Vanessa*: "Five thousand guineas in her purse: / The doctor might have fancied worse. . .' (*CP* 147).

25. Swift described the approaching loss of Stella to Sheridan as the loss of "that Conversation which could only make it [life] tolerable" (W 3:2).

26. Sophie Shillitoe Smith, *Dean Swift*, 260–61.

27. Hardy, *The Conjured Spirit*, 151.

CHAPTER 4

1. Orrery, *Remarks*, 168. This image is echoed at the end of the nineteenth century by Leslie Stephen, who refers to Swift as "this self-appointed sultan" (*Swift*, 121–22).

2. Montagu, *Complete Letters*, 3:56n.

3. Montagu, *Complete Letters*, 1:158.

4. Orrery never overcame his father's distrust, as is symbolized by the father's leaving his valuable library to his alma mater rather than to his son. See Fróes's introduction to Orrery, *Remarks*, 14–18. For Lady Mary, see Halsband's introduction to her *Complete Letters*, xiii–xvii.

5. Rumbold, *Women's Place in Pope's World*, 134.

6. Montagu to Lady Bute, Jan. 28 [1753], *Complete Letters*, 3:22.

7. These five exist only as Swift's preserved drafts (W 3:325n).

8. Alice Anderson Hufstader remarks the "numerous ladies who were flattered to be taken in hand by so truculent a tutor" (*Sisters of the Quill*, 157).

9. Doody, "Swift Among the Women," cited here in *Critical Essays on Jonathan Swift*, ed. Frank Palmeri (New York: G. K. Hall, 1993), 13–37.

10. Graddol and Swann, *Gender Voices*, 171.

11. Bourdieu, "The Economics of Linguistic Exchange," 646.

12. As a man of thirty-two, Swift wrote a series of resolutions titled "When I come to be old" that reveal his awareness of his predilection for young women. The very first resolution is "not to marry a young woman." Another is "not to keep young company unless they really desire it." And still another is a partial recasting of the first: "Not to hearken to flatteries, nor conceive I can be beloved by a young woman" (*PW* 1:xxxvii); cf. chapter 2, n. 6.

13. Patrick Delany, *Observations*, 218. See Brathwait, *The English Gentlewoman*, 41: "What is spoken of Maids, may be properly applyed by an usefull consequence to all women: *They should be seene, and not heard.*" James Fordyce, whose *Sermons to Young Women* were reprinted numerous times beginning in 1766, offered women the following advice: "Your business chiefly is to read Men, in order to make yourselves agreeable and useful" (162).

14. Pilkington, in her *Memoirs* (passim), has left the fullest account of the elderly dean playing this role.

15. Orrery, *Remarks*, 168.

16. *Boutade*, according to the *OED*, means "a sally, a sudden outburst or outbreak." The first citation for this definition is Bacon, 1614, but the list also includes Swift's *A Tale of a Tub* (1704) 4:67: "His first boutade was to kick both their wives . . . out of doors." The meaning in eighteenth-century French is somewhat different: "a caprice or sally of wit and humor" (*Dictionnaire de L'Académie Française*, Quatrième Édition, 1762).

17. Mary Delany, *Autobiography and Correspondence*, 1:602.

18. In this same time period Swift also expressed to Pope the idea of finding a substitute for a dear one. He wrote, "I am told poor Mrs. Pope is ill: Pray God preserve her to you, or raise you up as useful a friend" (W 3:213).

19. See Rawson, "Rage and Raillery"; he refers to "a simpering note of self-exculpation" and "a fond self-praise" in the characterization of Cadenus (187, 189).

20. *To Dean Swift*, By Sir Arthur Acheson (*CP* 377–78). Both recent editors of Swift's poems, Sir Harold Williams and Pat Rogers, agree that the poem was certainly the work of Swift himself (*PS* 3:876 and *CP* 793n).

21. See Barnett, *Swift's Poetic Worlds*, 45–111, for a discussion of Swift's poetic acts of self-representation. The Market Hill poems are treated on pages 57–67.

22. Orrery annotated his copy of *Death and Daphne* with the identification, "Lady Acheson, wife of Sir Arthur Acheson. Separated from her husband." Rogers comments that the Achesons were never "formally separated" (*CP* 819–20n).

23. Williams remarks that Orrery identified Daphne as Lady Acheson in an annotated copy of his *Remarks* in the Harvard College Library, MS Eng. 218.14 (*PS* 3:902). Rogers agrees: "There can be no doubt that this identification is the right one" (*CP* 820n).

24. Jaffe, "Swift and the 'agreeable young Lady,'" 134.

25. Jaffe, "Swift and the 'agreeable young Lady,'" 136.

26. Williams suggests that the poem was begun during the Market Hill period, laid aside, and completed in 1732–3 (*PS* 2:629). Apart from internal evidence, this is a plausible hypothesis if only because it seems unlikely that Swift would adduce the Market Hill relationship with Lady Acheson several years after his visits there ended.

27. For a discussion of Swift's satiric theory and practice in the poem, see Barnett, "Swift's Satiric Violence."

28. Mueller, "Imperfect Enjoyment at Market Hill," 53–54. Mueller argues that "Swift's impotent discourse proves to be a means of both domination and self-replication" (62).

29. Mueller, "Imperfect Enjoyment at Market Hill," 60.

30. This is the opinion of Pilkington's most recent editor, A. C. Elias, Jr. (P 1:xix). Harold Williams believes that "if some vivid colouring be removed the essential truthfulness of her picture remains" ("Swift's Early Biographers," 117). Elias remarks that Pilkington's Swift anecdotes are more reliable in volume 1 than in volume 3 ("Laetitia Pilkington on Swift," 133–37 and passim).

31. When Mary Pendarves arrived in Ireland in October of 1731, she described Pilkington as "a bosom friend of Dean Swift's" (Mary Delany, *Autobiography and Correspondence*, 3:301).

32. Doody, "Swift Among the Women," 17.

33. Tucker, *The Poetry of Laetitia Pilkington (1712–1750) and Constantia Grierson (1706–1733)*, 79–80. Further citations of Pilkington's poetry in the text will be to this edition.

34. Woolf, *The Common Reader*, 170.

35. Cited Stauffer, *The Art of Biography*, 103.

36. This attitude persists. Wayne Shumacker remarks that "Laetitia Pilkington and a few other vituperative women do their malicious best to bring their husbands into disrepute" (*English Autobiography*, 42).

37. Cibber's generous help to Pilkington is in ironic contrast to his treatment of his daughter, who, in circumstances similar to Pilkington's, wrote her own autobiography, *A Narrative of the Life of Mrs. Charlotte Charke* [1755].

38. Woolf, *The Common Reader*, 169. More recent women critics have also emphasized Pilkington's self-creation through writing. See Relke, "In Search of Mrs. Pilkington," 123; Turner, *Living by the Pen*, passim; and Spacks, *Imagining a Self*, who says of Pilkington, "Her prose converts her into a person of significance, defending her against the world's reluctance to take her seriously" (16). Susan Golding, in "Claiming the 'Sacred Mantle,'" describes Pilkington as "a nearly paradoxical combination of satirized writer trying to strike back and literary descendant trying to inherit 'the mantle'" (62).

39. Jelinek, *The Tradition of Women's Autobiography*, 35.

40. Claudia N. Thomas sees Pilkington as an early emulator of Pope who, as an adult, "discovered that while a girl might be caressed for precocity resembling Pope's, a woman had little chance of emulating his career" (*Alexander Pope*, 106).

41. Jerrold, *Five Queer Women*, 277.

42. Swift, Preface to *Poems on Several Occasions* (1734) in *BP*, 40.

43. Boswell, *Boswell's Life of Johnson*, 1:463. In "Thoughts on Various Subjects," Swift wrote in a similar vein, although evidently not for publication, that "a very little Wit is valued in a Woman; as we are pleased with a few Words spoken plain by a Parrot" (*PW* 4:247).

44. Piozzi, *Retrospection*, 2:352.

45. *Docile* here probably retains its more literal meaning of "teachable" rather than our modern sense of easily led or compliant.

46. Lonsdale, *Eighteenth-Century Women Poets*, 118.

47. Swift may have been unfair to Suffolk, since most historians agree that she had no influence whatsoever at court—and was disvalued accordingly. As Lord Hervey wrote of her in his *Memoirs of the Reign of George the Second*, "A mistress who could not get power was not a much more agreeable or respectable character than a minister who could not keep it" (1:53).

48. Sundon, *Memoirs*, 2:62, 69.

49. Sundon, *Memoirs*, 2:68.

50. The mystery of who wrote the letters appears never to have been solved. Barber was certainly the most likely suspect as the person having something to gain from it, but another possibility might be someone who wanted to embarrass Swift.

51. Mary Delany, *Autobiography and Correspondence*, 1:330, 407, 432, 554; 3:206.

52. She repeated this sentiment after her visit to Bath was over, writing to Swift, "I had more pleasure in her conversation than from any thing I met with at the Bath" (*C* 4:475).

53. In this list of "Swift's Friends Classed by their Character" (*C* 5:270–71) there are only two women, Mrs. Barber and Queen [Caroline]. The latter is among the ungrateful.

54. Tucker in *BP*, 30.

55. Krupat, "The Dialogic of Silko's 'Storyteller,'" 56–57.

56. Hibbert, *George III*, 182.

57. Mary Delany, *Autobiography and Correspondence*, 1:396–97.

58. Mary Delany, *Autobiography and Correspondence*, 1:407, 402, 396.

59. Dewes, *Mrs. Delany*, 203.

60. Cited in Reynolds, *The Learned Lady in England*, 362.

61. Burney, *Diary and Letters*, 1:461.

62. See Curran, *Dublin Decorative Plasterwork*, 21–23.

63. Hayden, *Mrs. Delany and Her Flower Collages*, 133. Today these extraordinary creations are in the British Museum.

64. Burney, *Diary and Letters*, 160.

65. Darwin, *The Botanic Garden*, 155–64.

66. Darwin, *The Botanic Garden*, 156n.

67. Cited in Wheeler, *Famous Blue-Stockings*, 80.

68. Mary Delany, *Autobiography and Correspondence*, 2:28.

69. Mary Delany, *Autobiography and Correspondence*, 1:333.

70. Mary Delany, *Autobiography and Correspondence*, 1:165.

71. Mary Delany, *Autobiography and Correspondence*, 2:333.

72. Cited in Hayden, *Mrs. Delany and her Flower Collages*, 39.

73. A record of her friendship with both Barber and Elstob can be found in her correspondence (Barber: *Autobiography* 1.330–31, 407, 432, and passim; Elstob: *Autobiography* 2:261–64, and passim). Pendarves's friendship with Barber continued until the latter's death in 1755.

74. Cited in Wheeler, *Famous Blue-Stockings*, 103.

75. Cited in Wheeler, *Famous Blue-Stockings*, 96.

76. I am grateful to Robert J. Barnett, Jr. for this translation and for pointing out the correct citation of this passage, given erroneously in the *Correspondence* as *Odes* 3.4.13. Swift's comment that he would have translated the lines "but my rhyming is fled with my health" recapitulates the letter's opening declaration that he has "grown sickly, weak, lean, forgetful, peevish, spiritless" (*C* 4:299, 297).

PART 2

1. In *The Lady's Dressing Room*, Strephon's motive for violating Celia's private space is never given.

2. Mary Delany, *Autobiography and Correspondence*, 1:525.

CHAPTER 5

1. Ehrenpreis comments about this text, "One remains startled to see Swift ignoring the duties of motherhood" (E 3:401).

2. See Swift's *A Proposal for Giving Badges to the Beggars*, in which he describes beggars who are not native to Dublin as "fitter to be rooted out off the Face of the Earth, than suffered to levy a vast annual Tax upon the City" (*PW* 13:139). As Claude Rawson remarks, "It was not unprecedented for writers on Irish affairs to toy more or less ambiguously with notions of large-scale extermination" (*Order from Confusion Sprung*, 144n).

3. Rawson, *God, Gulliver, and Genocide*, 230.

4. Defoe, *Some Considerations upon Street-Walkers with A Proposal for lessening the present Number of them* (1726), cited in Vivien Jones, *Women in the Eighteenth Century*, 70; see also Defoe's *Conjugal Lewdness*, 130, 230.

5. Flynn, *The Body in Swift and Defoe*, 40.

6. *A Vindication of the Rights of Woman*, in Wollstonecraft, *Works*, 5:217.

7. "A Physician," *The Pleasures of Conjugal Love Explained* (1740), in Vivien Jones, *Women in the Eighteenth Century*, 82.

8. Ellen Pollak, in *The Poetics of Sexual Myth: Gender and Ideology in the Verse of Swift and Pope*, does not treat maternity in either writer.

9. See Rumbold, *Women's Place in Pope's World*, 13. Noting Pope's love of tranquillity, Rumbold reflects that "it is hardly surprising that the women Pope loved best had either completed their families or never had children at all."

10. *An Epistle from Mr. Pope, to Dr. Arbuthnot*, in Pope, *Poems*, 612.

11. Mack, *Alexander Pope*, 366. Mack remarks that Pope's "consciousness of loss was acute" (547). When Swift's mother died, he made a brief comment in his account book and with this closed the subject.

12. See Chapter 2, for a discussion of Swift's efforts to memorialize various people.

13. Doody, "Swift Among the Women," 20.

14. Katharine M. Rogers notes that "hostile descriptions of motherhood . . . run through Swift's work" and that his "references to nurses are also invariably unpleasant" (*The Troublesome Helpmate*, 170, 170n).

15. John Nichols, in a note to Thomas Sheridan's *Life of Jonathan Swift, D. D.* [1784], maintains that Swift "retained his affection for Whitehaven to the last, as if it were his native place" (in Swift, *The Works of the Rev. Jonathan Swift, D. D.*, ed. Nichols, 10:80n). Having left at the age of four, Swift could have had only the sketchiest memory of Whitehaven. What must have remained instead was a positive emotion, associated more with the nurse than the place.

16. Abigail Swift's removal from Ireland to England is made more of a mystery by Ehrenpreis ("Appendix C: Swift's Maternal Grandfather," E 1:270), who believes that Abigail was born in Dublin in 1640 and had no personal ties with Leicestershire as her son stated in his autobiographical fragment, *Family of Swift* (*PW* 5:187–95). Since the cost of living was cheaper in Ireland and the young widow had limited means, there must have been some compelling reason for her to resettle herself and her young daughter in an unfamiliar place.

17. Johnston, *In Search of Swift*, 79.

18. In *The Works of Jonathan Swift, D.D.*, ed. Nichols, 10:105n; Patrick Delany, *Observations*, 72.

19. Thompson in Swift, *The Account Books of Jonathan Swift*, lv. Further, the list of letters in Swift's account book for 1708 and 1709, the only one mentioning his mother by name, "shows that they wrote each other once a month until the end of April."

20. Thompson in Swift, *Account Books*, lv.

21. Patrick Delany, *Observations*, 75.

22. Ehrenpreis asserts that in spite of her return to England, leaving him behind, "Swift continued to regard his mother with undiminished affection and respect" (*Personality of Swift*, 12). In the first volume of his biography, however, he admits that no direct evidence of Swift's attitude toward his mother exists except for the note on her death, where he finds that Swift's "affection and respect for Abigail Swift are delivered with intense feeling" (1:28–29).

23. Doody, "Swift and Women," 90; see also Nokes: "The evidence suggested that she neglected him in an age where neglect of children was not the invariable rule that has sometimes been claimed" (N 9).

24. Ehrenpreis, *Personality of Swift*, 12.

25. Nichols in Swift, *The Works of the Rev. Jonathan Swift*, 10:105.

26. Nichols in Swift, *The Works of the Rev. Jonathan Swift*, 10:105.

27. Bacon, "Of Married and Single Life," *Essayes*, 24–25.

28. These are matters that Swift routinely remarks on in the *Journal to Stella*, seldom mentioning a marriage without referring to the couple's antecedents and fortunes. His comment on the marriage of Lord Raby to the daughter of Sir H. Johnson is typical: "He has threescore thousand pounds with her, ready money; besides the rest at the father's death" (*JS* 351). See also his letter to Jane Waring (Varina) in which, after much talk of their respective fortunes, he asks, "Are you in a condition to manage domestic affairs, with an income of less (perhaps) than three hundred pounds a year?" (W 1:142).

29. Bowers, *Politics of Motherhood*, 22.

30. Alex. Niccholes, *A Discourse of Marriage and Wiving, & of the greatest Mystery therein contained: How to chuse a good Wife from a bad* (1615), in *The Harleian Miscellany*, 2:155–61, has a chapter on this subject.

31. Crawford, "The Construction and Experience of Maternity," 8.

32. Niccholes, *A Discourse of Marriage and Wiving*, in *Harleian Miscellany*, 2:146.

33. Niccholes, *A Discourse of Marriage and Wiving*, in *Harleian Miscellany*, 2:145.

34. Gataker, *A Good Wife Gods Gift*, 35, 34.

35. 1 Timothy 2:15, *King James Bible*.

36. Timothy Rogers, *The Character of a Good Woman*, 28.

37. Cf. Niccholes's advice not to choose a wife who is "too dwarfish a Size and Kindred to store thee with a Generation of Pigmies, Dwarfs, Half-men, that want the Majesty and Power of Height and Strength, and the Comeliness a good Stature is, for the most Part, wedded unto" (*Harleian Miscellany*, 2:147).

38. Susan Gubar, in "The Female Monster in Augustan Satire," notes the resemblance of this figure to other "negative emblem[s] of motherhood," Spenser's Error in *The Faerie*

Queene and Milton's Sin in *Paradise Lost*. Terry Castle comments: "One could hardly ask for a more flagrant image of a threatening gynocriticism" ("Women and Literary Criticism," in *Boss Ladies, Watch Out!*, 6).

39. Gulliver himself briefly adopts a quasi-maternal posture toward a three-year-old male Yahoo whom he catches and tries to quiet. In infant fashion the child wets Gulliver's clothes and wriggles free, earning the epithet of "odious Vermin" (*PW* 11:265–66).

40. See, in particular, Swift's comments about nurses in *Directions to Servants* (*PW* 13:64); cf. note 14.

41. See Rawson, *God, Gulliver, and Genocide*, chapter 2, especially 92–108, for a discussion of this image.

42. Boucé, "The Rape of Gulliver Reconsidered," 103.

43. Boucé is quite ingenious in suggesting possible couplings of Gulliver, both with the Lilliputian lady who fancies him and the maids of honor (102–3). He speculates that "if Gulliver may be placed astride the maid of honour's nipple, it is not inconceivable he may likewise be positioned on her erect clitoris, and stimulate it into orgasm" (103).

44. Rawson, *God, Gulliver, and Genocide*, 178.

45. In another example Rawson cites, the flayed woman and the dissected beau of *A Tale of a Tub* (*PW* 1:109), there is something closer to parity (*God, Gulliver, and Genocide*, 180). Nevertheless, the effect of *flay'd* is stronger than *stript*, even if in the context the two terms refer to the same thing.

46. Crook, *A Preface to Swift*, 139.

47. According to Gabrielle Palmer, "public suckling was accepted" (*Politics of Breastfeeding*, 123), yet Swift, with his fastidiousness about the female body, might well have been repulsed by it.

48. Ruth Perry observes that "the breast seems to have represented for eighteenth-century women the mutually exclusive nature of motherhood and sexual desire.... Either a woman sent away her children to nurse ... and resumed her earlier social and sexual identity, or she gave herself over to the business of mothering" ("Colonizing the Breast," 228–29). Patricia Crawford, in "The Sucking Child," writes that "men were in general unwilling to forego sexual pleasure for the sake of the relationship of mother and child" (30). Pier Paolo Viazzo also suggests that breast-feeding was "a chore which to many appeared animal-like and disgusting" ("Mortality, Fertility, and Family," 168). For further explanations, see Palmer, *Politics of Breastfeeding*, 123–27. I am indebted to Birgit Pretzsch for the insight that men might have been repulsed by leaky breasts.

49. Valerie Fildes states that "in England, wet nursing reached its height in the seventeenth and early-eighteenth centuries" (*Wet Nursing*, 79).

50. Steele, in *The Ladies Library*, 157.

51. Fildes, *Breasts, Bottles and Babies*, 98. These adjurations increased during the course of the century.

52. The anonymous writer of *The Parliament of Women* (1684), a satire on women, concludes his indictment with the invention of a *Projector* who "had found a way to make the men give Suck ... which would be a great ease to the Women, and take a World of trouble off their Hands" (140).

53. Flynn, *The Body in Swift and Defoe*, 102.

54. Gowing, *Common Bodies*, 52.

55. Yalom, *A History of the Breast*, 5.

56. See my discussion of *The Last Speech and Dying Words of Ebenezor Elliston* and similar examples in the conclusion.

57. Bowers points out that Anne chose as the text of her coronation sermon Isaiah 49:23, "Kings shall be thy nursing-fathers, and their queens thy nursing-mothers," as a

move from "literal to symbolic motherhood to engender royal authority" (*Politics of Motherhood*, 50).

58. Linda A. Pollock, *Forgotten Children*, 124–42. Pollock reports that the high rate of infant mortality seems to have increased parental anxiety over their children's illness, while the death of a child produced a "searing grief" (127, 133, 137). Roy Porter and Dorothy Porter, in *In Sickness and in Health*, write: "The fact that life was so precarious for babies did not preclude the most intense affections being lavished upon them: maybe the reverse" (78). See also Hufton, *The Prospect Before Her*, 209–10.

59. William Makepeace Thackeray remarks that "even more contemptible in his eyes than a lord's chaplain, is a poor curate with a large family" (*The English Humourists*, 31).

60. *Journal to Stella*, ed. Scott, 441n.

61. Thackeray, *The English Humourists*, 32n. Angus McInnes believes that Masham was less important than Swift thought: "Harley had already won the Queen's good opinion, and Abigail Hill was simply an additional channel" (*Robert Harley*, 100).

62. Allestree, *The Ladies Calling, Part II*, 205–6. A passage from *The Ladies Library* has almost identical wording: "The doating affection of the *Mother* is frequently punish'd with the untimely Death of the *Children*; or if not with that, 'tis many Times with a severer Scourge, they live *to grieve her Eyes & to consume heart* to be ruinous to themselves, and Afflictions to their Friends, and to force their unhappy *Mothers* to that sad Exclamation, *blessed are the Wombs which bare not*" (II:189). Kenrick, *The Whole Duty of a Woman*, 72, is even more absolute in its warning to mothers: "Dote not on the idol of thy womb, for the extreme fondness of a mother is as dangerous as the violence of her hate. Thy darling shall be taken from thee in the excess of thy love; or if it lives, it shall grieve thine eye and consume thine heart, it shall bring a curse upon thee, and not a blessing."

63. A similar comparison can be made between Swift's letters to Mrs. Whiteway on the death of her eldest son (*C* 4:460–61, 463–64) and Thomas Sheridan's to Swift on the same subject (*C* 4:464). Sheridan writes: "God Almighty support his poor mother; for none else can give her consolation under such a dreadful affliction."

64. Ehrenpreis remarks that Swift "knows that she [Stella] agrees with him that Mrs. Walls shows no dedication to motherhood and already has a bigger family than she can look after" (*The Lady of Letters*, 21).

65. Pilkington relates that Swift's housekeeper, Mrs. Brent, told her that when he avoided having to take a coach, "the Money a Coach would have cost him, he gave to a poor Man" (P 36).

66. This is a reference to the first child being male.

67. This concern is to be found throughout *A Proposal for Giving Badges to the Beggars* (*PW* 13:127–40) and *A Modest Proposal* (*PW* 12:107–18).

68. Ehrenpreis remarks "the theme of motherhood" in the essay, which he ascribes rather implausibly to "an unconscious preoccupation with Stella's failure to marry and have children" (E 3:630).

69. Flynn, *The Body in Swift and Defoe*, 164–65.

70. Francus, "'A-Killing Their Children With Safety,'" 276.

71. In his unsparing attention to dehumanizing detail, the modest proposer is a forerunner of the Nazis, who documented their real-life cruelty to mothers and children so efficiently, so bureaucratically, and so unapologetically.

72. For a reprise of contemporary sources for this idea see Wittkowsky, "Swift's *Modest Proposal*," 78 and passim; see also Landa, "*A Modest Proposal* and Populousness," and Appleby, *Economic Thought and Ideology*.

73. Locke, *Two Treatises of Government*, 2:42.

74. Other restatements of this idea occur throughout Swift's Irish Tracts of the 1720s and 30s. See *PW* 12:22, 66, 90, 136.

75. Cited in Wittkowski, "Swift's *Modest Proposal*," 104.

76. "Persons of Quality" in Lilliput appropriate a suitable amount of money for each child, and "these Funds are always managed with good Husbandry, and the most exact Justice" (*PW* 11:63).

77. The Earl of Nottingham had thirty children by his second wife, of whom ten died young and seven were stillborn (*JS* 2:397n). Paula R. Backscheider notes that Defoe's wife had seventeen children in nineteen years, only three of whom lived beyond infancy (*Daniel Defoe*, 500). Roy Porter observes that "up to one in five babies died in their first year; perhaps one in three infants died—of various fevers—before the age of five" (*English Society in the Eighteenth Century*, 27).

CHAPTER 6

1. Essex, *The Young Ladies Conduct*, 107.

2. Higgins, "The Reactions of Women," 178.

3. For a full discussion of male authority over the property of wives, see Staves, *Married Women's Separate Property*.

4. McKeon, "Historicizing Patriarchy," 300. See also Ezell, *The Patriarch's Wife*, especially chapter 5.

5. Noddings, *Women and Evil*, 61–62.

6. Overbury, *Miscellaneous Works*, xxxvii.

7. Gataker, *A Good Wife Gods Gift*, 57. Gataker's sermon conveys that "House or Inheritance" were the usual motivations for marriage. Swift in his resolutions "When I come to be old" (1699) vows not to marry a young woman and, continuing in Latin, "to hate and shun those who pursue an inheritance" (*PW* 1:xxxvii).

8. Niccholes, *A Discourse of Marriage and Wiving*, in *The Harleian Miscellany*, 2:143.

9. Whately, *Bride-Bush*, 60.

10. Tertullian, *De Cultu Feminarum* 1.1, cited in Ruether, *Religion and Sexism*, 157.

11. Brinsley, *A Looking-Glasse for Good Women*, 7.

12. Niccholes, *A Discourse of Marriage and Wiving*, in *The Harleian Miscellany*, 2:156.

13. *A Dialogue Concerning Women*, 20.

14. Heywood, *Gynaikeion*, 3:120.

15. Rogers believes that the spots are "pock-marks" or perhaps "an excess of patches (beauty-spots)" (*CP* 826n). I think they are more apt to be freckles, since the same kind of complexion that produces a freckled neck is likely to produce a freckled face. The analogy with the leopard's spots would thus be more accurate.

16. The *OED* has no definition that corresponds to that of Rogers: "a girl who is common and rather loose, but not actually a prostitute" (*CP* 826n).

17. George P. Mayhew notes that Swift visited John Rochefort almost annually between 1715 and 1721 (*Rage or Raillery*, 47).

18. Nancy Armstrong erroneously describes Swift as one of many writers who "tried their hands at writing conduct books for women" (*Desire and Domestic Fictions*, 65). Swift's *Letter* was intended to be a private communication to an individual and was never published by him.

19. *Swift's Autograph MSS 1723*. HM1599, Huntington Library.

20. See Haraway, *Primate Visions*, for a discussion of the questionable status of women as fully human. Simone de Beauvoir argues that men view women as a "hybrid, midway

between the human which man is and the natural world which he is not" (cited in Barnes, "Simone de Beauvoir and Later Feminism," 11).

21. In particular, Chapone, *Letter to a New-Married Lady*, 109, and More, *On Conversation*, in *The Lady's Pocket Library*, 19.

22. Although it may follow naturally from Swift's relegation of women to another species. See the Marchioness de Lambert's *Advice of a Mother to her Daughter* (first translated into English in 1722), cited in Vivien Jones, "The Seductions of Conduct," 129. The text begins: "The world has in all ages been very negligent in the education of daughters . . . as if the women were a distinct species." George Savile refers to women who talk impertinently as "chattering Monkeys" (Halifax, *The Lady's New-years Gift*, 106).

23. Laqueur, *Making Sex*, 4.

24. Laqueur, *Making Sex*, 62.

25. Hill, *Women Alone*, 82.

26. Cf. Heywood, *Gynaikeion*, 4:164: "Alas, how swiftlie doth Age with wrinkles steale upon you, and then where is that admiration it [beauty] before attracted."

27. Mary Wollstonecraft regards the education of women as a step toward their participation in public life (*A Vindication of the Rights of Woman*, in *Works*, 5:218–19). For a reading of Swift's and Wollstonecraft's similarities in this area, see Venturo, "Concurring Opponents." More radically, Anne Ingram, Viscountess Irwin, saw nurture, rather than nature, as all-powerful:

> In education all the difference lies;
> Women, if taught, would be as bold and wise
> As haughty men, improved by art and rules.
> (*An Epistle to Mr. Pope*, 745, lines 3–35)

28. Defoe, *An Essay upon Projects*, 112. James Sutherland comments that "to his contemporaries his Academy for Women probably seemed the wildest of all his projects" (*Defoe*, 55).

29. Backscheider, *Daniel Defoe*, 501–2.

30. Montagu, letter of March 6 [1753], *Complete Letters*, 3:25. Lady Mary made a number of such bitter comments, among them: "[There is] hardly a character in the World more despicable or more liable to universal ridicule than that of a Learned Woman" (1:45).

31. Fénelon, *Instructions for the Education of a Daughter*, 6, 2–3.

32. Defoe, *The Complete English Tradesman*, 367.

33. Stone, *The Family, Sex, and Marriage*, 136 and passim. Milton frequently expresses similar views in his divorce tracts when he argues against a narrow definition of marriage in terms of sexuality and reproduction. In *The Doctrine and Discipline of Divorce* he writes, "In Gods intention a meet and happy conversation is the chiefest and the noblest end of marriage" (8).

34. Perry, "Colonizing the Breast," 215–16.

35. Swift was hardly alone in his exasperation with such women. The popular eighteenth-century clergyman James Fordyce, whose *Sermons to Young Women* went through many editions, complained that "we are never safe in the company of a critic" (116). He went on to characterize the speech of a group of impertinent ladies as "the noisy, empty, trivial chatter of everlasting folly—it is too much for human patience to sustain" (119).

36. See *A Proposal for giving Badges to Beggars, April 22, 1737* (*PW* 13:127–40).

37. Cited in Fletcher, *Gender, Sex and Subordination*, 415–16.

38. Swetnam, *The Araignment*, 210.

39. Lawrence E. Klein critiques the idea that space was gendered in an absolute sense, associating women completely with the domestic sphere: "Women were found in all sorts of places that . . . were public" ("Gender and the Public/Private Distinction," 103). He also notes that "the degree to which in practice families actually adhered to 'separate spheres' ideology remains the subject of much debate" (101). This is a useful warning in terms of eighteenth-century society; Swift, however, seems committed to the traditional view.

40. See Margaret King, "Book-lined Cells," 66: "Not quite male, not quite female, learned women belonged to a third amorphous sex."

41. Later in the century, Dr. Johnson has a similar, albeit milder, fantasy about women who break a social rule: "Were a woman sitting in company to put out her legs before her as most men do, we should be tempted to kick them in" (Boswell, *Life of Johnson*, 53–54). Johnson would probably not have given in to such a temptation; he would have made a tart remark instead. Roy Porter reminds us that in Swift's time "criminals were publicly whipped, pilloried, and hanged. . . . People were not squeamish about inflicting or bearing physical pain" (*English Society in the Eighteenth Century*, 31).

42. Richardson, *Pamela*, 4:294. Pamela does go on to say, "I ought to beg pardon for this my presumption, for two reasons. First, Because of the truly admirable talents of this writer; and, next, Because we know not what ladies the ingenious gentleman may have fallen among in his younger days."

43. Jerome, Ep. 117. The translation is by F. A. Wright (*Select Letters of St. Jerome*, 387, 389).

44. Karen Armstrong, *The Gospel According to Woman*, 67.

45. Anne Finch, "The Introduction," ll. 9–15.

46. Phillips, *Swiftiana*, 2:2. Harold Williams describes these verses along with others as "attributed to Swift with slender justification" (*PS* 3:1145). Unlike the other examples from *Swiftiana*, this one sounds very much like Swift.

47. Gataker, *A Good Wife Gods Gift*, 23.

48. This is the second definition, after "prostitute," given by the *OED*.

49. Christine Rees provides the useful datum that the tulip is regarded as "the harlot of the garden" ("Gay, Swift, and the Nymphs of Drury-Lane," 16).

50. Gowing, *Common Bodies*, 32.

51. Concern over such unsanctioned unions culminated in the controversial 1753 Marriage Act, which required that those under the age of twenty-one have parental consent to marry. See Outhwaite, *Clandestine Marriage in England*, for a full discussion.

52. Daniel Rogers, *Matrimoniall Honour*, 83.

53. Daniel Rogers, *Matrimoniall Honour*, 88.

54. Scott, "Memoirs of Jonathan Swift, D.D.," 45n.

55. Trumbach, *Rise of the Egalitarian Family*, 97.

56. Outhwaite notes that "opposition to private marriages came from many quarters" (*Clandestine Marriage in England*, 51).

57. Trumbach, *Rise of the Egalitarian Family*, 101.

58. Such a position was hardly unique to Swift. Mary Astell wrote of a socially inferior husband that his attractions could hardly compensate for "all the advantages" a woman of quality would have to renounce on his account (*Some Reflections upon Marriage*, 12).

59. Defoe had a similar reaction to such cases. In *Conjugal Lewdness* he writes of a widow in her fifties marrying a younger man, "perhaps her Servant, her Book-keeper, or her late Husband's Steward, or some meaner Person. . . . if any Man is displeased at my calling this by the Name of Matrimonial Whoredom, let him find a better Name for it, if he can" (232–33).

60. Boyle, *Swift as Nemesis*, 43.

61. I include "natural order" to cover Swift's belief that D——y had no merits of person to recommend him to Lady S——, a condition he carries to an extreme in the Laputan episode.

62. The web of relationship encompassed more than just the two old schoolfellows. Pratt knew Vanessa and had been a trustee of Bartholomew Vanhomrigh's estate. Swift was also friendly with Pratt's brother, Captain John Pratt, and had some business dealings with him (see W 1:287, 288n).

63. In the list of "Swift's Friends Classed by their Character" the "Dean of Down, Pratt" receives the designation "ungrateful" (C 5:270).

64. Ball describes Pratt as "a man of fortune and highly cultured taste" (in Swift, *The Correspondence of Jonathan Swift, D.D.*, 4:83n).

65. According to Ball, Pratt succeeded in that aim at least: his daughter Elizabeth married Alexander Swift (in Swift, *The Correspondence of Jonathan Swift, D.D.*, 6:214).

66. Rather than marrying an ensign, which Rogers describes as "the lowest form of officer life (*CP* 721n), Lady Philippa married "Michael Connel of London, M.D." (W 2:405n). David Woolley suggests that her father's support for an Irish bank that Swift opposed led to "the dislike" found in the poem (W 2:405n).

67. Allestree, *The Ladies Calling*, 44. Richard Steele, whose *Ladies Library* echoes Allestree on many points, also takes widows to task for enjoying their liberty since women were made to be in subjection (256).

68. Hufton, *The Prospect Before Her*, 59.

69. *The Parliament of Women*, 34–35.

70. Staves, *Married Women's Separate Property*, 36–37. As Staves comments, "Although men can see the necessity of supporting the women who belong to them so long as the women do belong to them, they dislike seeing what they regard as their assets going to support another man's woman" (36).

71. Swift may have read some version of the life of Thecla of Antioch, who was accused of sorcery and condemned to be devoured by wild beasts but was spared by the lion. Hayley concludes his retelling of the story (*A Philosophical, Historical and Moral Essay*, 2:143–52) with the lion lacking the power "to violate the sacred body of a virgin. . . . So truly admirable is virginity that even lions revere it!" (2:149–50).

72. DePorte, "Night Thoughts in Swift," 648.

73. Roger Thompson describes as "something of a cliché by the early eighteenth century the punch-line of William Byrd's character of a female prude: 'She is now going to visit her child by her uncle's coachman'" (*Women in Stuart England and America*, 49). See Byrd, *Another Secret Diary*, 288.

74. O'Faolain and Martines, *Not in God's Image*, 137.

75. Hill, *Women, Work, and Sexual Politics*, 181. See Hair, "Bridal Pregnancy in Rural England," 239–40; and Outhwaite, *Clandestine Marriage in England*, 61: "Pre-nuptial pregnancy probably contributed significantly to the attractions of the eighteenth-century licence system in the provinces." Horace Walpole remarks that nine hundred of the fourteen hundred women married by the minister of the Savoy Chapel were said to be pregnant (*Memoirs of King George II*, 2:124).

76. Stallybrass, "Patriarchal Territories," 124.

77. Stallybrass, "Patriarchal Territories," 124, describing Rabelais.

78. Charles Greg Kelley believes that the poem moves from comic to compassionate ("Dismembered Beauty," 105). For other such readings, see my discussion of this poem in Chapter 7.

79. Baudelaire, *Les Fleurs du Mal*, 2.

80. Murry, *Jonathan Swift*, 439.

81. For the unfortunate lives of actual prostitutes in Swift's time, see Trumbach, *Heterosexuality and the Third Gender*, 135–68. "Prostitutes," he writes, "were subjected to public scorn, imprisonment, and whipping. . . . And they had to endure random public violence" (136).

82. Cf. Essex, *The Young Ladies Conduct*: "Preserve the strictest Modesty in all your private Intercourse; for let a Husband's Inclinations be never so Vicious, he is always pleas'd with Virtue; and in the main, delights in Cleanliness, Decorum, and delicacy of Behaviour" (100).

83. Rosslyn, "Deliberate Disenchantment," 296.

84. See Barnett, "Voyeurism as Entrapment," 56–57.

85. *Cassinus and Peter* was originally published in a pamphlet with *A Beautiful Young Nymph Going to Bed* and *Strephon and Chloe* on December 5, 1734 (*CP* 830).

86. Theweleit, *Male Fantasies*, 1:340.

87. Beauvoir, *The Second Sex*, 536.

88. Weil, *Political Passions*, 143–44. Astell in *Some Reflections upon Marriage* describes married women as the property of their husbands (12).

89. When Swift writes about a woman he likes, Lady Acheson, women's love of finery becomes part of the comic plot. In *The Revolution at Market-Hill* Lady Acheson is rendered helpless by a pair of "embroidered high heel shoes" which make it impossible to walk (*CP* 397). *To Janus* represents Lady Acheson trusting in velvet and lace to maintain her youth and beauty in the new year (*CP* 365).

90. Ehrenpreis uses terms like "ferocity," "desperate . . . futility," and "frantic violence" to describe the essays of this time (E 3:611, 612, 613).

91. This piece was not published during Swift's lifetime, perhaps, Davis believes, because Swift was too despondent at that time (*PW* 12:xvii). This would not explain why he failed to publish it later since he did write and publish *A Modest Proposal* after that date.

92. The question of manliness in Swift most often takes the form of concern about "effeminate" behavior. Men, he felt, were subject to this danger from various quarters. Soft living among the nobility, he wrote in the *Intelligencer* (no. 9), was "producing gradually a more effeminate Race" (*PW* 12:53), and the introduction of Italian opera had opened the door to "*Italian Effeminacy* " (*PW* 12:53, 37).

93. Charlotte Sussman remarks that the spread of tea drinking led Jonah Hanway (*An Essay on Tea*, 1756) to a "nightmare vision of social equality, in which all members of society believe themselves equal because of their equal capacity to consume" (*Consuming Anxieties*, 26). Swift is much more concerned with the effect of importation on the Irish economy.

94. Purkiss, "Material Girls," 74. Discussing a popular misogynist text, Joseph Swetnam's *The Araignment of Lewd, Idle, Froward and Unconstant Woman* (1615), Purkiss notes that Swetnam repeatedly castigates women for their capacity to spend money: "The point, however, is that woman spends money on her *own* desires, 'toys,' 'banqueting' and female pride" (74).

CHAPTER 7

1. Chapone, *A Matrimonial Creed*, in *Works*, 2:118–19.

2. John Gregory, *A Father's Legacy to His Daughters*; Chapone, *Letter to a New-Married Lady*, 109. Further page references to this edition will be given parenthetically in the text.

3. Chapone, *A Matrimonial Creed*, in *Works*, 2:121.

4. Boswell, *Boswell's Journal of a Tour to the Hebrides*, 170.

5. Doody, "Swift Among the Women," 34.

6. Castle, "Women and Literary Criticism," in *Boss Ladies, Watch Out!*, 3.

7. Montagu, *Lady Mary Wortley Montagu: Essays and Poems*, 273–76.

8. Lonsdale accepts Samuel Shepherd's attribution of the anonymously published poem to Miss W—— (*Eighteenth-Century Women Poets*, 129). However, the description of a gentleman's study might have been attributed to a woman to balance the male view of the lady's dressing room. There is no evidence for the author's sex other than Shepherd.

9. Phillips, *Swiftiana*, 1:12.

10. Berwick, *The Reputation of Jonathan Swift*, 53.

11. See, for example, Norman O. Brown, *Life Against Death*; Greene, "On Swift's 'Scatological Poems'"; and Gilmore, "The Comedy of Swift's Scatological Poems."

12. Most notably in Doody, "Swift Among the Women," 13–37. See also Donna Landry, *The Muse of Resistance*.

13. Crow, "Swift and the Woman Scholar." While this movement from Swift as misogynist to Swift as friend of women is generally chronological, Flynn's *The Body in Swift and Defoe* is an exception, an original reading of Swift's misogyny produced during the period of second-wave feminist criticism.

14. Gilbert and Gubar, *The Madwoman in the Attic*, 31.

15. Gilbert and Gubar, *The Madwoman in the Attic*, 138.

16. Katharine M. Rogers, *The Troublesome Helpmate*, 168. Although Rogers adumbrated the "harshness of Swift's misogyny" (172), she found aspects of his attitude that would reappear more than a decade later in her work as evidence of a favorable appraisal: Swift "never patronized women"; he "genuinely respected their minds and characters" (174).

17. Wyrick, *Jonathan Swift and the Vested Word*, 149.

18. Nussbaum, *The Brink of All We Hate*, 108.

19. Nussbaum, *The Brink of All We Hate*, 113.

20. *Gulliver's Travels* might be offered as an exception to this rule, but in those passages where Gulliver indicts the customs and behavior of Englishmen, he clearly uses "men" comprehensively to refer to both sexes.

21. Katharine M. Rogers, *Feminism in Eighteenth-Century England*, 61.

22. Katharine M. Rogers, *Feminism in Eighteenth-Century England*, 61–62. The argument that "the rejection—or the suppression—of femininity must be an irredeemably misogynist position" has been made by Penelope Wilson in "Feminism and the Augustans: Some Readings and Problems" (191).

23. Katharine M. Rogers, *Feminism in Eighteenth-Century England*, 61.

24. Katharine M. Rogers, *The Troublesome Helpmate*, 168.

25. Rabb, "The Manl(e)y Style," 126.

26. Rabb, "The Manl(e)y Style," 128. She might have added Richard I. Cook, whose book *Jonathan Swift as a Tory Pamphleteer* fails to mention Manley at all.

27. For a similar case of the critical establishment turning away from unpalatable ideas about Swift, see Andrew Carpenter's introduction to *Cadenus & Swift's Most Valuable Friend*, xiii, xv: "For most established Swiftians of the day—even Irvin Ehrenpreis ... there was no need to question the received truth about Swift's parentage. ... Though the establishment itself was aware of its failure to investigate these sides of Swift's life, it could not afford to acknowledge the failure in public."

28. *Journal to Stella*, ed. George A. Aitken, 92n.

29. Fabricant, "The Shared Worlds of Manley and Swift," 158.

30. Rabb reviews mostly late-twentieth-century work on Manley ("The Manl(e)y Style," 150). See also McDowell, *The Women of Grub Street*, 217–84 and passim.

31. Ballaster, "Manl(e)y Forms, 236.

32. Vendler, *Poets Thinking*, 5.

33. Salvaggio, *Enlightened Absence*, 80. Further page references will be given parenthetically in the text.

34. Blake, *The Marriage of Heaven and Hell*, xvii. Milton's lack of "knowing it" is certainly debatable. To make *Paradise Lost* work as a narrative Satan has to be a compelling and understandable, albeit evil, figure.

35. Frye, *The Anatomy of Criticism*, 57.

36. Vendler, *Poets Thinking*, 5.

37. Vendler, *Poets Thinking*, 5.

38. Freud's oft-quoted but apocryphal remark, "sometimes a cigar is only a cigar," suggests the need to differentiate between one sort of meaning and another, but in actual psychoanalytic criticism such commonsense distinctions are seldom made. Freud himself said that other addictions are *always* substitutes for masturbation, the "primary addiction" (*Complete Letters of Sigmund Freud to Wilhelm Fliess*, 287).

39. Swift's suggestion of sexual activity between bodies so grossly different in size, both here and in Brobdingnag, is meant to titillate.

40. Freud supposedly remarked to Marie Bonaparte, "The great question that has never been answered and which I have not yet been able to answer, despite my thirty years of research into the feminine soul, is 'What does a woman want?'" The sole authority for this is Ernest Jones, *Sigmund Freud: Life and Work*, 2:468.

41. Salvaggio invokes Luce Irigaray, Hélène Cixous, and Julia Kristeva to establish woman's role as other, but one does not need French feminism to make this case. St. Paul and St. Augustine, along with other early church fathers, furnish ample evidence of this attitude and are more relevant to Swift's intellectual formation.

42. Woolf, *A Room of One's Own*, 102.

43. Kelly, *Swift and the English Language*, 19.

44. Cf. Mueller: "Orthodox and subversive voices—masculine and feminine voices—vie for authority in Swift" ("Imperfect Enjoyment at Market Hill," 57). Mueller, however, is referring to actual voices in the poetry, not voices she must read into Swift's own voice.

45. Jaffe, "Swift and the 'agreeable young Lady,'" 150.

46. Jaffe, "Swift and the 'agreeable young Lady,'" 155.

47. Butler, *Gender Trouble*, 2.

48. See Barnett, "Voyeurism as Entrapment," 57.

49. G. V. Bennett remarks that the "records of Church courts after 1661 abound in the moral offences of the laity: adultery, fornication, begetting bastard children, and blasphemy" (*The Tory Crisis*, 7). Nokes observes as "an axiom of Swift's social philosophy that social ills have their origins in moral failings" ("Swift and the Beggars," 221).

50. Carol Barash, review of *The Body in Swift and Defoe*, 327.

51. Laura Brown, *Ends of Empire*, 177. Further page references will be given parenthetically in the text.

52. See Landa's "Swift's Economic Views and Mercantilism" for a persuasive discussion of Swift's ideas on mercantilism in terms of England and Ireland.

53. See my discussion of this idea in Chapter 6.

54. Vendler, *Poets Thinking*, 5.

CONCLUSION

1. Swift, *The Correspondence of Jonathan Swift, D. D.*, ed. F. Elrington Ball, 6:147. In this period Swift wrote many letters to Whiteway expressing concern for her health.

2. Erin Mackie believes that Swift finds women "no more inherently defective than men." However, she qualifies, "they are more open to debasement because they are more

open to exchange on a market where value has gone awry" ("'The anguish, toil, and pain, Of gathering up herself again,'" 6).

3. Wilson, "Feminism and the Augustans," 191.

4. Daniel Rogers, *Matrimonial Honour*, 281.

5. Haigh, *Elizabeth I*, 22.

6. Most recently, Aravamudan, *Tropicopolitans*, 14.

7. Welsh, *Strong Representations*, 9.

8. McKeon, "Historicizing Patriarchy," 307.

BIBLIOGRAPHY

Acworth, Bernard. *Swift*. London: Eyre & Spottiswoode, 1947.

[Allestree, Richard.] *The Ladies Calling in Two Parts*. Oxford: At the Theatre, 1677.

Amussen, Susan Dwyer. *An Ordered Society: Gender and Class in Early Modern England*. Oxford: Basil Blackwell, 1988.

Appleby, Joyce. *Economic Thought and Ideology in Seventeenth-Century England*. Princeton: Princeton University Press, 1978.

Aravamudan, Srinivas. *Tropicopolitans: Colonialism and Agency, 1688–1804*. Durham: Duke University Press, 1999.

Armstrong, Karen. *The Gospel According to Woman: Christianity's Creation of the Sex War in the West*. Garden City, N.Y.: Doubleday, 1987.

Armstrong, Nancy. *Desire and Domestic Fictions: A Political History of the Novel*. New York: Oxford University Press, 1987.

Arnold, Bruce. "Jonathan Swift: Some Current Biographical Problems." In Real and Stover-Leidig, *Reading Swift*, 39–48.

Astell, Mary. *Some Reflections upon Marriage*. 4th ed. London: William Parker, 1730.

Backscheider, Paula R. *Daniel Defoe: His Life*. Baltimore: Johns Hopkins University Press, 1989.

Bacon, Sir Francis. *The Essayes or Counsels, Civill and Morall*. Edited by Michael Kiernan. Cambridge, Mass.: Harvard University Press, 1985.

Ballaster, Rosalind. "Manl(e)y Forms: Sex and the Female Satirist." In Brant and Purkiss, *Women, Texts and Histories 1575–1760*, 217–41.

Barash, Carol. Review of *The Body in Swift and Defoe*. *Eighteenth-Century Studies* 27 (1993–94): 327.

Barber, Mary. *The Poetry of Mary Barber*. Edited by Bernard Tucker. Lewiston, Maine: Edwin Mellen Press, 1992.

Barnes, Hazel E. "Simone de Beavoir and Later Feminism." *Simone de Beauvoir Studies* 4 (1987): 5–34.

Barnett, Louise K. *Swift's Poetic Worlds*. Newark: University of Delaware Press, 1981.

———. "Swift's Satiric Violence." In *Enlightened Violence: Violent Enlightenment,* edited by Manfred Engel and Gerald Gillespie. Paris: Honoré Champion, forthcoming.

———. "Voyeurism as Entrapment in Swift's Poetry." In *Reader Entrapment in Eighteenth Century Literature,* edited by Carl R. Kropf, 45–62. New York: AMS Press, 1992.

Baudelaire, Charles. *Les Fleurs du Mal.* Edited by Jacques Crépet and Georges Blin. Paris: Librairie José Corti, 1942.

Beauvoir, Simone de. *The Second Sex.* Translated by H. M. Parshley. New York: Knopf, 1953.

Beddoes, Thomas, M.D. *Hygeia: or Essays Moral and Medical.* 3 vols. Bristol: R. Phillips, 1802.

Bennett, G. V. *The Tory Crisis in Church and State 1688–1730: The Career of Francis Atterbury, Bishop of Rochester.* Oxford: Clarendon Press, 1975.

Berkeley, George-Monck. *Literary Relics.* 2nd ed. London: T. Kay, 1792.

Berwick, Donald. *The Reputation of Jonathan Swift 1781–1882.* New York: Haskell House, 1965.

Blake, William. *The Marriage of Heaven and Hell.* Oxford: Oxford University Press, 1975.

[Blount, T.] *Glossographia: or a Dictionary, Interpreting all such Hard Words . . . By* T. B. London: Humphrey Moseley, 1656.

Bond, Donald F., ed. *The Tatler.* 3 vols. Oxford: Clarendon Press, 1987.

Boswell, James. *Boswell's Journal of a Tour to the Hebrides with Samuel Johnson.* Edited by Frederick A. Pottle. New York: McGraw-Hill, 1961.

——— *Life of Johnson.* Edited by George Birkbeck Hill, revised by L. F. Powell. 6 vols. Oxford: Clarendon Press, 1934.

Boucé, Paul-Gabriel. "The Rape of Gulliver Reconsidered." *Swift Studies* 11 (1996): 98–114.

Bourdieu, Pierre. "The Economics of Linguistic Exchange." Translated by Richard Nice. *Social Science Information* 16 (1977): 645–68.

Bowers, Toni. *The Politics of Motherhood: British Writing and Culture 1680–1760.* Cambridge: Cambridge University Press, 1996.

Boyle, Frank. *Swift as Nemesis: Modernity and Its Satirist.* Stanford: Stanford University Press, 2000.

Brant, Clare, and Diane Purkiss, eds. *Women, Texts and Histories 1575–1760.* London: Routledge, 1992.Brathwait, Richard. *The English Gentlewoman.* London: B. Alsop & T. Fawcet, 1631.

Brathwait, Richard. *The English Gentlewoman.* London: B. Alsop & T. Fawcet, 1631.

Brinsley, John. *A Looking-Glasse for Good Women.* London: Ralph Smith, 1645.

Brown, Laura. *Ends of Empire: Women and Ideology in Early Eighteenth-Century English Literature.* Ithaca: Cornell University Press, 1993.

Brown, Norman O. *Life Against Death.* Middletown, Conn: Wesleyan University Press, 1959.

Burney, Fanny. *The Diary and Letters of Frances Burney, Madame D'Arblay.* Revised and edited by Sarah Chauncey Woolsey. 2 vols. Boston: Roberts Brothers, 1880.

Butler, Judith. *Gender Trouble: Feminism and the Subversion of Identity.* New York: Routledge, 1990.

Byrd, William. *Another Secret Diary of William Byrd of Westover.* Edited by Maude H. Woodfin, translated by Marion Tinling. Richmond, Va: Dietz Press, 1942.

Carpenter, Andrew. "Introduction." In *Cadenus & Swift's Most Valuable Friend: Two Books on Jonathan Swift by Sybil le Brocquy,* xi–xxii. Dublin: Lilliput Press, 2003.

Castle, Terry. *Boss Ladies, Watch Out! Essays on Women, Sex, and Writing*. New York: Routledge, 2002.

Cave, Richard. "Dramatising the Life of Swift." In *Irish Writers and the Theatre*, edited by Masaru Sekine, 17–32. Gerrards Cross: Colin Smythe, 1986.

Chapone, Hester. *Letter to a New-Married Lady*. London: John Sharpe, 1822.

———. *The Works of Mrs. Chapone*. 4 vols. Boston: W. Wells & T. B. Wait, 1809.

Charke, Charlotte. *Narrative of the Life of Mrs. Charlotte Charke*. London: Constable, 1929.

Clifford, James L., and Louis A. Landa, eds. *Pope and His Contemporaries: Essays presented to George Sherburn*. Oxford: Clarendon Press, 1949.

The Concise Dictionary of European Proverbs collected by Emanuel Strauss. London: Routledge, 1998.

Connery, Brian A. "Self-Representation and Memorials in the Late Poetry of Swift." In *Aging and Gender in Literature*, edited by Anne M. Wyatt-Brown and Janice Rossen, 141–63. Charlottesville: University of Virginia Press, 1993.

Cook, Richard I. *Jonathan Swift as a Tory Pamphleteer*. Seattle: University of Washington Press, 1967.

Cordry, Harold V. *The Multicultural Dictionary of Proverbs*. Jefferson, N.C.: McFarland, 1997.

Cowper, William. Surgeon. *The Anatomy of Humane Bodies*. Oxford and London: Sam. Smith, Benj. Walford, Printers to the Royal Society, 1698.

Craig, Maurice James, ed. *The Legacy of Swift: A Bi-Centenary Record of St. Patrick's Hospital, Dublin*. Dublin: Sign of the Three Candles, 1948.

Craik, Henry. *The Life of Jonathan Swift*. 2 vols. London: Macmillan, 1894.

Crawford, Patricia. "The Construction and Experience of Maternity in Seventeenth-Century England." In *Women as Mothers in Pre-Industrial England: Essays in Memory of Dorothy McLaren*, edited by Valerie Fildes, 3–29. London: Routledge, 1990.

———. "The Sucking Child." *Continuity and Change* 1 (1986): 23–52.

Crook, Keith. *A Preface to Swift*. London: Longman, 1998.

Crow, Nora. "Swift in Love." In Real and Stover-Leidig, *Reading Swift*, 48–64.

———. "Swift and the Woman Scholar." In Mell, *Pope, Swift, and Women Writers*, 222–238.

Curran, C. P. *Dublin Decorative Plasterwork of the Seventeenth and Eighteenth Centuries*. New York: Transatlantic Arts, 1967.

Curtis, Laura Ann, ed. *The Versatile Defoe: An Anthology of Uncollected Writings by Daniel Defoe*. Totowa, N.J.: Rowan and Littlefield, 1979.

Darwin, Erasmus. *The Botanic Garden*. London: Jones & Company, 1824.

Davis, Herbert. *Stella: A Gentlewoman of the Eighteenth Century*. New York: Macmillan, 1942.

Defoe, Daniel. *The Complete English Tradesman, in Familiar Letters*. Vol. 1. London: Charles Rivington, 1726.

———. *Conjugal Lewdness; or, Matrimonial Whoredom*. (London: T. Warner, 1727.) Facsimile edition. Gainesville: Scholars' Facsimiles & Reprints, 1967.

———. *An Essay upon Projects*. Edited by Joyce D. Kennedy, Michael Seidel, and Maximillian E. Novak. New York: AMS Press, 1999.

———. *Meer Nature Delineated: or, a Body without a Soul*. London: T. Warner, 1726.

Delany, Mary. *The Autobiography and Correspondence of Mary Granville, Mrs. Delany*. Edited by Lady Augusta Llanover. 3 vols. 1st series. London: Richard Bentley, 1861.

Delany, Patrick. *Observations upon Lord Orrery's Remarks on the Life and Writings of Dr. Jonathan Swift*. London: W. Reeve, 1754.

DePorte, Michael. "Night Thoughts in Swift." *Sewanee Review* 98 (1990): 646–63.

Dewes, Simon. *Mrs. Delany*. London: Rich & Cowan, n.d.

A Dialogue Concerning Women, Being a Defence of the Sex. Written to Eugenia. London: R. Bentley and J. Tonson, 1691.

Dictionary of National Biography. Edited by Leslie Stephen. 63 vols. London: Smith, Elder, 1887.

Doody, Margaret Anne. "Swift and Women." In *The Cambridge Companion to Jonathan Swift*, edited by Christopher Fox, 87–111. Cambridge: Cambridge University Press, 2003.

———. "Swift Among the Women." In *Critical Essays on Jonathan Swift*, edited by Frank Palmeri, 13–37. New York: G. K. Hall, 1993.

Downie, J. A. "'The Coffee Hessy Spilt' and Other Issues in Swift's Biography." In Real and Stover-Leidig, *Reading Swift*, 65–75.

———. *Robert Harley and the Press: Propaganda and Public Opinion in the Age of Swift and Defoe*. Cambridge: Cambridge University Press, 1979.

Dr. S———'s Real Diary. London and Dublin: n.p., 1715.

Du Boscq, Jacques. *The Compleat Woman*. Translated by N.N. London: Thomas Wykes, 1639.

Ehrenpreis, Irvin. *The Personality of Swift*. Cambridge, Mass: Harvard University Press, 1958.

———. *Swift: The Man, His Works, and the Age*. Vol. 1, London: Methuen, 1962; vols. 2 and 3, Cambridge, Mass.: Harvard University Press, 1967, 1983.

Ehrenpreis, Irvin, and Robert Halsband. *The Lady of Letters in the Eighteenth Century*. Los Angeles: William Andrews Clark Memorial Library, University of California, 1969.

Elias, A. C., Jr. "Laetitia Pilkington on Swift: How Reliable Is She?" In *Walking Naboth's Vineyard: New Studies on Swift*, edited by Christopher Fox and Brenda Tooley, 127–42. Notre Dame: University of Notre Dame Press, 1995.

Essex, John. *The Young Ladies Conduct: or, Rules for Education, Under several Heads; with Instructions upon Dress, both before and after Marriage. And Advice to Young Wives*. London: John Brotherton, 1722.

Ezell, Margaret J. M. *The Patriarch's Wife: Literary Evidence and the History of the Family*. Chapel Hill: University of North Carolina Press, 1987.

Fabricant, Carole. "The Shared Worlds of Manley and Swift." In Mell, *Pope, Swift, and Women Writers*, 154–78.

Feingold, Richard. *Moralized Song: The Character of Augustan Lyricism*. New Brunswick, N.J.: Rutgers University Press, 1989.

Fénelon, François de Salignac. *Instructions for the Eduction of a Daughter*. Translated and revised by Dr. George Hickes. London: Jonah Bowyer, 1707.

Fildes, Valerie A. *Breasts, Bottles and Babies: A History of Infant Feeding*. Edinburgh: Edinburgh University Press, 1986.

———. *Wet Nursing: A History from Antiquity to the Present*. Oxford: Basil Blackwell, 1988.

Fildes, Valerie A., ed. *Women as Mothers in Pre-Industrial England. Essays in Memory of Dorothy McLaren*. London: Routledge, 1990.

Finch, Anne, Countess of Winchilsea. *The Poems of Anne Countess of Winchilsea*. Edited by Myra Reynolds. Chicago: University of Chicago Press, 1903.

Fletcher, Anthony. *Gender, Sex and Subordination in England 1500–1800*. New Haven: Yale University Press, 1995.

Flynn, Carol Houlihan. *The Body in Swift and Defoe*. Cambridge: Cambridge University Press, 1990.

Fordyce, James. *Sermons to Young Women.* A New Edition. Philadelphia: Thomas Dobson, 1787.

Francus, Marilyn. "'A-Killing Their Children With Safety': Maternal Identity and Transgression in Swift and Defoe," In Kittredge, *Lewd & Notorious,* 258–82.

Fraser, Antonia. *The Weaker Vessel.* New York: Knopf, 1984.

Freeman, A. Martin, ed. *Vanessa and Her Correspondence with Jonathan Swift.* Boston: Houghton Mifflin, 1921.

Freud, Sigmund. *The Complete Letters of Sigmund Freud to Wilhelm Fliess, 1887–1904.* Edited by J. M. Masson. Cambridge, Mass.: Harvard University Press, 1985.

Fritz, Paul, and Richard Morlon, eds. *Woman in the Eighteenth Century and Other Essays.* Toronto: Samuel Stevens Hakkert, 1976.

Frye, Northrop. *The Anatomy of Criticism.* Princeton: Princeton University Press, 1957.

Gataker, Thomas. *A Good Wife Gods Gift: and A Wife Indeed. Two Marriage Sermons.* London: Fulke Clifton, 1623.

Gilbert, Sandra M., and Susan Gubar. *The Madwoman in the Attic: The Woman Writer and the Nineteenth-Century Imagination.* New Haven: Yale University Press, 1979.

Gillis, John R. *For Better, For Worse: British Marriages, 1600 to the Present.* New York: Oxford University Press, 1985.

Gilmore, Thomas B., Jr., "The Comedy of Swift's Scatological Poems." *PMLA* 91 (1976): 33–43.

Glass, D. V., and D. E. Eversley, eds. *Population in History: Essays in Historical Demography.* London: Edward Arnold, 1965.

Glendinning, Victoria. *Jonathan Swift: A Portrait.* New York: Henry Holt, 1998.

Gold, Maxwell. *Swift's Marriage to Stella.* New York: Russell and Russell, 1967.

Golding, Susan. "Claiming the 'Sacred Mantle': The Memoirs of Laetitia Pilkington." In Kittredge, *Lewd & Notorious,* 47–68.

Gowing, Laura. *Common Bodies: Women, Touch and Power in Seventeenth-Century England.* New Haven: Yale University Press, 2003.

Graddol, David, and Joan Swann. *Gender Voices.* Oxford: Basil Blackwell, 1989.

Gregory, Alyse. "Stella, Vanessa, and Swift." *Nineteenth-Century and After* 113 (June 1933): 755–64.

Gregory, John. *A Father's Legacy to His Daughters* [1774]. In *The Lady's Pocket Library.*

Greene, Donald. "On Swift's 'Scatological' Poems." *Sewanee Review* 75 (1967): 672–89.

Gubar, Susan, "The Female Monster in Augustan Satire." *Signs* 3 (1977): 380–94.

Gumperz, John J. *Discourse Strategies.* Cambridge: Cambridge University Press, 1982.

Haigh, Christopher. *Elizabeth I.* London: Longman, 1988.

Hair, P. E. H. "Bridal Pregnancy in Rural England in Earlier Centuries." *Population Studies* 20.2 (1966): 233–43.

Halifax, 1st Marquis of [George Savile] *The Lady's New-years Gift: or, Advice to a Daughter.* London: Randal Taylor, 1688.

Halsband, Robert. "Women and Literature in 18th Century England." In Fritz and Morlon, *Woman in the Eighteenth Century,* 55–71.

Haraway, Donna. *Primate Visions: Gender, Race and Nature in the World of Modern Science.* New York: Routledge, 1989.

The Harleian Miscellany: or, a Collection of Scarce, Curious, and Entertaining Pamphlets and Tracts . . . Found in the late Earl of Oxford's Library. 8 vols. London: T. Osborne, 1744.

Hardy, Evelyn. *The Conjured Spirit: A Study in the Relationship of Swift, Stella, and Vanessa.* London: Hogarth Press, 1949.

Hayden, Ruth. *Mrs. Delany and Her Flower Collages.* London: British Museum Press, 1992.

Hayley, William. *A Philosophical, Historical, and Moral Essay on Old Maids*. 3 vols. Dublin: White, Byrne, Cash, and Moore, 1786.

Hervey, John, Lord Hervey. *Memoirs of the Reign of George the Second*. Edited by John Wilson Croker. 2 vols. London: John Murray, 1848.

Heywood, Thomas. *Gynaikeion: or Nine Bookes of Various History Concerned Women*. London: Adam Islip, 1624.

Hibbert, Christopher. *George III: A Personal History*. New York: Basic Books, 1998.

Higgins, Patricia. "The Reactions of Women, with Special Reference to Women Petitioners." In *Politics, Religion and the English Civil War*, edited by Brian Manning, 178–222. New York: St. Martin's Press, 1974.

Hill, Bridget. *Women Alone: Spinsters in England 1660–1850*. New Haven: Yale University Press, 2001.

———. *Women, Work, and Sexual Politics in Eighteenth Century England*. Oxford: Basil Blackwell, 1989.

Hill, Bridget, ed. *Eighteenth-Century Women: An Anthology*. London: George Allen & Unwin, 1984.

Homer. *The Odyssey*. Translated by Robert Fitzgerald. Garden City, N.Y.: Doubleday, 1961.

Hufstader, Alice Anderson. *Sisters of the Quill*. New York: Dodd, Mead, 1978.

Hufton, Olwen. *The Prospect Before Her: A History of Women in Western Europe*. Vol. 1: *1500–1800*. New York: Knopf, 1996.

———. "Women Without Men: Widows and Spinsters in Britain and France in the Eighteenth Century." *Journal of Family History* 9 (Winter 1984): 355–376.

Ingram, Anne, Viscountess Irwin. "An Epistle to Mr. Pope. Occasioned by his Characters of Women." *Gentleman's Magazine* 6 (1736): 745.

Jackson, R. Wyse. *Swift and His Circle: A Book of Essays*. Dublin: Talbot Press, 1945.

Jaffe, Nora Crow. *The Poet Swift*. Hanover, N.H.: University Press of New England, 1977.

———. "Swift and the 'agreeable young Lady, but Extremely Lean.'" In *Contemporary Studies of Swift's Poetry*, edited by John Irwin Fischer and Donald C. Mell, Jr., 149–58. Newark, University of Delaware Press, 1981.

Jameson, Anna. *Memoirs of the Loves of the Poets* [1829]. Freeport, NY: Books for Libraries Press, 1972.

Jelinek, Estelle C. *The Tradition of Women's Autobiography: From Antiquity to the Present*. Boston: Twayne, 1986.

Jerome. *Select Letters of St. Jerome*. Translated by F. A. Wright. London: William Heinemann, 1954.

Jerrold, Walter and Clare. *Five Queer Women*. London: Brentano, 1929.

Johnson, Maurice. *The Sin of Wit: Jonathan Swift as a Poet*. Syracuse: Syracuse University Press, 1950.

Johnson, Samuel. *Lives of the English Poets*. Edited by George Birkbeck Hill. 3 vols. 2nd ed. Oxford: Clarendon Press, 1958.

Johnston, Denis. *In Search of Swift*. Dublin: Hodges Figgis, 1959.

Jones, Ernest. *Sigmund Freud: Life and Work*. 2 vols. London: Hogarth Press, 1955.

Jones, Vivien. "The Seductions of Conduct: Pleasure and Conduct Literature." In *Pleasure in the Eighteenth Century*, edited by Roy Porter and Marie Mulvey Roberts, 108–32. New York: New York University Press, 1996.

Jones, Vivien, ed. *Women in the Eighteenth Century: Constructions of Femininity*. London: Routledge, 1990.

———. *Women and Literature in Britain 1700–1800*. Cambridge: Cambridge University Press, 2000.

Jordan, W. K. *The Charities of London 1480–1660*. London: George Allen & Unwin, 1960.

Karian, Stephen. "Swift's Epitaph for Stella? A Recently Discovered Document." *Swift Studies* 16 (2001): 109–13.

Kelley, Charles Greg. "Dismembered Beauty: A Swiftian Presentation of the False Members." *Swift Studies* 16 (2001): 98–108.

Kelly, Ann Cline. *Jonathan Swift and Popular Culture: Myth, Media, and the Man*. New York: Palgrave, 2002.

———. *Swift and the English Language*. Philadelphia: University of Pennsylvania Press, 1988.

[Kenrick, William.] *The Whole Duty of Woman*. By a Lady, written at the desire of a noble Lord. London: n. p., 1753.

King, Gregory. *Natural and Political Observations and Conclusions upon the State and Condition of England in 1696*. Edited by George Chalmers. London: n.p., 1810.

King, Margaret. "Book-lined Cells: Women and Humanism in the Early Italian Renaissance." In *Beyond their Sex: Learned Women of the European Past*, edited by Patricia H. Labalme, 66–90. New York: New York University Press, 1980.

Kittredge, Katharine, ed. *Lewd & Notorious: Female Transgression in the Eighteenth Century*. Ann Arbor: University of Michigan Press, 2003

Klein, Lawrence E. "Gender and the Public/Private Distinction in the Eighteenth Century: Some Questions about Evidence and Analytic Procedure." *Eighteenth-Century Studies* 29 (1996): 97–109.

Krupat, Arnold. "The Dialogic of Silko's 'Storyteller.'" In *Narrative Chance: Postmodern Discourse on Native American Indian Literatures*, edited by Gerald Vizenor, 55–68. Albuquerque: University of New Mexico Press, 1989.

The Ladies Library. Written by a Lady. Published by Mr. Steele. London: Jacob Tonson, 1714.

The Lady's Pocket Library. Philadelphia: Mathew Carey, 1792.

Landa, Louis A. "*A Modest Proposal* and Populousness." *Modern Philology* 40 (1942): 161–70.

———. "Swift's Economic Views and Mercantilism." *ELH* 10 (1943): 310–35.

Landry, Donna. *The Muse of Resistance: Laboring-Class Women's Poetry in Britain, 1739–1796*. Cambridge: Cambridge University Press, 1990.

Laqueur, Thomas. *Making Sex: Body and Gender from the Greeks to Freud*. Cambridge, Mass: Harvard University Press, 1990.

Le Brocquy, Sybil. *Cadenus*. Dublin: Dolmen Press, 1963.

———. *Swift's Most Valuable Friend*. Dublin: Dufour Editions, 1968.

Lecky, W.E.H. "Biographical Introduction." In *The Prose Works of Jonathan Swift*, edited by Temple Scott. 1: xiii–xci. London: George Bell and Sons, 1897.

Lein, Clayton D. "Jonathan Swift and the Population of Ireland." *Eighteenth-Century Studies* 8 (1974–75): 431–53.

Locke, John. *Two Treatises of Government*. Edited by Peter Laslett. 2 vols. Cambridge: Cambridge University Press, 1991.

Longe, Julia G., ed. *Martha, Lady Giffard: Her Life and Correspondence (1664–1722)*. London: George Allen, 1911.

Lonsdale, Roger. *Eighteenth-Century Women Poets: An Oxford Anthology*. Oxford: Oxford University Press, 1990.

Lyons, John O. *The Invention of the Self: The Hinge of Consciousness in the Eighteenth Century*. Carbondale: Southern Illinois University Press, 1978.

Mack, Maynard. *Alexander Pope: A Life*. New York and New Haven: W. W. Norton and Yale University Press, 1985.

Mackie, Erin. "'The anguish, toil, and pain of gathering up herself again': The Fabrication of Swift's Women." *Critical Matrix* 6 (1991): 1–7.

Mahony, Robert. *Jonathan Swift: The Irish Identity*. New Haven: Yale University Press, 1995.

———. "Swift's Modest Proposal and the Rhetoric of Irish Colonial Consumption." *1650–1850: Ideas, Aesthetics, and Inquiries in the Early Modern Era* 4 (1998): 205–14.

[Makin, Bathsua.] *An Essay to Revive the Antient Education of Gentlewomen* (1673). Augustan Reprint Society Publications, no. 202. Los Angeles: William Andrews Clark Memorial Library, 1980.

Manch, Joseph. "Jonathan Swift and Women." *The University of Buffalo Studies* 16 (February 1941): 130–214.

Mandeville, Bernard. *A Treatise of the Hypochondriack and Hysterick Diseases* [1711]. 3rd ed. London: J. Tonson, 1730.

Mason, William Monck. *The History and Antiquities of the Collegiate and Cathedral Church of St. Patrick, near Dublin*. Dublin: printed for the author, 1819.

Masson, David. *The Three Devils: Luther's, Milton's, and Goethe's*. London: Macmillan, 1874.

Mayhew, George P. *Rage or Raillery: The Swift Manuscripts at the Huntington Library*. San Marino, Calif.: The Huntington Library, 1967.

McDowell, Paula. *The Women of Grub Street: Press, Politics, and Gender in the London Literary Marketplace 1678–1730*. Oxford: Clarendon Press, 1998.

McInnes, Angus. *Robert Harley, Puritan Politician*. London: Victor Gollancz, 1970.

McKeon, Michael. "Historicizing Patriarchy: The Emergence of Gender Difference in England, 1660–1760." *Eighteenth-Century Studies* 28 (1995): 295–322.

Mell, Donald C., ed. *Pope, Swift, and Women Writers*. Newark: University of Delaware Press, 1996.

Meynell, Alice. *Essays*. London: Burns Oates & Washbourne, 1930.

Milton, John. *The Doctrine and Discipline of Divorce: Restor'd to the Good of Both Sexes. . . in Two Books*. London: n.p., 1644.

———. *Tetrachordon: Expositions upon the foure chief places in Scripture, which treat of Mariage, or nullities in Mariage*. London: n.p., 1643.

Montag, Warren. *The Unthinkable Swift: The Spontaneous Philosophy of a Church of England Man*. London: Verso, 1994.

Montagu, Lady Mary Wortley. *The Complete Letters of Lady Mary Wortley Montagu*. Edited by Robert Halsband. 3 vols. Oxford: Clarendon Press, 1965–67.

———. *Lady Mary Wortley Montagu: Essays and Poems and Simplicity, A Comedy*. Edited by Robert Halsband and Isobel Grundy. Oxford: Clarendon Press, 1977.

Mueller, Judith C. "Imperfect Enjoyment at Market Hill: Impotence, Desire, and Reform in Swift's Poems to Lady Acheson." *ELH* 66 (1999): 51–70.

Mumford, Lewis. *The City in History: Its Origins, Its Transformations, and Its Prospects*. New York: Harcourt Brace Jovanovich, 1961.

Murry, John Middleton. *Jonathan Swift: A Critical Biography*. London: Jonathan Cape, 1954.

Neville, Henry. *A Parliament of Ladies: With Their Lawes Newly Enacted*. London: n.p., 1647.

Newman, Bertram. *Jonathan Swift*. Boston: Houghton Mifflin, 1937.

Newstead, Christopher. *An Apology for Women: or, Womens Defence*. London: Rr. Whittakers, 1620.

Nichols, John. *Literary Anecdotes of the Eighteenth Century*. Edited by Colin Clair. Carbondale: Southern Illinois University Press, 1967.

Noddings, Nel. *Women and Evil*. Berkeley: University of California Press, 1989.

Nokes, David. *Jonathan Swift, A Hypocrite Reversed*. Oxford: Oxford University Press, 1985.

———. "Swift and the Beggars." *Essays in Criticism* 26 (1976): 218–35.

Novak, Maximilian E. "Swift and Defoe: Or, How Contempt Breeds Familiarity and a Degree of Influence." In Real and Vienken, *Proceedings of The First Münster Symposium on Jonathan Swift*, 157–73.

Nussbaum, Felicity. *The Brink of All We Hate: English Satires on Women, 1660–1750*. Lexington: University of Kentucky Press, 1984.

O'Faolain, Julia, and Lauro Martines. *Not in God's Image: Women in History from the Greeks to the Victorians*. New York: Harper & Row, 1973.

Oliphant, Mrs. M. O. W. *Historical Characters of the Reign of Queen Anne*. New York: Century Company, 1894.

Orrery, John Boyle, Earl of. *Remarks on the Life and Writings of Dr. Jonathan Swift*. Edited by João Fróes. Newark: University of Delaware Press, 2000

Outhwaite, R. B. *Clandestine Marriage in England, 1500–1850*. London: Hambledon Press, 1995.

Overbury, Sir Thomas. *Miscellaneous Works*. Edited by E. F. Rimbault. London: Smith, 1856.

The Oxford English Dictionary. 2nd ed. 20 vols. Oxford: Clarendon Press, 1989.

Palmer, Gabrielle. *The Politics of Breastfeeding*. London: Pandora, 1988.

The Parlament of Women. With the merry Lawes by them newly Enacted. London: J. Wright, 1640.

The Parliament of Women. London: John Melford, 1684.

Peake, Charles. "Swift's Birthday Verses to Stella," In Real and Vienken, *Proceedings of the First Münster Symposium on Jonathan Swift*, 175–86.

Perry, Ruth. "Colonizing the Breast: Sexuality and Maternity in Eighteenth-Century England." *Journal of the History of Sexuality* 2 (1991): 204–34.

Phillips, Richard, ed. *Swiftiana*. 2 vols. London: Richard Phillips, 1804.

Pilkington, Laetitia. *The Memoirs of Mrs. Laetitia Pilkington*. Edited by A. C. Elias, Jr. 2 vols. Athens: University of Georgia Press, 1997.

Piozzi, Hester Thrale. *Retrospection*. 2 vols. London: J. Stockdale, 1801.

Pollak, Ellen. *The Poetics of Sexual Myth: Gender and Ideology in the Verse of Swift and Pope*. Chicago: University of Chicago Press, 1985.

———. "Swift Among the Feminists." In *Critical Approaches to Teaching Swift*, edited by Peter Schakel, 65–75. New York: AMS Press, 1992.

Pollock, Linda A. *Forgotten Children: Parent-Child Relations from 1500 to 1900*. Cambridge: Cambridge University Press, 1983.

Pope, Alexander. *The Poems of Alexander Pope*. Edited by John Butt. New Haven: Yale University Press, 1963.

Porter, Roy. *English Society in the Eighteenth Century*. London: Penguin, 1982.

Porter, Roy, and Dorothy Porter. *In Sickness and in Health: The British Experience 1650–1850*. London: Fourth Estate, 1988.

Powys, Llewelyn. *Cup-Bearers of Wine and Hellebore*. Girard, Kans.: Haldeman-Julius, 1924.

Purkiss, Diane. "Material Girls: The Seventeenth-Century Woman Debate." In Brant and Purkiss, *Women, Texts and Histories 1575–1760*, 69–101.

Quintana, Ricardo. *The Mind and Art of Jonathan Swift*. Oxford: Oxford University Press, 1936.

Rabb, Melinda Alliker. "The Manl(e)y Style: Delariviere Manley and Jonathan Swift." In Mell, *Pope, Swift, and Women Writers*, 125–53.

Rawson, C. J. *God, Gulliver, and Genocide: Barbarism and the European Imagination, 1492–1945.* Oxford: Oxford University Press, 2001.

———. *Order from Confusion Sprung: Studies in Eighteenth-Century Literature from Swift to Cowper.* London: Allen & Unwin, 1985.

———. "Rage and Raillery and Swift: The Case of *Cadenus and Vanessa.*" In Mell, *Pope, Swift, and Women Writers,* 179–91.

Real, Hermann J. *Securing Swift: Selected Essays.* Dublin: Maunsel, 2001.

Real, Hermann J., and Helgard Stover-Leidig, eds. *Reading Swift: Papers from the Fourth Münster Symposium on Jonathan Swift.* Munich: Wilhelm Fink, 2003.

Real, Hermann J., and Heinz J. Vienken, eds. *Proceedings of The First Münster Symposium on Jonathan Swift.* Münster: Wilhelm Fink Verlag, 1985.

Rees, Christine. "Gay, Swift, and the Nymphs of Drury-Lane." *Essays in Criticism* 23 (1973): 1–21.

Relke, Diana M. A. "In Search of Mrs. Pilkington." In *Gender at Work: Four Women Writers of the Eighteenth Century,* edited by Ann Messenger, 114–49. Detroit: Wayne State University Press, 1990.

Reynolds, Myra. *The Learned Lady in England 1650–1760.* Boston: Houghton Mifflin, 1920.

Richardson, Samuel. *Pamela; or Virtue Rewarded.* 4 vols. Philadelphia: J. B. Lippincott, 1902.

Rogers, Daniel. *Matrimoniall Honour: or, the mutuall Crowne and comfort of godly, loyall, and chaste Marriage.* London: Th. Harper for Philip Nevil, 1642.

Rogers, Katharine M. "The Feminism of Daniel Defoe." In Fritz and Morlon, *Woman in the Eighteenth Century,* 3–24.

———. *Feminism in Eighteenth-Century England.* Urbana: University of Illinois Press, 1982.

———. *The Troublesome Helpmate: A History of Misogyny in Literature.* Seattle: University of Washington Press, 1966.

Rogers, Timothy. *The Character of a Good Woman, Both in a Single and Marry'd State.* London: John Harris, 1697.

Ross, John F. *Swift and Defoe: A Study in Relationship.* Berkeley: University of California Press, 1941.

Rosslyn, Felicity. "Deliberate Disenchantment: Swift and Pope on the Subject of Women." *The Cambridge Quarterly* 23 (1994): 293–302.

Ruether, Rosemary Radford, ed. *Religion and Sexism: Images of Woman in the Jewish and Christian Traditions.* New York: Simon and Schuster, 1974.

Rumbold, Valerie. *Women's Place in Pope's World.* Cambridge: Cambridge University Press, 1989.

Salvaggio, Ruth. *Enlightened Absence: Neoclassical Configurations of the Feminine.* Urbana: University of Illinois Press, 1988.

Scott, Walter. "Memoirs of Jonathan Swift, D.D." Vol. 1 of *The Works of Jonathan Swift,* edited by Sir Walter Scott, 2nd ed .

Shakespeare, William. *Shakespeare's Sonnets and A Lover's Complaint.* Edited by Stanley Wells. Oxford: Clarendon Press, 1985.

Sheridan, Thomas. *The Life of the Rev. Dr. Jonathan Swift.* 2nd ed. London: J. F. & C. Rivington, 1787.

Shumacker, Wayne. *English Autobiography: Its Emergence, Materials, and Form.* Berkeley: University of California Press, 1954.

Smith, Frederik N. "Dramatic Elements in Swift's *Journal to Stella.*" *Eighteenth-Century Studies* 1 (1968): 332–52.

Smith, Sophie Shilleto. *Dean Swift.* New York: G. P. Putnam, 1910.

Spacks, Patricia Meyer. *Gossip*. New York: Knopf, 1985.

————. *Imagining a Self: Autobiography and Novel in Eighteenth-Century England*. Cambridge, Mass.: Harvard University Press, 1976.

Stallybrass, Peter. "Patriarchal Territories: The Body Enclosed." In *Rewriting the Renaissance: The Discourses of Sexual Difference in Early Modern Europe*, edited by Margaret W. Ferguson, Maureen Quilligan, and Nancy J. Vickers, 123–42. Chicago: University of Chicago Press, 1986.

Stauffer, Donald A. *The Art of Biography in Eighteenth Century England*. Princeton: Princeton University Press, 1941.

Staves, Susan. *Married Women's Separate Property in England, 1660–1833*. Cambridge, Mass.: Harvard University Press, 1990.

Stephen, Leslie. *Swift*. New York: Harper & Brothers, 1898.

Stone, Lawrence. *The Family, Sex, and Marriage in England, 1500–1800*. New York: Harper & Row, 1977.

Sundon, Lady Charlotte Clayton. *Memoirs of Viscountess Sundon, Mistress of the Robes to Queen Caroline*. Edited by Katherine Byerley Thomson. 2 vols. London: Henry Colburn, 1847.

Sussman, Charlotte. *Consuming Anxieties: Consumer Protest, Gender, and British Slavery, 1713–1833*. Stanford: Stanford University Press, 2000.

Sutherland, James. *Defoe*. London: Methuen, 1937.

Swetnam, Joseph. *The Araignment of Lewd, Idle, Froward, and Unconstant Women (1615)*. Edited by F. W. Van Heertum. Nijmegen: Cicero Press, 1989.

Swift, Deane. *An Essay upon the Life, Writings, and Character of Dr. Jonathan Swift*. Facsimile of 1755 London edition. Hildesheim, Georg Olms, 1968.

Swift, Jonathan. *The Account Books of Jonathan Swift*. Edited by Paul V. Thompson and Dorothy Jay Thompson. Newark: University of Delaware Press, 1984.

————. *The Collected Poems*. Edited by Joseph Horrell. Cambridge, Mass: Harvard University Press, 1958.

————. *The Correspondence of Jonathan Swift, D.D.* Edited by F. Elrington Ball. 6 vols. London: G. Bell and Sons, 1910–14.

————. *The Correspondence of Jonathan Swift*. Edited by Harold Williams. 5 vols. Oxford: Clarendon Press, 1963–65.

————. *The Correspondence of Jonathan Swift, D.D.* Edited by David Woolley. 4 vols. Frankfurt am Main: Peter Lang, 1999–.

————. *Jonathan Swift: The Complete Poems*. Edited by Pat Rogers. New York: Penguin Books, 1983.

————. *Journal to Stella*. Edited by George A. Aitken. London: Methuen, 1901.

————. *Journal to Stella*. Edited by Walter Scott. 2 vols. London: Routledge & Sons, n.d.

————. *Journal to Stella*. Edited by Harold Williams. 2 vols. Oxford: Clarendon Press, 1948.

————. *Letter to a Young Lady on her Marriage. Swift's Autograph Mss 1723*. HM1599, Huntington Library, San Marino, Calif.

————. *Letters and Journals of Jonathan Swift*. Edited by Stanley Lane-Poole. London: Kegan Paul, Trench, 1885.

————. *The Poems of Jonathan Swift*. Edited by Harold Williams. 2nd ed. 3 vols. Oxford: Clarendon Press, 1958.

————. *The Poetical Works of Jonathan Swift with a Memoir by the Rev. John Mitford*. 3 vols. London: George Bell, 1894.

————. *The Prose Works of Jonathan Swift*. Edited by Herbert Davis. 14 vols. Oxford: Clarendon Press, 1937–68.

————. *The Works of Dr. Jonathan Swift*. Edited by John Hawkesworth. 12 vols. London: W. Bowyer et al., 1768.

————. *The Works of Jonathan Swift*. Edited by Sir Walter Scott. 2nd ed. 19 vols. Boston: Houghton Mifflin, 1883.

————. *The Works of the Rev. Jonathan Swift, D. D., Dean of St. Patrick's, Dublin, arranged by Thomas Sheridan, A. M.* Revised edition by John Nichols. 24 vols. London: J. Johnson, et al., 1803.

Taylor, Coley B. *Mark Twain's Margins on Thackeray's Swift*. New York: Gotham House, 1935.

Thackeray, W. M. *The English Humourists of the Eighteenth Century*. New York: Harper & Brothers, 1854.

Theweleit, Klaus. *Male Fantasies*. Vol. 1: *Women, Floods, Bodies, History*. Translated by Stephen Conway. Minneapolis: University of Minnesota Press, 1987.

Thomas, Claudia N. *Alexander Pope and His Eighteenth-Century Women Readers*. Carbondale: Southern Illinois University Press, 1994.

Thompson, Roger. *Women in Stuart England and America: A Comparative Study*. London: Routledge & Kegan Paul, 1974.

Trumbach, Randolph. *Heterosexuality and the Third Gender in Englightenment London: Sex and the Gender Revolution*. Vol. 1. Chicago: University of Chicago Press, 1998.

————. *The Rise of the Egalitarian Family: Aristocratic Kinship and Domestic Relations in Eighteenth-Century England*. New York: Academic Press, 1978

Tucker, Bernard, ed. *The Poetry of Laetitia Pilkington (1712–1750) and Constantia Grierson (1706–1733)*. Lewiston, N.Y.: Edwin Mellen Press, 1996.

Turner, Cheryl. *Living by the Pen: Women Writers in the Eighteenth Century*. London: Routledge, 1992.

[V. W.] *The Ladie's Blush: or, the History of Susanna, the Great Example of Conjugal Chastity*. London: Robert Robinson, 1673.

Vendler, Helen. *Poets Thinking*. Cambridge, Mass.: Harvard University Press, 2004.

Venturo, David F. "Concurring Opponents: Mary Wollstonecraft and Jonathan Swift on Women's Education and the Sexless Nature of Virtue." In Mell, *Pope, Swift, and Women Writers*, 192–202.

Viazzo, Pier Paolo. "Mortality, Fertility, and Family." In *Family Life in Early Modern Times 1500–1789, The History of the European Family*, edited by David I. Kertzer and Marzio Barbagli, vol. 1, 157–87. New Haven: Yale University Press, 2001.

Virgil. *P. Vergilii Maronis Eclogae*. Edited by H. E. Gould. New York: St. Martin's Press, 1967.

Wall, Richard. "Women Alone in English Society." *Annales de Démographie historique* (1981): 303–17.

Walpole, Horace. *Anecdotes of Painting in England 1760–1795*. Edited by Frederick W. Hilles and Philip B. Daghlian. 5 vols. New Haven: Yale University Press, 1937.

————. *Horace Walpole's Correspondence*. Edited by W. S. Lewis. 48 vols. New Haven: Yale University Press, 1937–83.

————. *Memoirs of King George II*. Edited by J. Brooke. New Haven: Yale University Press, 1985.

————. *Reminiscences*. Oxford: Clarendon Press, 1924.

Watkins, Susan Cotts. "Spinsters." *Journal of Family History* 9 (1984): 310–25.

Weil, Rachel. *Political Passions: Gender, the Family and Political Argument in England 1680–1714*. Manchester: Manchester University Press, 1999.

Welsh, Alexander. *Strong Representations: Narrative and Circumstantial Evidence in England*. Baltimore: Johns Hopkins University Press, 1992.

Whately, William. *Bride-Bush: or, A Direction for Married Persons*. London: Thomas Man, 1619.

Wheeler, Ethel Rolt. *Famous Blue-Stockings*. London: Methuen, 1910.

Wilde, Lady [Jane Francesca]. *Notes on Men, Women, and Books*. London: Ward & Downey, 1891.

Wilde, William R. *The Closing Years of Dean Swift's Life*. 2nd ed., rev. Dublin: Hodges & Smith, 1849.

Wilkes, Wetenhall. *Letter of Genteel and Moral Advice*. In Jones, *Women in the Eighteenth Century*, 29–35.

Williams, Harold. "Swift's Early Biographers." In Clifford and Landa, *Pope and His Contemporaries*, 114–28.

Williams, Howard. *English Letters and Letter-Writers of the Eighteenth Century*. First Series. London: George Bell, 1886.

Wilson, Penelope. "Feminism and the Augustans: Some Readings and Problems." In *Jonathan Swift*, edited by Nigel Wood, 182–95. London: Longman, 1999.

Wittkowsky, George. "Swift's *Modest Proposal*: The Biography of an Early Georgian Pamphlet." *Journal of the History of Ideas* 4 (1943): 75–104.

Wollstonecraft, Mary. *The Works of Mary Wollstonecraft*. Edited by Janet Todd and Marilyn Butler. 7 vols. New York: New York University Press, 1989.

Woodbridge, Linda. *Women and the English Renaissance: Literature and the Nature of Womankind, 1540–1620*. Urbana: University of Illinois Press, 1984.

Woods, Margaret. "Swift, Stella, and Vanessa." *The Nineteenth Century and After* 74 (December 1913): 1230–47.

Woolf, Virginia. *Collected Essays*. 4 vols. New York: Harcourt, Brace & World, 1967.

———. *The Common Reader*. New York: Harcourt, Brace, 1925.

———. *A Room of One's Own*. New York: Harcourt, Brace & World, 1929.

Woolley, James. "Friends and Enemies in *Verses on the Death of Dr. Swift*." *Studies in Eighteenth-Century Culture* 8 (1979): 205–25.

———. "Thomas Sheridan and Swift." *Studies in Eighteenth-Century Culture* 9 (1979): 93–114.

Wrigley, E. A. "Marriage, Fertility, and Population Growth in Eighteenth-Century England." In *Marriage and Society: Studies in the Social History of Marriage*, edited by R. B. Outhwaite, 137–85. London: Europa, 1981.

Wrigley, E. A., and R. S. Schofield, *The Population History of England, 1541–1871*. Cambridge, Mass.: Harvard University Press, 1981.

Wyrick, Deborah Baker. *Jonathan Swift and the Vested Word*. Chapel Hill: University of North Carolina Press, 1988.

Wyse, Jackson R. *Swift and His Circle: A Book of Essays*. Dublin: Talbot Press, 1945.

Yalom, Marilyn. *A History of the Breast*. New York: Knopf, 1997.

Zimmerman, Don H., and Candace West. "Sex Roles, Interruptions and Silences in Conversation." In *Language and Sex: Difference and Dominance*, edited by Barrie Thorn and Nancy Henley, 105–29. Rowley, Mass.: Newbury House, 1975.

INDEX